READING

What can be measured?

Second Edition

Roger Farr
Indiana University

Robert F. Carey
Rhode Island College

An IRA/Elva Knight Research Fund Monograph

1986

International Reading Association, Inc.
800 Barksdale Road   Newark, Delaware 19714

INTERNATIONAL READING ASSOCIATION

Copyright 1986 by the
International Reading Association, Inc.

Library of Congress Cataloging-in-Publication Data

Farr, Roger
  Reading: What can be measured?
  (An IRA/Elva Knight research fund monograph)
  Includes bibliographies.
  1. Reading—Ability testing. 2. Reading comprehension—
Ability testing. I. Carey, Robert. II. International Reading As-
sociation. III. Title. IV. Series.
LB1050.46.F374   1986   428.4   85-28078
ISBN 0-87207-805-1
Second Printing, December 1986

Contents

Foreword

O ne way or another, most educators must deal with educational assessment and the most frequently assessed behavior is reading. Indeed, in many schools, reading assessment—in the form of standardized testing—continues for several years after formal reading instruction stops. Regardless of one's philosophical approach to teaching in general, or to teaching reading in specific, measurement issues must be addressed if only because of the amount of time and money spent on testing. The assessment of reading performance is now a multimillion dollar a year endeavor and all those who read this monograph should be awed by the profound social implications inherent in this mammoth educational enterprise. Putting into practice the information contained in this excellent monograph can only help reading education.

The title of this monograph, *Reading: What Can Be Measured?* asks a question. The answers to that question should provoke thoughtful reflection for educators, for reading researchers (their research almost always involves testing), for test makers, for school administrators, and for policymakers.

Classroom teachers and administrators who read this volume will gain answers to the question, "What can be measured in reading?" They also will learn that the *why* in assessment is just as important as the *what*. They will learn that communicating clearly to their various constituencies (and to one another) about *why* they are assessing reading performance is vital.

Test makers who read the volume will understand the importance of integrating the latest scientific knowledge of measurement with the most recent findings about reading acquisition, reading competence, and reading performance. There is much yet to be done. The reading achievement tests of the early 80s look far too much like those published in previous decades.

Policymakers who read this monograph—particularly the chapter on accountability—will be less likely to judge a school, a school district, or even a state solely on the basis of standardized test performance while ignoring the corresponding increase in high school dropouts which *may* account for the increase in test performance. Policymakers will learn why many of the simple solutions (like state mandated assessment) to complex educational problems fail.

The coverage of reading research as it relates to measuring reading achievement is comprehensive and objective. It will be widely used as a reference tool. *Reading: What Can Be Measured?* should be widely shared. It is an excellent monograph.

Alden J. Moe
Louisiana State University

An overview

This monograph is a revision of the 1969 edition which organized and described the research literature related to reading measurement published to that time. The 1986 revision attempts to bring that research summary up to date. Neither the earlier edition of the text nor this revision has attempted to be comprehensive, since the volume of research on the measurement of reading is too extensive. Rather, both editions have selectively reviewed and summarized the research that was determined to be of greatest importance and relevance in illuminating the issues and problems in reading measurement.

There are two major themes that are evident throughout the manuscript. The first is that those who use reading tests often fail to consider why they are testing before they begin to ask what should be tested and how to test. Fundamental questions regarding the definition of reading and concerns as to whether reading can be measured at all usually are not raised by those who are eager to quantify students' reading abilities. As we developed this revision, we often felt that a book should be written entitled, *Reading: Why Should It/Can It Be Measured?* After that book had been read by curriculum leaders in the schools, they would be ready for a book entitled, *Reading: What Can Be Measured?* Because this idea was not feasible we attempted to raise the more fundamental issues throughout this single monograph.

The second theme we have emphasized is the need for improved selection and interpretation of reading tests. Test scores are too often relied on as the only measure of the quality of a child's reading or of a reading program. We believe that the misuses of tests, especially by educational policy makers, significantly diminish any value test results may have for improving education.

There are three major content additions in this second edition. We have added a complete chapter on accountability and reading assessment. Much of this chapter focuses on the development and use of minimum competency tests, an issue seldom mentioned at the time of the first monograph.

The second addition is a discussion of the assessment of word recognition skills in reading. The earlier monograph did not include any studies on the assessment of word recognition skills. The position taken at that time was that reading was "comprehension" and word recognition skills were skills that *might* help someone learn to read, but they should not be considered reading. The number of comments regarding that omission have caused us to include the topic in this volume. Despite this inclusion, we were struck by the paucity of research regarding the assessment of word recognition skills.

The third content addition is not an entirely new section. Rather, it is a more extensive treatment of issues related to the assessment of reading comprehension. The extensive amount of research in the past decade devoted to increasing understanding of reading comprehension should, we believe, be reflected in improved measures of reading comprehension.

The monograph is addressed to those who direct reading programs at various levels — state, district, and individual schools. We have attempted to describe for this group some of the major problems with the assessment of reading, and to provide guidelines for the improved use of reading tests. Pre and inservice teachers and curriculum leaders should be primary audiences for the book. School administrators, state education department personnel, and school board members also should be interested. The book will provide an introduction to the researcher who is generally unfamiliar with the area of reading assessment. Serious researchers, especially those who are familiar with the area of reading assessment, will find that most of the topics in this book are not considered in adequate depth for their needs.

RF
RC

Acknowledgments

T his second edition of *Reading: What Can Be Measured?* could not have been completed without the assistance and hard work of several people. It should be emphasized that the opinions expressed and the interpretations of the research are the responsibility of the authors. However, we would be remiss if we did not acknowledge the important contributions of several people. One person who provided considerable assistance was Larry Rayford. Larry not only gathered research articles, checked references, and edited every chapter, but he also provided considerable assistance in the revision of several chapters. Bruce Tone also edited a number of chapters and helped with the conceptualization of several others.

The editorial staff at IRA headquarters also provided guidance and assistance. The revision of the monograph was fostered by Lloyd Kline who was the Director of Publications when the revision was launched. Jennifer Stevenson, who succeeded Lloyd, continued to provide valuable support. Romayne McElhaney took on the task of the final editing of the manuscript and guided it through to final production.

Without the help of all of these people we would have found it very difficult to complete our work. We would also like to thank the International Reading Association for providing a grant to assist us in the task of updating the monograph.

Roger Farr
Robert Carey

1

Reading measurement in perspective

This first chapter begins with a statement of the authors' perspective about the role of testing in educational practice. It is followed by an overview of the historical context of reading assessment. A third section outlines the most important issue in the field – the validity of reading tests. The validity issues introduced in this section are discussed in greater detail throughout the monograph. A final section provides a set of recommendations regarding the way tests are used.

Reading assessment in perspective

The perspective that focuses the review of the literature in this monograph considers testing exclusively within the broader concept of evaluation. While there are numerous definitions of evaluation, most have in common the process of collecting a wide variety of information for decision making. Thus, evaluation is often defined as the process of collecting information for making decisions (Stufflebeam, 1971). Tests are merely one means of collecting information and therefore are not synonymous with evaluation.

The test as a part of evaluation

Too often a school district evaluation is nothing more than the administration and interpretation of several different tests including norm referenced, criterion referenced, and teacher made tests. The practice of using tests as a total evaluation program predominates in schools today and is one of the major causes of reading test misuse. In order to use tests intelligently—and there are many times when it would be more intelligent not to use tests at all—consideration must be given to the use which will be made of the test results.

This means that the validity of any test must be determined in relation to the use that will be made of the results. Tests do not possess validity as some inherent quality. A test may be valid for a particular educational decision when it is used with other information, but no test is valid for all purposes. This perspective places the emphasis for better test use on the explicit understanding of the purposes for which particular tests can be used. Both the developers and consumers of tests must indicate the educational decisions they face before designing or selecting a test.

The field of evaluation has undergone much reformulation in the past several decades. The result has been a proliferation of approaches and models for conducting evaluation studies (Popham, 1975). When the first edition of this monograph was published, evaluation was considered primarily to be an activity to determine how "good" something was. More traditional evaluation specialists have, according to Scriven (1973), argued that the most effective role evaluation can serve is to ascertain whether results match objectives.

The most important developments in evaluation have been 1) the focus on decision making as the purpose for conducting an evaluation, 2) the acknowledgment that both process and product information are important for educational decision making, 3) the use of a variety of information collected continuously, and 4) an approach to evaluation that has allowed both the goals of the evaluation and the issues studied to emerge from the context. While a thorough discussion of each of these developments is beyond the scope of this monograph, each development will be considered in its implications for the development and use of reading tests.

If decision making is the focus of evaluation, as it should be, the first concern must be with clearly stating the educational decisions to be made. Decision making as the central rationale for evaluation broadens the focus of evaluation from merely labeling something as good or bad to producing information that can improve what is being evaluated. Most evaluators today consider the act of evaluating only to determine whether a program is adequate or inadequate to be a waste of time. What one wants to know is how to improve the program regardless of how good or how bad it is. What is true about programs is also true in the evaluation of individual students. The emphasis should be on obtaining information for planning instruction and not on labeling.

Once the need to make a specific educational decision has been determined, consideration must be given to the information that is needed to provide the basis for making the decision. Almost always the information that is needed will include descriptions of the present state of the program, how it is viewed by those involved in its implementation, its successes, its failures, and any problems experienced in implementing it. The point is that a wide variety of information is needed for making educational decisions.

Once it has been determined what information is needed, the search for the best ways to collect that information can begin. Tests are one way of collecting information, but they may not be the best way. To determine if a particular test (or any test) is the best way to collect the information, three criteria need to be considered: 1) Will this test provide the information that is really needed? That is, does the test sample from the domain of behaviors of pertinent interest and does the test provide a realistic context (one that is like the situation in which the real reading behaviors will occur)? 2) Does the test provide a convenient and nonthreatening means of collecting the needed information? 3) Does the sample of behaviors included on the test cover enough different situations to insure that the results will be both valid and reliable?

The focus on decision making brings into prominence the need for both process and product information. If decisions about how to improve a program are to be made, one certainly needs more information than just the results of the program. It is vital to know how the program is functioning. To rely only on product information for making program improvements would be shortsighted.

An analogy about the plant manager who wants to improve the production of widgets illustrates why process information is essential. The manager wants to make more widgets at a lower cost per unit. If the only information he has consists of the results of widget production, he will not know how to improve production. He also needs information about how the plant is functioning. Without such information he has no way of determining if changes in production methods or procedures are needed. The concern with process as well as product information has given rise to the terms formative and summative evaluation. These terms have been used to separate the important considerations of process evaluation (formative) from those of outcome evaluation (summative).

The need for process information with respect to reading assessment emphasizes the need for a thorough understanding of the reading process and assessments that will provide information about those reading processes. There are, however, very few tests available that provide any information about the processes a reader goes through while reading. Most tests provide various kinds of product information, and the test user must infer the reading processes from that product information. Most tests that claim to provide process information merely provide product information for a wide range of assumed reading subskills. This subskill product information is then purported to be useful in interpreting a reader's processes. There is little evidence to support the claims of such reading process tests. In fact, there is ample evidence supporting the fact that the reading process is much more than the mastery of a set of separate subskills as assessed by a set of product tests.

To stress that decision making requires a variety of information does not imply that a test cannot provide any of the information that is needed or that scattered information should be collected in place of tests. Evaluation requires a thoughtful consideration of all of the information needed and a search for the best ways to collect that information.

Decision making evaluation should also provide the opportunity for issues to emerge from the context in which the evaluation is being conducted. No matter how sensitive the analysis of needed information and the determination of ways to get it, an inflexible determination of issues can mask important and even crucial issues related to program improvement. If such issues have been overlooked, they are almost certain to emerge from a responsive evaluation. If the evaluation is static, however — particularly if it relies only on a test or a set of tests — there is little chance for the identification of emerging issues. Thus, the focus on evaluation as the broader concept in which tests should be considered, and on evaluation as a decision making process, emphasizes that the validity of tests can be considered only in relation to test use.

Test use is the most important issue for the test consumer

> Too often, we ask how to measure something without raising the question of what we would do with the measurement if we had it. We want to know *how* without thinking of *why*. I hope I may say without impiety, seek ye first for what is right for your needs, and all these things shall be added to you as well. (Kaplan, 1964, p. 214)

The admonition set forth by Kaplan delineates the most serious problem in the development and use of reading tests. The development of better tests is hampered because test users expect far too much from the tests they administer and attempt to interpret; and the more enthusiastic test authors and publishers have encouraged the view that tests can solve most of the ills that face education.

The primary concern with the use of tests is the validity of the uses test users would have them serve. Tests must be considered as nothing more and nothing less than the sampling of behaviors. The sample of behaviors produced by a test may or may not provide some of the information needed to make an educational decision. That is, a test may be partially valid for some purposes and totally invalid for others. It is never the case that the results of any test would, unaccompanied by other information, provide all the needed information for even a single educational decision. The fact that the valid use of tests relies on consumers selecting and using tests only when those tests meet their specific needs does not absolve test publishers and authors from clearly delineating the specific purposes for which their tests may be used and, more importantly, those decisions for which they should not be used.

Often the misuse of tests comes at the point of score interpretations as opposed to misselections of tests. That is, the data produced by a test selected to produce information for one decision is inappropriately applied to other analyses. Such inappropriate use of results affects, or even provokes, subsequent decision making. No more glaring or unfortunate example of this phenomena can be cited than the Scholastic Aptitude Test (SAT). The use of the SAT to predict college level expected performance may be debatable but, accepting that use, SAT scores have come to be used in a grossly inappropriate way that exerts a dynamic influence on the public evaluation of education and predicates serious and expensive educational decisions. When the SAT results for high school seniors are released each year, they produce media headlines. If the SAT results reveal an average decline of as few as three standard score points (equivalent to about a third of a raw score point), the editorial writers lament the declining state of American education.

Perhaps no other single use of tests so dramatically demonstrates their potential for misuse. One does not need to know much about tests to question the wisdom of arriving at a conclusion about the improvement of American education on so limited an information base. The SAT is a test designed to determine which students might be successful in colleges and universities. It is taken by only about half of the nation's high school seniors—primarily those who are in the top half of their classes. Yet the decline on the SAT seems to have given rise to a host of simpleminded solutions to the "problem" identified by the SAT decline. Examples of such solutions include the administration of minimum competency tests and the teaching of isolated phonics in first grade. Results of the SAT score reports are the primary source of evidence for the provocative but undirected alarm sounded in *A Nation at Risk*. This misuse of SAT results was discussed by Farr and Olshavsky (1980).

Reading assessment: A time of change

The measurement field in general, and the area of reading assessment in particular, have been the subject of significant changes in the past two decades. These two decades have witnessed the National Right to Read Effort, Reading Is Fundamental (RIF), the U.S. Office of Education's Basic Skills Program, *Sesame Street* and *The Electric Company*, Head Start, Follow Through, the Elementary and Secondary Education Act (including Chapters I and III), and a host of other programs designed to eliminate the stigma of illiteracy (Chall, 1983). With all of these programs has come the mandate to evaluate their effectiveness and impact. Most often this has meant the increased use of tests, quite often reading tests.

But testing programs to determine accountability, even without the impetus of new instructional programs, also have exploded on the educational scene. The National Assessment of Educational Progress (NAEP) and the myriad of state and local school district minimum competency testing programs are prime examples. There is no question that the administration and use, or misuse, of reading tests in 1984 has increased significantly over the use of tests fifteen years ago when the first edition of this monograph was published.

The disturbing tendency to rely solely on tests for evaluation that informs decision making has been offset somewhat by another important change. The direction of reading research conducted in the past decade has focused on reading as a cognitive process, and has been stimulated by a variety of researchers in psychology, linguistics, semiotics, and education. The eclectic synthesis of this process revealing work has much to recommend to those who develop and use tests.

Testing in schools: Rooted in accountability and the quest for a science of education. Testing in American schools got into full swing shortly after the turn of the century. Tests were first used as a means to evaluate the effectiveness of schools, a use of tests which has been noted here as widespread today. And, as they are today, test results were often used as the sole criterion by which to judge the worth of the schools. Levine (1976) points out that the results of tests used in a school survey in 1911 became a major factor "in the political assault on the schools in communities all over the United States" (p. 232).

The beginning of the widespread use of tests in schools in 1915 was related to the so-called "scientific movement" in education. The scientific movement, particularly the emphasis in the hard sciences on quantifiable results, was an attempt to bring the techniques of the hard sciences to the benefit of education. One of the education leaders of the period tied the need for the increased use of educational tests directly to measurement in the physical sciences. Thorndike (1918) wrote:

> Whatever exists at all exists in some amount…This is obviously the same general creed as that of the physicist or chemist or physiologist engaged in quantitative thinking….And, in general, the nature of educational measurements is the same as that of all scientific measurements. (pp. 16-17)

The emphasis on testing grew rapidly. In fact, by 1917 eighteen U.S. cities had research organizations within their school systems constructing, administering, and interpreting tests (Levine, 1976). In addition, the widespread use of group testing of enlistees in World War I further encouraged the development and use of tests. As Gould (1981) notes, it also led to rampant misuse.

Test developers of the time firmly believed in Thorndike's statement that if something existed, it existed in some amount and therefore, could be measured. Many test developers also believed that mental ability was primarily inherited and immutable. This led to some of the most blatant misuses of tests the country has ever witnessed.

Gould (1981) points specifically to the interpretation of the mental ability tests given to World War I inductees. Robert M. Yerkes convinced the U.S. Army to administer a mental test to all Army recruits. The results of the tests revealed that the average mental age of the recruits was slightly over 13 years. Since it had been previously determined that a "moron" was anyone with a mental age of between 7 and 12 years, Yerkes proclaimed that almost half of the draftees were morons. He went on to conclude that feeblemindedness must be of much greater occurrence in the general population than previously determined.

Gould described how Yerkes' findings influenced the thinking of even the most learned men of the time. In a speech entitled "Is America Safe for Democracy?" the chair of the psychology department at Harvard stated:

The results of the Army tests indicate that about 75 percent of the population has not sufficient innate capacity for intellectual development to enable it to complete the usual high school course. (McDougall, quoted in Gould, 1981, p. 224)

The misuse of mental testing was not restricted to the Army. H.H. Goddard, the Director of the Training School for Feebleminded Girls and Boys in Vineland, New Jersey, was also convinced that he could accurately measure mental ability. Like Yerkes, he was positive about the strong hereditary influence in the development of mental ability and was very outspoken in his belief that the "racial health" of the nation was threatened by the existence of morons. Unlike some of his contemporaries who saw the solution to the problem in sterilization programs, Goddard believed that those labeled as morons should be set apart from society in colonies where they could be prevented from reproducing (Gould, 1981).

With such profound faith in the validity of test scores, it is no wonder that the use of tests developed rapidly. Another factor that encouraged the use of tests was the chaos brought about by the Industrial Revolution. Up to the time of the Industrial Revolution, the United States was based on local autonomy and informal arrangements. However, it was found that, with the growth of big cities and big industry, such arrangements led to corruption. The corruption referred to was the way in which people were appointed to various positions and how jobs were secured. It was felt that the use of tests would help to identify talent and potential regardless of social background. Tests were seen as the great equalizer of educational and economic opportunity. It is interesting to note that today tests are often criticized because they are unfair barriers to opportunities—a significant change in attitudes about tests in fifty years.

Today testing permeates almost every aspect of social development in the United States. Tests are given to determine if one is fit to be a firefighter, a real estate agent, a baseball umpire, or a lawyer. The U.S. Armed Services continue to be extensive users of tests. It has been estimated that 95 percent of the people in the United States have taken a standardized test at some time or other, and that most people have taken several such tests. The cost of this extensive testing is not trivial. Estimates of testing costs are hard to determine accurately; however, one estimate places the annual cost at $1.32 for every man, woman, and child in the country (Anderson, 1982).

Testing in schools: A well accepted fact. The use of tests in schools is ubiquitous. Anderson (1982) explained why.

In 1975 Houts estimated that in the United States each student receives from six to twelve full batteries of achievement tests during the years from kindergarten through high school. This estimate did not even take into account specialized achievement testing, locally developed diagnostic tests, testing done through the National Assessment of Educational Progress, or competency tests now in effect in many states. Given a 1978 population of about 48 million 5 to 17 years old, the number of tests administered to elementary and secondary school students each year must be in the hundreds of millions. (p. 232)

Anderson further estimates that average students may spend two to six hours each year taking tests throughout their elementary and secondary school years, and students in compensatory or special education programs may experience two to three times more testing. This does not include, of course, the tests which accompany textbooks and instructional programs used in schools, nor does it include teacher made tests that are administered often on a weekly basis, and sometimes even on a daily basis.

Annual standardized testing programs in school systems abound. Anderson (1982) suggests that their use is almost universal. She cites a 1976 study in Michigan which revealed that 93 percent of the schools in the state had a regular standardized testing program.

There is certainly no doubt that teachers, administrators, and the public have come to rely on extensive amounts of testing in schools. One wonders why any school system, be it local or state, needs to consider any additional testing to determine the reading levels of students and their fitness for graduation. There is almost certainly enough testing information already available if it were used properly.

Resnick (1982) cogently summarized some of the reasons that tests are so widely used:

Standardized testing enjoys the support not only of the organized groups which have fostered its development—psychologists, school administrators, and publishers alike—but of public agencies, state and federal, and of taxpayers, whose contributions help to support our localized school systems. Public support for testing has grown out of a desire to keep our schools accountable for their costs and their educational quality. At the same time, testing has met a variety of other needs in the organization of schools and their interface with colleges and universities. The present wave of controversy would have to wash very high to erode a base of use and support that has grown considerably in size and character over the past three-quarters of a century. (p. 174)

The major issues for the next decade: Predictable from present events.
Certainly, no more significant event in education has occurred in the past

decade than the multitude of reports commenting on the quality of education. This spate of reports captured public attention and, for a while, was a major media event. The quality of education was an issue that was both promoted and used by politicians at all levels of government. An editorial in the *Louisville Courier-Journal* (1980) entitled, "Tests Hold Keys to School Improvement" is exemplary of the faith Americans seem to have in the use of tests as the primary evidence regarding the quality of education. Not only did this editorial proclaim that tests could provide important information so the public could hold the schools accountable, it went on to describe the importance of tests in diagnosing students' abilities. It seems that the American public has had a love affair with tests for over fifty years.

In commenting on some of the implications of the report *A Nation at Risk,* Hogan (1983) said that the report "calls for more testing: more frequent testing, more kinds of tests in more different fields, and paying more attention to the test results." Hogan concluded, "Testing plays a prominent role in the Commission's plan for remedying the currently perceived problems—heady prospects for the measurement field."

It seems safe to conclude that the next decade will not witness a decline in the amount of testing in the schools. Indeed, indications are that there will be even more testing, especially testing to monitor the success and failure of educational systems. In few of the recent education reports are there any discussions of the misuses of tests, nor are there any discussions of the kinds of improvements that need to be made in both the development of tests and the use of test results. It almost seems that the authors of the reports, particularly of *A Nation at Risk*, have provided their assessment of the failure of American education and have outlined their particular improvement plan. However, they have left the assessment of that improvement to the Scholastic Aptitude Test and other standardized tests which are now in widespread use in every school district in the nation.

Despite the fact that tests are widely used and the critics seem to be calling for more tests, controversy has always surrounded the use of tests. In a major report on testing in schools (Tyler & White, 1979), the authors listed four major uses and four major criticisms of tests:

Major Uses of Current Tests
1. *Tests are used to hold teachers, schools, and systems accountable.* Many principals, superintendents, and other educational authorities use test scores, particularly achievement tests, as a rough gauge of the adequacy of the performance of a teacher, a school, or a larger administrative unit.

2. *Tests are used to make decisions concerning individual students.* Educational authorities use the same tests when placing individual students in special programs and classes and in counselling them on plans for future education and careers.

3. *Tests are used to evaluate educational innovations and experimental projects.* Government agencies, private foundations, and school systems sponsor experimental projects in American schools and seek to evaluate these projects through the use of standardized achievement tests.

4. *Tests are used to provide guidance to teachers in the classroom.* Test makers and the educators who select published tests for use in schools exert influence directly and indirectly on teachers in the classroom. Direct influence is exerted by the choice of subtests to measure the strengths and weaknesses of students in particular component skills. The indirect influence results when tests are used for accountability.

Major Criticisms of Current Tests

1. *Tests do not reflect the full range of student cultural backgrounds and thus lead to decisions that are unfair to minority students.* The underlying logic of standardized testing requires that a given test performance must have the same meaning for all children or groups of children being assessed or compared.

2. *Current standardized tests have only limited value for holding teachers, schools, and school systems accountable for the quality of education.* The use of current standardized tests to evaluate the effectiveness of education is under attack by educators and other persons concerned with education. They argue that the educational objectives tested often differ from what the school is seeking to teach.

3. *Tests exercise a limiting effect on classroom teaching.* Several national educational groups have called for a moratorium on testing. It is argued that standardized tests have no positive direct usefulness in guiding instruction, and their indirect influence — implicitly laying down goals and standards — disrupts or blocks teaching.

4. *Tests are too narrow in scope to provide for fair evaluation of new approaches to teaching.* Evaluation is an important part of the present effort to improve education, because without full evaluation an educational experiment loses most of its meaning. But crit-

ics maintain that the narrowness and inflexibility of published tests with regard to curriculum make them unsuitable for evaluation of new and potentially valuable approaches to teaching. (pp. 7-11)

The summary provided by Tyler and White seems to reinforce the notion that testing will continue to be a major factor in education but that controversy will continue to accompany test use. The controversy is easy to understand when one considers the vital decisions about peoples' lives that test results are used to determine: Who will get to go to which college or university? Who will/will not be graduated from high school? Which teachers will be considered exemplary or unqualified? Which schools/school districts/state education programs will be labeled "adequate"? Which students will be labeled "remedial learners"? The consequences of such decisions have impact on all aspects of education, and the impact of such decisions on an individual's life is sometimes monumental.

It follows that testing will continue to spark attention and controversy in the coming decades. The attention may be the call for more testing, as happened with the recent calls for testing of teachers and students in an attempt to improve education. Or it may be a call for a ban on testing. In 1973, for example, the response of the National Education Association to the problems with testing was a call for a moratorium on the use of standardized tests in schools (Coffman, 1974). When Florida passed a statewide minimum competency law, the legal cases that followed led to a judicial ruling to delay the use of the tests to deny a student a high school diploloma. The ruling was based primarily on the belief that the Florida testing program was unconstitutional because it perpetuated the effects of past discrimination and because it was implemented without an adequate phase-in period (Haney, 1980).

In July 1972, an editorial appeared in the *Los Angeles Times* stating that, "Much time, effort, and money have been wasted in California on administering reading tests whose results are not only misleading but damaging." The editorial went on to attack tests on the grounds that 1) test revisions are dependent on sales; 2) norms are not appropriate to certain population groups; 3) test scores often reflect testwiseness; 4) honest students, those who leave blanks when they are not sure of an answer, may not score as well as students who guess when they do not know; and 5) students who are motivated will do better than those who are not motivated. The editorial concludes:

We would undoubtedly upgrade the level of reading in California if we would divert the money spent on testing to building better reading programs, supplying teachers with more and better books, and training teachers in the use of more effective approaches. Of course, smaller classes would help. (Chasman, 1972)

Despite the obvious merits of the improvements called for in the editorial, it is almost certain that a public call for more testing would follow to find out if "all the money being spent on the changes in education were producing any measurable results." And probably, a short time later, we would discover another editorial calling for a moratorium on testing—and so the cycle seems to go.

The issue should not be whether tests should or should not be used; they are almost as sure a part of the educational makeup of school systems as are death and taxes to every citizen. The issue, therefore, should be how to make better use of tests, which may mean significantly reducing the amount of testing, eliminating the significant misuses of tests and test results, and developing alternative strategies for collecting the information needed for educational decision making.

In commenting on the conflicting views of testing, Haney (1980) points out that a federal judge in California ruled that standardized tests of intelligence are invalid and biased, while a Florida federal judge ruled that a standardized test has not been shown to be biased or invalid. Haney suggests that the controversy over testing goes much farther than just the issue of testing.

The differences derive from deeper underlying assumptions about the relative rights and prerogatives of individuals versus those of state agencies and institutions, about the different social functions served by standardized testing, and at root from underlying differences in educational and social philosophies. (p. 647)

The need for better test use was summed up by Coffman (1974) in his reaction to the NEA call for a moratorium on standardized testing:

I've questioned the desirability of calling a complete moratorium on standardized testing in the schools: to interrupt the data collection process while we perfect our evaluation system is to create a critical information gap. But I see nothing wrong at all with encouraging a moratorium on the use of test scores to label children rather than to guide their learning, to classify teachers rather than to identify points where teachers may be helped to become more effective, to pull the wool over the eyes of the public rather than to generate questions about how a school system might go about doing an even better job. Let's not spend too much time deploring the NEA's resolution; let's get on with the business of meeting their demands for better tests, better reporting systems, and wiser test use. (p. 6)

There are several other issues significant enough to note in the continuing controversy over the increasing use of tests. These include the continuing emphasis of many educators on the importance and value of informal testing, the use of test development techniques which attempt to assess underlying traits, and the use of microcomputers for test administration and record keeping.

The call for more informal testing has come primarily from educators concerned with the language arts area, particularly reading, for a number of years. Informal tests are highly effective as diagnostic tools that can guide instruction. The response to this call has been lamentably meager. The actual use of informal tests in most schools is minimal, and little attention has been paid to the development of informal techniques that could be used either to supplement or supplant the use of standardized tests. In fact the search for alternatives has not produced much that is new (Lennon, 1981). The research related to the informal assessment of reading is reviewed in Chapter 5.

The list of alternatives usually offered includes observation schedules, anecdotal records, work products, interviews, contracts, and "whole-child" assessment. All of these have been discussed and reviewed in the measurement field for decades. The problem is that they have not been refined and developed, they have not been presented to teacher education programs, and they have not been generally accepted by teachers. We have much to do if we expect informal testing to make its important contribution to the improvement of assessment in schools.

The use of test development approaches which assess underlying traits are referred to as *latent trait models.* The basic assumption of these models is that tests can assess basic traits if the test item selection techniques are based on a statistical model that relates each item to a basic underlying scale. Latent trait approaches have become quite popular in the past several years (Urry, 1977; Marcos, 1977; Frederiksen, 1979). This topic is dealt with in more detail elsewhere in this monograph, but it is important to note here that the use of latent trait models has been claimed to be "an emerging trend in the field of testing that will make possible important advances in efficiency and accuracy of measurement" (Frederiksen, 1979).

The use of microcomputers in the measurement field is certain to expand in the decade ahead. The entire Summer 1984 issue of *Educational Measurement: Issues and Practice* was devoted to microcomputers. Included were articles on using microcomputers to develop tests, administer tests, and assess achievement and instruction. The potential uses of microcomputers include the development of tailor made tests, the creation of item banks, the immediate scoring of tests, the storage of test data, the analysis of test performance, and the development of immediate instructional prescriptions.

Many experimental microcomputer testing programs have been developed to meet these needs. Brzezinski (1984) claims that it will be a long time (if ever) before each teacher has a microcomputer to use for classroom based testing and before students will routinely take tests on classroom microcomputers. She does predict, however, that increasingly sophisticated test analysis packages, increased graphics capability, and increased integration of the various components of a complete school testing program are almost sure to influence the immediate future of test administration programs in schools.

Whatever the next few decades hold for the development of tests and the use of test results, it is the validity of the test that will remain the crucial issue. All of the sophisticated computer programs, the advanced statistical programs, and the new approaches to assessment will be so much useless paraphernalia without a better understanding of the behaviors we call reading and more inventive ways to understand those behaviors.

The crucial reading assessment issue: Validity

Validity is discussed throughout this monograph. These discussions are concerned in one way or another with four issues. The first is whether a test actually assesses a particular behavior. The issue strikes at the heart of the meaning of validity and poses such questions as: What do we really understand reading to be? How is reading similar to other language behaviors? How can reading be assessed in a realistic context?

The second issue grows out of the first and is concerned with whether any single test can validly assess all that one may need to know, or want to know, about a child's reading behaviors. This second issue raises questions about the use of test results. For example, can any test really tell us how well a child can read when he or she really wants to accomplish some purpose? Can a test score, by itself, tell us everything we need to know about a child's reading ability?

The third issue concerns what is to be done with the test results. That is, what educational decision does one want to make, and does a particular set of test results help with that decision? This issue raises questions about the criterion levels of tests, the interpretation of norm referenced scores such as grade equivalents, and the meaning and interpretation of informal test results.

The fourth validity issue focuses on the misunderstanding and misuse of test results. This issue raises questions about both educators' and the public's understanding and use of test results.

Do reading tests really measure reading? To determine if tests actually measure reading, we must first ask: What is reading? If reading is defined as an activity in which human beings engage themselves for specific reasons as part of their everyday lives, the answer to the first question is "No!" At best, tests can provide some indication of how someone reads, but the relationship of such indications to actual reading behaviors must be inferred. Despite what one often reads in research articles, reading is not what reading tests test. If test consumers understood, accepted, and acted on the basis of this basic fact, we might witness significant improvements in the use of reading tests.

It must be understood that tests are activities to engage examinees in behaviors that are like what they do in everyday life. But tests are not reality. The testing conditions, the purposes for reading, the examinees' attitudes toward tests (and even toward school) all influence test performance. More importantly, the selection of the particular response mode that comprises the test may be more or less like the real reading behaviors that are of interest.

Throughout this monograph the discussion of the behaviors assessed by tests are considered in relation to the real behaviors of reading. Of course, the search for the elusive definition of reading continues. We are still unsure about the basic processes that comprise reading, and we are still debating the process of decoding (some would rather say "recoding") a printed message. Most of all we are very unsure about the skills that should be taught to beginning readers, the sequence in which those skills should be taught, or even whether any separate skills of reading need to be taught.

In order to measure any behavior, it is first necessary to know the basic components of that behavior. Factor analytic studies of reading tests (Davis, 1941; Traxler, 1941; Holmes, 1962; Holmes & Singer, 1964, 1966) were attempts to define reading in past decades. These studies were tied to the manipulation of the results of existing tests. Raygor (1966) criticized all such factor analytic studies because they were completely dependent on the validity and reliability of the tests used to gather the data. These factor analytic researchers were obviously in agreement with the idea that reading is what the reading tests test, and that all one has to do is arrange the parts of this behavior by manipulating the data generated by the test results.

More recent studies have attempted to explain the reading behaviors of readers. One of the most influential researchers to use this approach is

Goodman (1969). He views reading as a form of information processing that occurs when an individual selects and chooses from the information available in an attempt to decode graphic messages. Continuing research by Goodman and others has provided a better understanding of the reading process.

Results of research on the reading process are in obvious conflict with the contents of many standardized reading tests. The tests assess separate reading skills as if these separate parts made up the total of reading behavior. Research on the reading process indicates that reading cannot be fractionated into a set of separate skills; to do so is to misunderstand reading behavior. Additionally, many tests attempt to assess mastery of these skills though research indicates that the concept of the mastery of reading is anathema to a constantly developing behavior.

One of the points that must be remembered in considering validity is that test behavior involves skill in both the reading behavior being tested and in the particular task used to assess that behavior. Some tests seem to be more heavily weighted with test taking behaviors. For example, on many tests of phonics skills, capable readers may not be able to perform the particular test task. It is not that the examinees cannot read; it is just that they cannot do what the test asks. Perhaps they did not learn to read using a structured phonics approach and thus are not able to perform the tasks on a phonics test, even though the children can read quite well. Surely the validity of such tests for these users should be questioned.

The goal of too many test developers and too many test consumers is to get a student's reading performance narrowed down to a single score. This emphasis on a single score is epitomized in a story told by Kaplan:

> One of the subjects of Kinsey's study of sexual behavior in the human male afterwards complained bitterly of the injury to his masculine ego. "No matter what I told him," he explained, "he just looked me straight in the eye and asked, 'How many times?' " Insofar as the objection is well taken it rests on the "no matter what." Plainly the subject felt that what he had done was incomparably more significant than the frequency of its performance; there are surely cases where this attitude is justified, even if it is scientific significance that is in question. The principle, "Let's get it down to something we can count!" does not always formulate the best research strategy; "Let's see now, what have we here?" may point to a more promising program. (1964, p. 121)

It seems obvious that more valid assessments of reading will grow out of attempts to better understand "what we have here" as we try to understand the reading process. As we consider the complexities of the reading process, we will need to remember that "real reading" occurs in a "real world." Our measurement, if it is to be valid, must consider whether a reader has established useful reading habits, whether what has been read can be applied to the reader's problems, and whether newly acquired information can be integrated with what is already known by the reader.

A second crucial validity problem: How much a single test can reveal. Another of the important validity problems that has existed almost since the first time standardized tests were used in this country is the assumption that a test score tells all there is to know about a person or a program. Gould (1981) describes how single test scores were used in the 1920s and 1930s to label people as mental defectives, and how such labeling led to their sterilization. It is still common for people to be labeled mentally retarded, learning disabled, or dyslexic from the results of a single test score. The debate about the value of labeling notwithstanding, it is illogical and invalid to make any important educational decision on the basis of information as limited as a single test score.

In evaluating the quality of our nation's schools, many critics take the SAT scores as the prime criterion – perhaps the only criterion – for judgment. In evaluating school districts, the annual release of the test scores to local newspapers has become the evidential basis for discussion of school district quality. And state legislatures pass legislation calling for minimum competency tests, seeming to suggest that all would be right with the schools if students could pass certain tests.

Researchers, school administrators, and the general public debate the meaning of test score increases or decreases as if test results were all there was to know about the schools. By the 1960s, data produced by tests were held in such high regard that the public tended to look on tests as absolute evaluations rather than the limited indicators they are. On the other hand, the public seemed to ignore other encouraging indicators regarding the quality of education: average grades completed for the U.S. population; the increasing number of high school graduates; the rapidly increasing numbers and percentages of minority children completing twelve years of school; and the significant increases in library circulation, book buying habits, and magazine publication and circulation (Cole & Gould, 1979).

There are many kinds of information needed to judge the quality of a school system or the reading development of an individual child. The need for more valid information raises a question that has been debated continuously by measurement specialists: "Aren't there some things which are intrinsically immeasurable?"

Kaplan (1964) answers this question quite cogently: "For my part, I answer these questions with an unequivocal 'No.' I would say that whether we can measure something depends, not on the thing, but on how we have conceptualized it, on our knowledge of it, and above all on the skill and ingenuity which our inquiry can put to use."

Kaplan's position does not mean that we can indeed measure everything, but that we should try to understand all those behaviors that are important to what we do measure. If we ignore certain aspects of a reading program or a child's reading by arguing that some things cannot be measured, we will limit our understanding and our ability to plan effective instruction.

If, in fact, we measure only what can be easily measured, we are putting on blinders. If we ignore what cannot be measured or assign it an arbitrary quantitative label, we are being dishonest. If we argue that some things cannot be measured easily and thus ignore them, we are being naive. If we claim that what cannot be measured does not exist, we are being stupid. The valid use of tests for educational decision making mandates that we understand that there is more information needed than can be gathered from test results.

Reading tests can only indicate how well a child reads from a limited perspective, under a limited set of conditions, and with a limited set of responses. Chittenden and Bussis (1972) have discussed the use of observations and work samples as appropriate material for evaluation. Campbell (1974) has argued that quantitative knowing should be leavened by qualitative knowing. Whether quantitative and qualitative are different ways of knowing is immaterial; the point is that we need to collect appropriate information that reveals the complexity of a child's reading so we can understand how to teach that child. Hiding behind a single test score will only mask what we really need to know.

Madaus (1983) summed up the naivete that seems to surround the use of tests as a basis for educational policy:

> By mandating tests, policy makers create an illusion that educational quality is synonymous with performance on the tests. People are told that more and more pupils pass the tests and therefore are competent to face the demands of our society; that once again the high school diploma has meaning; that at last we have truth in labeling education. The philosophy underlying this illusion is utilitarian—overly concerned with social efficiency at the expense of the wider and deeper aspects of education. (p. 24)

A third major validity problem: The criterion level for successful performance. This problem exists with both norm referenced and criterion referenced tests, but is more prevalent with criterion referenced tests since these tests are designed to determine if examinees can perform specific tasks.

The traditionally accepted differences between criterion referenced and norm referenced tests seem to indicate that criterion referenced tests can better serve instructional decision making needs. Criterion referenced tests are closely related to the familiar concept of a mastery test. The purpose of such a test is to measure achievement of a specific behavior and often to make a specific decision. For example: Has Bill mastered the skills necessary to drive a car? Is Judy able to swim a mile? Has Chris mastered the essential beginning reading skills necessary to go on to the next phase of instruction? In each of these situations, the criterion is definite and the student are assessed to determine whether they can complete the task.

A norm referenced test is also concerned with assessing behaviors and making decisions, but the decisions are of a comparative nature. For example: How good a driver is Bill compared with Judy? Is Judy an adequate swimmer for her age and size? How good is Chris' reading skill development compared to other students at his grade level?

Are there two different types of tests or is there one test with two different types of scores derived from the test? In the preceding examples, Bill has to demonstrate his driving ability, Judy has to be able to swim, and Chris has to read on both the norm referenced and the criterion referenced versions of the tests. The differences are not in two different types of tests but rather in the different interpretations or scores derived from the tests.

The emphasis on criterion referenced tests has been positive in that test developers have been more explicit about the behaviors their tests assess. Scores have been developed that indicate whether examinees can perform specific tasks, and teachers have been able to gather comparable classroom observation since the criterion referenced tests more explicitly delineate the behaviors included on them.

There are, however, several validity problems that need to be considered in the use of criterion referenced tests. One of these problems explains why early test developers moved to norm referenced scores rather than criterion referenced scores. They did so because reading is such a complex behavior and little was known about it at the time these tests were first developed in the 1920s. It was difficult then, as it is today, to get reading specialists to agree on the specific subskills of reading or to define exactly what reading vocabulary is or to state specifically how many sight words children should know before they can begin reading a preprimer or to decide how many phoneme/grapheme matches indicate a child has mastered this skill.

The point here is that the development of criterion referenced tests has not solved any of the problems of defining reading, the subskills that comprise the process, or the number of test items that indicate mastery of a skill. They have just simplified the results and have made it seem that such questions have been answered.

Criterion referenced concepts have been built into the minimum competency tests that have gained increasingly widespread popularity in the past decade. The development of these tests, which are generally pitched toward the lowest level of reading ability, are the result of the public's misunderstanding of the decline on higher level reading tests such as the Scholastic Aptitude Tests.

The question is, can minimum competency tests help people become more critical, creative readers—readers who can identify and respond to nuance, mood, and tone and who can spot a strong or weak argument when they read? There is a whole set of similar questions that ought to be addressed if the minimum competency movement is to have any positive impact on education. The most important of these include:

- Is it necessary to test millions of children observed daily in the classroom in order to identify those very few who cannot read well?
- How are the minimum levels of the tests to be determined? How closely do these levels match what is taught in the classroom? Is the minimum competency movement changing curricula in any significant way? If so, is designing curricula to conform to the tests what we really want or ought to be doing?
- Can minimum competency tests actually assess the reading act, which theorists are just now beginning to define convincingly?
- Other than determining which children will repeat instruction (that is, will fail the test), can minimum competency testing produce information that teachers can apply to specific instruction? Can such tests yield other than gross distinctions?
- How autocratic is the data being produced by minimum competency testing in educational decision making? Is it a contributing indication in a broader evaluation program that incorporates teacher judgment? What impact, if any, has the minimum competency movement had on other kinds of educational evaluation?

The fourth validity problem: The misunderstanding and misuse of test results. This validity problem again emphasizes that test validity is determined by test use. If they are properly used, tests can be useful supplements to the information base needed for planning instruction, estimating students' reading development, and evaluating a school district's success in achieving stated goals. Information for planning instruction is an essential need; assessing students' achievement is important if the value of various teaching methods are to assessed; and the importance of assessment for determining a school district's success in meeting its goals is vital if continued support from the taxpayers is expected.

If the need for information is so great, why is there continuous controversy concerning the misuses of tests? There seem to be four major reasons which, taken together, define test misuse and misunderstanding:

1. Tests are sometimes (perhaps often) administered when there is no clearly stated purpose for administering them.
2. Tests are often viewed as the sole criterion on which to judge the success of a program.
3. Specific tests, which might provide some information regarding some behaviors, are often used to assess the achievement of all goals.
4. Test results are released to the news media and the public without accompanying information.

These four misuses of tests and test results are sufficient justification for anyone to oppose the continued use (misuse) of tests in schools. Examples of such misuses are rampant, but a few will suffice. In a speech before a learned educational association, Chall (1983) (a respected leader in the reading field) stated that, "Further evidence for the low state of literacy among high school students comes from the steady decline in SAT verbal scores." Whatever the decline on the SAT indicates, it does not, as Chall suggests, indicate a decline in literacy. The reading levels demanded of an examinee to get a score slightly above a chance level score on that test are quite high. Research has indicated that even students who score at low levels on the SAT are very good readers as measured by more traditional high school reading tests (Farr, Courtland, & Beck, 1984).

Another example of test misuse concerns the public's interpretation of grade equivalent scores from norm referenced tests. Levine (1976) states that many educators and the public believe there really is such a thing as "second grade reading achievement, and that every second grade child should meet or exceed that standard." The examples of such misuses could fill volumes. These misuses must be eliminated.

Recommendations for improved test use

Many books include a set of recommendations at the end of the final chapter. The importance of improved test usage, however, dictates that this monograph begin with recommendations. Later chapters will provide additional recommendations related to the specific content of the chapter which they follow, or are further explications of the recommendations provided here.

These recommendations are put forth with the full understanding that testing in our schools is not going to lessen – it will most likely increase. It is further contended that, when used carefully, tests scores may lead to decisions considering some incremental value that makes them more dependable than decisions made without this information. The authors of this monograph had planned to develop their own particular list of recommendations. However, a conference on testing sponsored by the U.S. Department of Health, Education and Welfare and the National Institute of Education (1979) developed recommendations which we feel cannot be improved. The conference and the resulting report were the products of thirty-one participants concerned with teaching and educational administration and policy, with research and development relevant to education, with educational testing, with various areas of educational content, and with information handling technology. These recommendations follow.

Testing for Tracking and Instructional Grouping

1. No important decision about an individual's educational future should be based on a single test score considered in isolation. This should hold true for tests that purport to measure educational achievement as well as for tests that purport to measure aptitudes or disabilities. Scores ought to be interpreted within the framework of a student's total record, including classroom teachers' observations and behavior outside the school's situation, taking into account the options available for the child's instruction.

2. If a school or school district institutes testing to guide placement decisions, it is imperative that the faculty, parents, and all others playing a role in placement decisions be instructed in interpreting test data and understanding their limitations.

3. Careful attention should be given to the question of the instructional validity of ability grouping decisions. Schools should make a continuing effort to check on the educational soundness of any plan they use for grouping or classifying students or for individualizing instruction. Regular monitoring should be instituted to insure that

instruction is contributing to the child's growth over a broad spectrum of abilities. Beyond that, special attention should be paid to determining which kinds of children thrive best in alternative programs. Assignment policies should be revised if there is any evidence that pupils being assigned to narrower or less stimulating programs are progressing more slowly than they would in regular instruction.

4. Because the concept of instructional validity is only now being articulated, we strongly urge that the National Institute of Education and other agencies with interests in this matter encourage research and demonstration projects in:

(a) The development and use of tests as diagnostic instruments for choosing among alternative teaching programs the one most appropriate to a given student's mental traits or abilities (that is, matching aptitudes and instructional instruments);

(b) The development and use of tests to assess current learning status as it relates to a child's ability to move on to more complex learning tasks.

Testing in Special Education

1. There is little justification for making distinctions and isolating children from their cohorts if there is not a reasonable expectation that special placement will provide them with more effective instruction than the normal instruction offers. The fundamental challenge in dealing with children who seem ill adapted to most regular instruction is to devise alternative modes of instruction that really work.

2. Skepticism about the value of tests in identifying children in need of special education has probably been carried too far; people making those decisions should, whenever practicable, have before them a report on a number of professionally administered tests, in part to counteract the stereotypes and misconceptions that contaminate judgmental information.

3. We recommend against the use of rigid numerical cutoff scores (applying to a test, a set of tests, or any other formula) as the basis for decisions about mental retardation and special education.

The Use of Tests in Certifying Competence

1. Fair and accurate assessment of competencies includes: clear specification of the kinds of academic and other skills that are to be mas-

tered; methods of evaluation that are tied closely to those skills, e.g., tests with high content validity and construct validity; a reasonable justification of the pass/fail cutoff point that takes cognizance of community expectations; many opportunities to retake the test; gradual phasing in of the program so that the teachers, students, and community can be prepared for it; and stability of requirements, both in content and difficulty level, so that standards are known and dependable.

2. Since the desired result of minimum competency testing is to encourage intensive efforts on the part of students and teachers to increase the general level of accomplishments in the schools, the tests should be introduced well in advance of the last year of high school in order to provide ample opportunity for schools to offer and students to take extra training geared to the problems revealed by the tests.

3. Above all, minimum competency programs must involve instruction as well as assessment. We can see little point in devoting considerable amounts of educational resources to assessing students' competencies if the information so gained is not used to improve substandard performance. Furthermore, schools should carry the burden of demonstrating that the instruction offered has a positive effect on test performance. Diagnosis without treatment does no good and, quite literally, adds insult to injury.

The Use of Tests in Policy Making and Management

1. Testing for survey and policy research purposes should be restricted to investigations that have a good chance of being used; testing should not degenerate into routine manipulations of data that are filed and forgotten. Moreover, any testing should be designed to collect adequately precise data with a minimum investment of effort (for example, when the purpose is system monitoring, sampling rather than administering the same long tests to every pupil every year).

2. Tests introduced for the purpose of guiding policy should be examined both before and after introduction for undesirable side effects, such as unintended standardization of curriculum or making a few subjects unduly important.

3. Surveys of performance of groups should emphasize performance descriptions and avoid comparisons between schools or school districts (*Testing, Teaching, and Learning*, 1979, pp. 178-181).

References

Anderson, B. Test use today in elementary and secondary schools. In A.K. Wigdor and W.R. Garner (Eds.), *Ability testing: Uses, consequences, and controversies, Part 2.* Washington, DC: National Academy Press, 1982.

Brzezinski, E.J. Microcomputers and testing: Where are we and how did we get there? *Educational Measurement: Issues and Practice,* 1984, *3,* 7-10.

Campbell, D.T. *Qualitative knowing in action research.* Kurt Lewin Award Address presented at the meeting of the American Psychological Association, New Orleans, September 1974.

Chall, J.S. *Literacy: Trends and explanations.* Award address presented at the American Educational Research Association, Montreal, April 1983.

Chasman, D. Reading tests called wasteful, damaging. *Los Angeles Times,* June 24, 1972.

Chittenden, E.A., and Bussis, A.M. Open education: Research and assessment strategies. In E.B. Nyquist and G.R. Hawes (Eds.), *Open education: A sourcebook for parents and teachers.* New York: Bantam Books, 1972.

Coffman, W.E. A moratorium? What kind? *Measurement in Education,* 1974, *5,* 1-7.

Cole, J.C., and Gold, C.S. *Reading in America 1978.* Washington, DC: Library of Congress, 1979.

Davis, F.B. Reporting test data in the media: Two case studies. *Reading Teacher,* 1972, *26,* 305-310.

Educational Measurement: Issues and Practice, 1984, *3,* 7-10.

Farr, R., Courtland, M.C., and Beck, M. Scholastic Aptitude Test performance and reading ability. *Journal of Reading,* 1984, *28,* 208-214.

Farr, R., and Olshavsky, J.E. Is minimum competency testing the appropriate solution to the sat decline? *Phi Delta Kappan,* 1980, *61,* 528-530.

Frederiksen, N. Some emerging trends in testing. In R.W. Tyler and S.H. White (Eds.), *Testing, teaching and learning.* Washington, DC: U.S. Department of Health, Education and Welfare and National Institute of Education, 1979.

Goodman, K.S. Analysis of oral reading miscues: Applied psycholinguistics. *Reading Research Quarterly,* 1969, *5,* 9-30.

Gould, S.J. *The mismeasure of man.* New York: W.W. Norton, 1981.

Haney, W. Trouble over testing. *Educational Leadership,* 1980, 640-650.

Hogan, T.P. Measurement implications of "A Nation at Risk." *Educational Measurement: Issues and Practice,* 1983, *2,* 32.

Holmes, J.A. Speed, comprehension, and power in reading. In E.P. Bleismer and R.C. Staiger (Eds.), *Problems, programs, and projects in college adult reading.* Yearbook of the National Reading Conference, 1962, *11,* 6-14.

Holmes, J.A., and Singer, H. *The substrata factor theory: Substrata factor differences underlying reading ability in known groups at the high school level.* Final report covering contracts No. 538, sae-8176 and 538A, sae-8660. Washington, DC: U.S. Government Printing Office, 1966.

Holmes, J.A., and Singer, H. Theoretical models and trends toward more basic research in reading. *Review of Educational Research*, 1964, *34*, 127-155.

Kaplan, A. *The conduct of inquiry.* San Francisco: Chandler, 1964.

Lennon, R.T. *A time for faith.* Presidential address, National Council on Measurement in Education annual meeting, Los Angeles, April 15, 1981.

Levine, M. The academic achievement test: Its historical context and social functions. *American Psychologist,* March 1976, 228-238.

Louisville Courier-Journal. Tests hold keys to school improvement, October 1, 1980, A 4.

Madaus, G.F. Test scores: What do they really mean in educational policy? Address presented to the National Consortium on Testing, Washington, DC, April 1983.

Marcos, G.L. Item characteristic curve solutions to three intractable testing problems. *Journal of Educational Measurement,* 1977, *14*, 139-160.

Popham, J.W. *Educational evaluation.* Englewood Cliffs, NJ: Prentice-Hall, 1975.

Raygor, A.L. Problems in the substrata factor theory. *Reading Research Quarterly,* 1966, *3*, 147-150.

Resnick, D. History of educational testing. In A.K. Wigdor and W.R. Garner (Eds.), *Ability testing: Uses, consequences, and controversies, Part 2.* Washington, DC: National Academy Press, 1982.

Scriven, M. Goal free evaluation. In E.R. House (Ed.), *School evaluation: The politics and process.* Berkley, CA: McCutchan, 1973.

Stufflebeam, D.L., et al. *Educational evaluation and decision making.* Itasca, IL: F.E. Peacock, 1971.

Thorndike, E.L. The nature, purposes and general methods of measurement of educational products. In G. Whipple (Ed.), *The measurement of educational products.* The Seventeenth Yearbook of the National Society for the Study of Education, Part 2. Bloomington, IL: Public School, 1918.

Tyler, R.W., and White, S.H. (Eds.). *Testing, teaching, and learning.* Washington, DC: U.S. Department of Health, Education and Welfare and National Institute of Education, 1979.

Tyler, R.W., and White, S.H. Chairman's preface, in R.W. Tyler and S.H. White (Eds.), *Testing, teaching and learning.* Washington, DC: U.S. Department of Health, Education and Welfare and National Institute of Education, 1979.

Urry, V.W. Tailored testing: A successful application of latent trait theory. *Journal of Educational Measurement,* 1977, *14*, 181-196.

2
Assessing reading comprehension: A research perspective

W ithin the community of reading researchers, theorists, and practitioners there exists very little agreement concerning any single aspect of the reading process. Controversy exists—about measurement, about the relevance of subskills, about developmental and related cognitive issues, about the adequacy of research paradigms, and about instruction. However, a single proposition has emerged within the past decade on which most reading professionals agree: The purpose of reading is comprehension.

Since the ready acceptance of such a notion depends to a large extent on one's definition of comprehension, even this statement is not without controversy. Some equate reading with the process of comprehension while others suggest it is the product of a hierarchy of lesser (but still vital) reading strategies. Yet even with this definitional penumbra it is clear that the profession has come to appreciate the central role of comprehension in the reading process. Evidence for this assertion lies in the quantity of comprehension research conducted and published during the past fifteen years. Understanding and supporting readers' comprehension of disparate texts has become a priority.

Definitional problems with respect to reading comprehension are vital issues in the assessment of reading comprehension. Virtually no one involved in reading research during the past decade or so underestimates the complexity of measuring comprehension. We no longer have the luxury of perceiving comprehension as one among an array of subskills, all of which can be accurately assessed within a uniform metric. Fortunately or unfortunately, we know too much about the interactive nature of readers and texts to attempt to provide simplistic answers. But do we know enough?

The question is moot. Political considerations require assessment, and educators must respond within reasonable limits. While a variety of assessment alternatives exists, it is clear that most autonomous educational units prefer cost effective methods of assessment. Thus the demand for the more "quick and dirty" alternatives perpetuates the assessment of processes and subprocesses considered by most reading professionals to be something less than the total process of reading comprehension. Still, important issues must be raised. Most of the potent issues in assessing comprehension have been with us for some time, as the history of reading comprehension assessment reveals.

Comprehension assessment: A brief historical perspective

A brief historical review of reading comprehension assessment suggests that educators, researchers, and test makers have attempted to find more valid and useful ways of assessing reading. Reading assessment is as old as the first mother or teacher who questioned and observed a child reading. The recent emphasis on the potential value of informal assessment in the classroom reminds us that formal testing is but one type of assessment and that to equate it with total assessment would be to adopt an unfortunately narrow perspective.

A limited outlook is promoted by the fact that the history of reading tests is more easily specified. However, although such a review covers only part of the picture, it does illustrate that the assessment issues brought into focus by recent research are not entirely new.

In 1913 Pintner reported a study which compared the oral and silent reading comprehension of fourth grade pupils. Pintner's method of measurement was to ask each child to read a passage and write down as much of it as could be remembered without looking back. Today some researchers continue to stress the necessity of understanding the relationship between short term memory and reading comprehension. Pintner's reproduction method, for example, is similar to the Silent Reading subtest of the Durrell Analysis of Reading Difficulty (1978) in which examinees read and then recite orally from memory. It is also closely related to the comprehension assessment of reading miscue analysis techniques (Goodman & Burke, 1972; Goodman & Burke, 1968, 1973) and the recent work of Harste, Burke, and Woodward (1981, 1983). The early emphasis on assessing the recall of what has been read is emphasized by Brown (1914), who discussed both the quantity and quality of reproduction as key factors in reading measurement.

Interestingly, the first published reading test, the Standardized Reading Paragraphs (Gray, 1915), contained no specific measure of reading comprehension. The Kansas Silent Reading Test (Kelly, 1916) appears to be the first test to attempt to assess reading comprehension. That test was not unlike current group verbal intelligence tests; even today some reading tests still bear a strong resemblance to so-called aptitude measures.

Four early reading comprehension tests were the Courtis Silent Reading Test, Monroe's Standardized Silent Reading Test, the Haggerty Reading Examination, and the Chapman Reading Comprehension Test. The Courtis test (n.d.) was timed; pupils were allowed three minutes to read as much as they could of a two page story. Then they were given five minutes to reread the passage broken into paragraphs, each followed by five yes/no questions.

Monroe's test (1919) was also timed. The examinee had four minutes to read a series of paragraphs. Five words appeared after each paragraph, and the examinee was instructed to underline the word that answered a question. The Speed and Accuracy subtest of the Gates-MacGinitie Reading Test (1964) employed a similar technique.

The Haggerty test (1920) used a vocabulary test, yes/no, and true/false questions to test sentence and paragraph comprehension. The Chapman test (1920) had the examinee read paragraphs to find and cross out a word which spoiled its meaning. The Gates-MacGinitie (1964) and the Stanford Achievement Test: High School Reading Test (Gardner, et al., 1965) used a technique reminiscent of Haggerty's by asking the examinee to select one word from four to finish blanks in sentences. The modified cloze technique of the Degrees of Reading Power test (American College Board, 1980) offers the examinee four choices for filling a blank in text scaled to actual reading materials used in instruction.

A key criterion mentioned by Brown (1914) but missing in early instruments was "quality of reading." Depending on how quality is defined, one might ask if it is found in today's comprehension measures. Many current instruments do test inferencing as a higher level skill requiring closer reading, but none has yet incorporated the reader's purpose for reading and no one has devised a way of determining how what is read is put to use afterward. Surely one's purpose for reading affects the quality of reading; most reading specialists now agree that using what one reads is a vital step in comprehension.

Earlier definitions of reading comprehension as a "thought-getting" process tended to emphasize literal recall. Buros (1938) noted that Joseph C. Dewey, in reviewing the 1934 Progressive Reading Tests, argued that although the test's authors claimed to measure interpretation and inference, the questions that attempted this were actually testing literal comprehension. In the same Buros volume, Spencer Shank had a similar criticism of the 1934 Traxler Silent Reading Test. Johnston (1981), however, argues that much of what we have considered literal comprehension could, in fact, be categorized as inferential.

Early reviews from Buros' *Nineteen Thirty-Eight Mental Measurements Yearbook* deal with other issues not yet resolved. In reviewing the 1931 Metropolitan Achievement Tests (Reading), Dewey praised that instrument's attempt to measure inference drawing, but also questioned whether portions of the tests did not measure intelligence in lieu of reading. Still a concern, this question has led to a few proposals that attempt to factor reasoning out of reading assessment (e.g., Royer & Cunningham, 1978; Tuinman, 1974).

Reviewing the Progressive Reading Tests, Ivan A. Brooker (in Buros, 1938) suggested that some items could be answered without relying on the passage. Likewise in Buros' *Sixth Mental Measurements Yearbook* (1965), Clarence Derrick claimed to be able to answer eight of nine questions on the Survey of Reading Achievement (1959) without looking at the passage. This concern about the passage-dependence of items is still prevalent today, and will be treated in more detail at a later point in this chapter.

The ongoing need to arrive at a dependable definition of comprehension was succinctly articulated in the 1965 Buros Yearbook by Lohnes in his review of the Sequential Tests of Educational Progress: Reading (1963):

> It is admitted that the tests measure a complex set of reading skills, but no evidence is forthcoming to support the contention that the chosen "five major reading-for-comprehension skills" are major components of reading ability, or that the STEP reading tests do actually "weight these five kinds of skills approximately equally." All we know is that a committee of authorities agreed on this breakdown of reading into component skills. With due respect for the committee, it would be highly desirable to have their judgments tested and supported by empirical evidence. (Lohnes, cited in Buros, 1938, p. 327)

Lohnes' comments exemplify the continuous concern that motivates the search for the elusive answer to the question, "What constitutes reading comprehension?" Without a definitive answer, the quest has led to the development of a multitude of reading comprehension measures which offer a variety of subskill mixes in attempts to subsume comprehension.

The period from the 1940s through the decade in which Lohnes wrote his review could be labeled the "era of subskills proliferation." The intent seemed to be to identify with the right set of skills in a persuasive balance that would somehow capture general endorsement. Across many of these tests, however, single subskills were labeled differently. Furthermore, some tests had similar labels for the same skill, but tested it with different types of questions.

A list of all of the subtests from available reading tests that appear to measure comprehension referenced over fifty different designations (Lennon, 1970). The tests that used these different labels were developed as if there were, in fact, a well known theoretical construct called "reading comprehension." This kind of assumption has fired the bulk of criticism of standardized tests' ability to diagnose—a concern which has generated much of the research for a universally acceptable model of comprehension. The recognition of this need, however, has long been jelling in educational circles around the writings of scholars like Bormuth (1970, 1973) and Schlesinger and Weiser (1970).

The sophistication of test developers and test reviewers has increased tremendously. They have become increasingly alert to the need to ask more probing questions about the theoretical constructs of reading comprehension and reading comprehension assessment. They have been able to provide more sophisticated technical data on reliability, validity, and norming procedures. The editing of test items also has improved dramatically. But the essential issue that obfuscates valid reading assessment remains the same. We are still asking, "What is reading comprehension?"

Parallel with this fundamental issue is understanding how we can measure what we believe are the specific behaviors indicative of the comprehension process. While research has yet to produce a definitive answer to the theoretical complexity of reading comprehension, it has informed effectively on certain aspects of the process and is now suggesting practical ways to tailor assessment to what we currently know about the comprehension process.

Various assessment approaches measure different behaviors

The information explosion in comprehension research has yielded a number of promising techniques for assessing a student's ability to comprehend a given passage. It should be noted again, however, that definitional problems still limit that assessment; no one has yet come close to developing an adequate performance based definition of reading comprehension. Almost everyone has an opinion, but empirical justification for these opinions does not point toward consensus.

There are a variety of approaches to measuring reading comprehension and each seems to have its followers as well as its critics. The major problem with reading comprehension tests is the use of test results. The misuse of tests arises primarily from the uncritical selection and use of tests, as well as from the general acceptance of test results as if the scores represented all that can be known, or needs to be known, about reading comprehension ability.

All reading comprehension tests are essentially nothing more than samples of indicators of "real reading." It is important to emphasize that point. Tests are not samples of actual reading; rather, they are merely indices of actual reading. Some tests seem to approximate more closely natural encounters with text than do others. All tests, however, rely on relatively limited samples of behavior gathered under limited conditions.

The problems with measuring reading comprehension are noted throughout this volume, but it is worth emphasizing here just a few of the more significant ones. There is, for example, the question of generalizability. On what basis can we assume that performance on one of these tests is an index of performance for other reading situations? Situations like those encountered during a reading comprehension test rarely exist outside of school. Is it possible that readers approach short narrative or expository passages quite differently than they do longer, naturally occurring texts? Decades of research have suggested that the answer is a vehement, "yes". Yet the tendency is still to equate achievement test performance with, say, the reading of a novel.

The ubiquity of comprehension tests suggests a sort of validity and, indeed, many members of the educational community, as well as the general public, have considerable faith in their particular test choices. Whether this faith is warranted is a question worthy of consideration; yet it is clear that conventional practice accepts the results of reading comprehension tests (regardless of the format for the test) as a valid index of a child's, a community's, even a nation's ability to comprehend.

Multiple choice tests

The most common form of comprehension assessment is the format which provides a relatively short reading passage followed by several multiple choice questions designed to assess reading comprehension. This format predominates on commercially developed reading comprehension tests as well as those developed as part of statewide minimum competency assessment. On most of these tests, examinees can look back at the text.

One needs to consider the history of mental measurement to understand fully the forces that have led to the general acceptance of the multiple choice format, but it seems safe to say that a number of historical, economic, and social forces have conspired to influence its prevalence in reading measurement (see especially Fleck, 1979; Gould, 1981). The passage/multiple choice technique appears to produce a clean, neat, scientific score, an attraction not easily overcome. There are serious limitations and problems with the "read the passage and choose the best answer to these questions" format, but it seems we are willing to ignore many of these problems for the sake of efficiency. Our awareness of the problem appears to have diminished as multiple choice tests of reading comprehension have gained ascendancy in our culture.

One of the major problems with the multiple choice format is the insistence on a single correct answer. Recent research has emphasized that reading comprehension is a constructive process and that meaning is as dependent on the reader as it is on the text. Thus, the single correct answer format provides a dilemma for authors of multiple choice tests. Even if a particular answer is agreed upon by a committee of experts, the possibility exists that a creative reader is capable of going beyond conventional implications of the passage to infer a response that is incorrect when measured against the single response anticipated and allowed. Developing a multiple choice test is, therefore, a difficult and tricky task. Anyone who has ever participated in the rather painstaking development of a good multiple choice test appreciates how difficult it is.

The efficiency of using standardized multiple choice tests to measure reading comprehension has made them an economic reality. They are perceived to be the most economical method of determining how well schools are doing their job. The limitations of the multiple choice measurement mode are often lost in a shuffle of debate arising from the data they produce.

The problems with multiple choice reading comprehension tests are not, however, merely a question of how the scores are reported and interpreted, although these are profound problems that affect great segments of society. The discussion here is aimed at the limitations of these tests. If multiple choice reading comprehension tests are used, it is essential that test consumers understand these limitations as they try to understand the reading abilities of those to whom they administer the tests.

The situation with the limitations of multiple choice tests is not unlike that in current reading research where a modest number of statistical tests are used to determine significance within, between, and among groups. All researchers learn the formal assumptions underlying each of these tests, some of which are exceedingly robust. When it comes time to face the practicalities of research, though, these constraints take a back seat to "getting the study done" and the assumptions are cavalierly violated.

Many of the problems with multiple choice tests are technical ones, having to do with notions of probability, statistics, and item generation. These problems are all widely known and are, or have been, much discussed in the professional literature (see especially Houts, 1977). Even larger questions loom, however, and these are generally questions of theory. Most multiple choice reading comprehension tests reflect grossly inadequate theories of cognition, language, and learning. Certainly, they reflect outdated theories of the reading process. As noted previously, there is no consensus regarding a definition of comprehension, but there are few reading theorists today who would condone a definition of comprehension as word based, a function of short term recall, or unidimensional.

On another level, the theories reflected in these tests are inadequate simply because they reflect what has become the conventional wisdom. Consider virtually any multiple choice test today and your most immediate interpretation might be that comprehension is clearly comprised of skills such as literal comprehension, and making inferences. Obviously, tests which fulfill this description reflect some aspect of subskill stratification theory and levels of comprehension. For measurement purposes, that is a very convenient theory since it lends itself well to quantification and, subsequently, to summative accountability (see Chapter 1).

It may be worth noting that it is not necessarily the content of these tests that flies in the face of advances in theory. It is the *form*. To use a multiple choice test of reading comprehension is necessarily to buy into a number of specific theoretical positions including theories about how people learn, how people remember, how language and learning go together, how people read, how we can measure learning, and how we can measure language. These are not trivial issues. In many ways, they are the questions which form the basis of education; yet the ubiquity and social dependence on such tests (and the theories embodied in the tests) suggest that these questions are settled. The conventional wisdom is so strong that making significant headway against these unexamined assumptions is almost impossible.

Cloze testing: An attempt to use context

Depending upon the source, the cloze procedure, which requires the examinee to supply words deleted from a text, should now be celebrating an anniversary of somewhere between fifty and one hundred years. Cloze has been with us for quite some time now; yet we are still trying to ascertain its position in the hierarchy of comprehension assessment.

The cloze technique has been used as a readability device (Bormuth, 1963, 1969), as a teaching technique (Bloomer, 1966), and as a test of reading comprehension. It has run into serious, albeit interesting, problems in each of these domains. Its problems as an assessment device are formidable, not the least of which is that we are unclear about exactly what it is that cloze measures. It appears that responses to cloze are more or less predictable depending on the specific content area, or at least the domain of inquiry. For example, a passage on marine biology, after having been deleted according to a prescribed pattern, is much more likely to require words from a common linguistic pool of responses than is, say, a 500 word passage from a travelogue.

Another problem often voiced by reading researchers is that cloze performance is clearly related to syntactic competence. This, however, should not be especially problematic in that all language systems are, of necessity, interactive. Still, it bothers some researchers to think that we may be using some sort of test of syntax as a test for comprehension since the two clearly are not isomorphic.

There is no denying that cloze performance correlates very highly with multiple choice test performance. Positive correlations of up to .90 can be found in the research literature for cloze in its "pure" form (i.e., every *nth* word deleted) as well as in its various mutations.

It is probably Bormuth's research (1968) which has done the most to influence the growing use of the cloze as an assessment of comprehension. This study, built on previous research (1963, 1967), indicates that cloze is an acceptable indicator of comprehension. The major argument for the use of the cloze technique is the existence of high reliability and correlational validity coefficients when using conventional multiple choice methods of test construction as the criterion. In other words, the appeal of cloze appears to have much to do with the possibility that it is cheaper and easier to construct, and it provides roughly the same assessment as multiple choice tests.

While Bormuth contended that comprehension is the factor that accounts for most of the variance in cloze test scores, Weaver and Kingston

(1963) held that comprehension is not the significant factor in cloze score variance. They suggest that cloze draws on a "special ability or aptitude for utilizing redundancy in a passage" and is "independent of verbal ability." Coleman and Miller (1968) reached somewhat the same conclusion when they suggested that cloze scores were heavily dependent upon the influence of the surrounding words on the excised word.

Rankin (1965) asserted that the kinds of words deleted were important, while Carroll (1972) concluded that syntax, rather than semantics, was the significant factor in cloze performance. He thought that cloze, as it is generally used, was "too crude" to measure comprehension. Horton's factor analytic study (1973), on the other hand, concluded that cloze tended to measure "the subject's ability to deal with the relationships among words and ideas."

Among the first to suggest another kind of problem with cloze was Page (1976), who perceived students' anxiety in responding to a "mutilated" passage they had never before encountered. As a consequence, he introduced the post oral reading cloze test and demonstrated its significant and persistent relationship not only to multiple choice comprehension test scores, but also its negative and persistent correlation to certain kinds of oral reading miscues. Page's results were affirmed in a number of studies, including those by Ganier (1976) and Carey (1978).

It seems safe to assume, then, that there exists a common measurement factor (in terms of shared variance) between cloze and conventional multiple choice tests of comprehension. This places the measurement specialist into somewhat of a quandry. Since we know there are problems with multiple choice tests, do we want to employ a device which correlates very highly with those tests? The issue gets more complicated if the equation is lengthened. For example, if we add another index of comprehension, this time from the miscue literature, that score too suggests some overlap with multiple choice tests. However, it also suggests some measurement overlap with cloze. There is some common ground among the three indicators, but is it the shared variance among all three that represents comprehension, or is comprehension only part of the overlap, or perhaps even none of it? (See Chapter 5).

The most rational approach to this problem is never to use only a cloze test as an index of comprehension—just as one should not rely only on multiple choice tests. It seems likely that some aspect of cloze performance taps into some part of comprehension performance, but to make decisions based on the use of cloze only is to make a less than informed choice.

Oral reading as an indication of reading comprehension

Oral reading has a long and influential history in American education. From round robin oral reading instruction to the research of Kenneth Goodman, much has been written about this practice as an artifact of the teaching and testing of reading. Today there are relatively few programs that are primarily assessed through oral reading, the most popular reason being that it requires too much time and money.

The limitations of oral reading as an index of comprehension are obvious and, in some ways, confusing; there are significant differences between oral and silent reading. Much careful research has been conducted on the relationships between oral and silent reading, and the question has yet to be settled. Goodman (1968) maintains there are no good alternatives; that oral reading miscues are our only "windows on the reading process." He has amassed a great deal of data to lend credibility to his claim (see especially Goodman & Burke, 1973).

Others have felt much the same as Goodman, although they did not necessarily espouse similar perceptions of the relationship between language and cognition. Gray (1915), for example, developed a series of oral reading tests, as have many other well known reading researchers and educators.

It is likely, however, that Goodman would balk at the notion that the miscue technique is a "test." He has used it primarily as a research device. Nor is it likely that the authors of the more popular version of the miscue technique, the Reading Miscue Inventory (Goodman & Burke, 1972), would be pleased to have their instrument labeled a test. Instead, the RMI is viewed by its developers as a general diagnostic and assessment device which provides a general profile of a reader's strengths and weaknesses, but which is not reducible to a single numerical index. The results of the RMI, or its parent the Goodman Taxonomy of Oral Reading Miscues, reveal patterns.

Miscue devices should not be confused with informal reading inventories which are derived from quite disparate ideas about the reading process. One of the most popular, Silvaroli's Classroom Reading Inventory (1976), was based upon notions of practicality in administration, but as Powell (1969) pointed out, it lacked any authoritative theoretical framework. Since it was not normed, it tended to lack both psychometric and theoretical rigor.

A number of researchers have also questioned the theoretical and methodological grounds of the RMI (Leu, 1981). But these kinds of criticisms have often misapprehended some of the basic psycholinguistic assumptions of the model underlying the instrument, or have been unaware of the relatively large body of supporting empirical data (Page, 1977).

While there is little doubt that oral reading will continue its history as a popular instructional strategy, there is some question as to its future in reading assessment. The erroneous tendency of the public to rely on standardized achievement test scores as indicators of specific abilities suggests that the popularity of oral reading assessment will only decline; currently, no standardized achievement test includes an oral reading index as part of a reading subscore.

Recall as a measure of reading comprehension

One of the perennial problems in reading comprehension measurement has been the confounding of comprehension and recall. Virtually everyone assumes that one need not have understood something to remember it, even when one has read it. Naturally, this ability diminishes with an increase in the length of the text. Still, verbal learning research has aptly demonstrated the formidable ability of human beings to remember nonsense. It is the reverse question that garners the interest and poses problems in psycholinguistic studies: If students have understood something, is it necessarily the case that they will remember it? It is obviously more likely that recall and comprehension support one another, and this too has been well researched. The problem for reading educators lies in the tendency to equate these two aspects of human information processing.

In fact, we might now add *process* to the grand triumvirate noted at the outset of this chapter. Everyone is in favor of process because it provides a focus for instruction. Product, on the other hand, seems to delimit instruction to a narrow set of goals. In like manner, everyone is in favor of goals rather than quotas. Still, when it comes time to respond to external demands, we have to admit that our ability to study the process of reading has not kept up with our good intentions, and we are forced to resort to the product as an index of the process.

Assessment controversies have practical significance for comprehension assessment

The implications of the various controversies underlying methods of comprehension assessment are of practical significance and must not be passed over lightly. The fundamental assumptions we bring to the measurement of comprehension have important ramifications for the design and implementation of instructional programs and for the types of educational environments to which large numbers of children are likely to be subjected.

The issues of prior knowledge and passage dependence

Comprehension tests appear to measure something like general ability, although this is clearly related to vocabulary (Coleman, 1971) and, perhaps more importantly, to IQ (Tuinman, 1979). If, however, we control statistically for ability and IQ, it can be shown that a large proportion of the remaining variance in comprehension can be attributed to the prior knowledge of the individual (Johnston & Pearson, 1982). This issue of prior knowledge is perhaps the most significant question to come out of the reading information explosion of recent years. How can prior knowledge be controlled or accounted for?

Johnston (1981, 1984) suggests that there are two alternatives to dealing with the problem of determining the influence of reader background, which also could be taken to mean the control of the *passage dependence* of reading comprehension test items. One alternative is to develop tests that are less dependent on prior knowledge, and another is to try to separate the influence of reader background from "raw comprehension ability" (Johnston, 1984). Johnston's suggestion is to eliminate the bias factor of background knowledge for individuals who are being assessed since it is at the level of an individual student, rather than a group of students, that the effect of background knowledge operates. Johnston's procedure would be to administer content knowledge tests (related to the content of a passage) prior to the administration of a reading comprehension test. The reading comprehension score would then be "adjusted" depending on the examinee's prior knowledge score on the content test.

While Johnston's procedure does seem to remove the influence due to prior knowledge, it seems to result in a test score that is biased in a different way. By removing the effects of background knowledge, Johnston denies that reading ability is the result of a combination of factors, including the reader's background knowledge.

An attempt to develop more passage dependent tests was proposed fifteen years ago by Schlesinger and Weiser (1970). They called for the development of reading comprehension tests by determining the explicit relationship of a test's items to the text on which they are based. They recommended a test development procedure referred to as *facet design*, which determined whether a reading comprehension test item required information primarily from the text or from the reader's background knowledge.

The passage dependence of reading comprehension test items may also depend on the particular aspect of reading comprehension being assessed. Literal comprehension test items seem to be tied more closely to the content of passages. On the other hand, both inferential and evaluative items seem to call on the reader to make greater use of prior knowledge.

Research has yet to establish the exact relationship between types of items and the aspect of comprehension they probe. Schreiner and Shannon (1980) found that multiple choice response items aided test takers in the literal recall of a reading selection's content more than just the question part of multiple choice, incomplete sentence questions. Multiple choice questions proved to be more helpful in stimulating literal comprehension than did free recall responses, but Schreiner and Shannon were not able to determine those aspects of the multiple choice questions that seemed to cue the readers to the content of the passages.

Other problems that limit the passage dependence of multiple choice test items may be solved by more careful item writing (Hanna and Oaster, 1980). For example, common reading comprehension test writing problems include writing the options for multiple choice items so they all provide feasible answers in terms of the passage content; or writing a test item so that the syntax of the correct response provides the possibilty of a student picking the right answer on the basis of how well the correct answer qualifies itself within the test item itself.

Making sure that the correct option is not the longest of the options also helps to eliminate the possibility of testwise students selecting that choice even when they are unsure of the correct answer. Popham and Husek's charge(1969) about "spurious factors" in norm referenced tests suggests the possibility of manipulating the appeal of the correct option in a variety of ways to produce test responses which will provide the maximum score variation that is the essence of developing a norm referenced test.

A testing technique that, at the surface, seems to guarantee passage dependence is cloze assessment. Those who disagree that cloze assessment develops test items that are more passage dependent argue that completing a cloze passage is just as dependent on a reader's background knowledge and language development as is performance on any multiple choice test.

Proponents of cloze contend that because words in text represent interrelated concepts, the ability of an examinee to complete a cloze task successfully is a valid measure of reading comprehension. Research on the cloze procedure has established that successfully completing 40 percent of the blanks in a passage in which every fifth word has been deleted is equivalent to achieving 75 percent comprehension on the content of the same passage (Bormuth, 1968; Duffelmeyer, 1983; Rankin & Culhane, 1969). Bormuth (1971) found that the percentage of correct cloze responses is somewhat higher with elementary grade level examinees than with secondary grade level examinees; however, Carver (1976) concluded just the opposite from his study. Even though the cloze technique seems to emphasize passage dependence some researchers have found it to be more reliable than multiple choice tests (Panackal & Heft, 1978), and others have found it to be less subject to score deteriorations on repeated test administrations (Anderson, 1974).

One test which has gained some general use and which uses a modified cloze item mode is the *Degrees of Reading Power* (DRP) (1980). The DRP is a criterion referenced reading test which assesses "a student's ability to process and understand nonfiction English prose passages written at various levels of difficulty or readability." The item format includes passages in which selected words have been omitted and replaced by blank lines. The examinee is to select from several choices the word which best completes the sentence.

The key concern related to passage dependence is how likely a student is to know the answer to an item from background knowledge. As Tuinman (1971) points out, because of the varying individual "levels of sophistication" of different readers, determining this is no easy task. The concern for passage dependence is, in turn, related to a concern about how "fair" the content of a test is in its familiarity across the different experiences of a broad spectrum of test takers from varying rural, urban, racial, educational, and socioeconomic backgrounds.

Since determining passage dependency is a matter of concern, it must be remembered that it is a concern that affects all types of reading comprehension items. Duffelmeyer (1980) found that the issue is as pertinent to free response type items as it is to multiple choice type items. The passage dependency research, however, has focused almost exclusively on multiple choice items. Duffelmeyer asserts that items based on factual information are somewhat more likely to be passage dependent than those requiring the examinee to infer responses. On the one hand, this position seems reasonable since involving background in reading comprehension is a sequencing act. At the same time, this suggests that passage information is also involved, even when background information is impacting on the examinee's response. Yet one might also expect background information to more readily allow a reader to get purely factual items correct without any reliance on the passage. Of course, this would depend on whether the factual items are based on information that might generally be known, or whether the information is relevant only to the particular reading selection on the test.

In analyzing the passage dependence of reading comprehension items on informal reading inventories, Marr and Lyon (1981) found that the item types that were least passage dependent were those that focused on general information in the text, those that tested vocabulary meaning, and those that called for affective responses. In an attempt to determine how much reader background knowledge affects the scores on a standardized test, Johns (1978) found that a group of fourth and fifth graders scored significantly above the chance level when given test items without the passages. Reading the passages before answering the items improved raw scores by 4 to 10 points. Johns noted that careful item development should help assure the passage dependence of items.

Another issue in the debate over passage dependence is whether completion of the test item actually constitutes a reading task by itself. In order to answer an item correctly, even without reading the passage, an examinee has to read the test item and the accompanying answer choices (in the case of multiple choice items) and then select the most appropriate answer. It seems reasonable to assume that examinees would not just read a question and select the best choice even when their background knowledge leads them to favor a particular answer. It also seems that many examinees would at least skim the passage to verify a particular answer choice. In any event, it may be most useful to consider the reading passages and the test items based on those passages as a total test task. That is, the passages and the items form a reading unit to which the examinee must respond.

Some interesting formulae have been developed to try to determine the passage dependence or independence of reading test items (Pyrczak, 1975 Tuinman, 1974). Into these Hanna and Oaster (1978) incorporated the consideration of reading difficulty. Applying the Hanna and Oaster method, Entin and Klare (1980) examined extant test data and found that items based on more difficult passages on the Nelson-Denny were less passage dependent than those based on easier passages; thus the former tended to contribute to a score reflecting "prior knowledge." Klare (1976) reported that prior knowledge tends to eliminate the effect of passage difficulty on reading test scores.

Study of the passage dependency of reading comprehension test items is motivated, of course, by the necessity to develop more valid tests. In the attempt to distinguish between the amount of knowledge a reader gains from reading a particular text and knowledge the reader brings to the text, passage dependency research needs to incorporate more thoroughly the theory and research which are helping to define and delineate the reading comprehension process. This would direct the focus of research not only to the strategies a reader uses in answering questions without the aid of a passage, but also to those strategies involved in actual comprehension, which seem to involve checking (affirming, contradicting, or evolving) and filing of ideas gained in reading in some memory or understanding scheme in the brain. As Johnston (1981) has argued, the developing theories of reading comprehension clearly indicate that such processing is so intricately dependent on reader background and experience that worrying about factoring those basic contributing aspects out of reading comprehension may be a moot issue.

In calling for more study and categorization of inferencing, Flood and Lapp (1978) acknowledged that background information is essential to drawing inferences; and Hanna and Oaster (1980) argued that passage dependence does not necessarily invalidate a test. Prentice and Peterson (1977) saw the need for passage dependency research to help develop a psycholinguistic definition of reading comprehension in which comprehension is the construction of meaning, not merely a passive discovery of meaning in text. Increasing the passage dependency, they suggested, might inhibit information processing strategies that are at the heart of the behavior being measured.

On the other hand, it is difficult to see how the evolving explanations of the role of reader background in comprehension can justify test items that cue on a single specific fact in a passage and force the student to draw on background in order to answer the item correctly. Some tests, for example, include with each passage at least one item similar to the following example:

> After a paragraph stating that the heat in a person's home went off in the winter, a completion item would require the examinee to tell why it went off. A set of possible completions based on experience (the fuel tank went dry, the fan in the furnace broke, etc.) would be acceptable as correct, but nothing in the paragraph would imply an exact cause.

Good item writing can assure that the examinee has comprehended how a concept, fact, or feeling is operating in or suggested by the particular text on which it is supposed to be based, even with the background knowledge that may operate in answering an item. Factual items can be made more passage dependent by coupling the particular fact that denotes the correct answer to some other fact that is stated in the text and is repeated in the item stem.

Despite Duffelmeyer's finding (1980) that factual based items tend to be more passage dependent than ones that require inferencing, probably it is more difficult to establish the absolute passage dependence for literal factual items. A stem that begins, "The writer says that..." may force verification within the passage, but if examinees know the literal fact, they will not have to read the text to get it correct. This point suggests a defense for tests that are balanced toward items requiring inferencing. Axelrod's study (1973) used symbols instead of words in passages. He concluded that inferencing items can be written so that students cannot answer them without knowing the meaning of key words that occur in the text.

Why should concern for the source of a reader's correct answer to a comprehension question be greater than for a vocabulary item based on a passage? Vocabulary items, in which the options are all possible meanings of the word, force the reader to read the word in the passage to see which meaning applies. This, however, tends to force an emphasis on relatively common words. Suppose a difficult and uncommon word is a key concept in a passage. It is reasonable to determine if the reader knows its meaning as a main idea of the passage. Does it make any difference if the examinee used the text to determine the appropriate meaning for the word or if the word was known from previous experiences—most likely reading experiences? Perhaps it is unreasonable to argue that drawing on experience in answering a reading test item contaminates the results more than does comprehending a passage by drawing on general vocabulary knowledge. If reading vocabulary is developed as an understanding of concepts from life experience that includes prior language experiences, then vocabulary knowledge and general background knowledge are, in effect, one and the same.

There is certainly a limit as to how far a reading test passage and its items can go in forcing the implementation of reader background in the reading process. Langer (1986) analyzed the lexical, syntactic, and rhetorical structures used in norm referenced reading comprehension tests. Her analysis supports the intricate role of background in comprehending reading test passages and the accompanying items. Langer argues that the understanding and knowledge a reader brings to a test ought not to be upset by seemingly illogical information.

Langer's study provokes serious consideration of the possibility that poor writing may be one influence that limits passage dependency, and suggests that readers who answer test items incorrectly may "never have the opportunity to demonstrate their understanding of the passage" because the cognitive demands of the test are unreasonable (p. 15). A "considerate" test, Langer argues, does not pack too many ideas into the passage even if, as the analysis found, such density attempts to simplify many of the concepts with techniques such as familiar analogies.

Langer also criticized 1) the tendency of passages to be "unknitted," that is, poorly organized and written; 2) items that force readers to hypothesize or make assumptions that are not corroborated in the passage; 3) passages that pretend to be of a particular genre but do not actually abide by the characteristics of that genre; and 4) passages that similarly contradict the reader's background by making generally unbelievable assertions that go unacknowledged as contrary to what is generally accepted as fact. Langer argued that "the strategies required for success on...such items do not bear a strong relation to the processes involved in constructive meaning making" (p. 33).

Along with a reader's background, it is the reader's purpose for reading that engages the necessary text. This same need assures that readers will be motivated to use all the process ability at their command (McConkie, Rayner, & Wilson, 1973).

The recognized importance of reader purpose obligates the test maker to determine ways to frame reading assessment passages with clear purposes (Rayford, 1984; Reynolds & Anderson, 1980; Rowe & Rayford, 1984). Readers' ability to comprehend is greatly enhanced or limited by their ability to grasp how the text at hand responds to their immediate needs. This awareness should have more real life relevance than "I better do my best on this test"—a point which relates instead to concerns about the impact of test environments (Spiro, 1977, 1980; Steffenson and Guthrie, 1980).

The Metropolitan Achievement Test (1985) attempts to relate a reader's background knowledge to a reading test passage by providing a "purpose question" at the beginning of each reading selection. The purpose question is intended to activate a reader's background knowledge prior to the reading of a test passage. The questions that follow the passage are related, either directly or indirectly, to the purpose question at the beginning. Thus, purpose questions "get readers into" the content and structure of the passage, and provide broad goals by drawing attention to the main purpose for reading the passage and for answering the questions which follow.

This type of prepassage questioning has been the focus of several recent investigations (Rowe & Rayford, 1984; Swenson & Kulhavy, 1974;

Wilhite, 1983) seeking to validate the use of purpose questions as adjunct aids to facilitate the reader's construction of meaning. These researchers have found that, in general, lower elementary grade level students respond somewhat differently than do secondary and college level students, and that more research is needed to determine the feasibility of purpose questions as an appropriate adjunct aid. If purpose questions do help the construction of reading tests which acknowledge the importance of reader background in comprehension, then research must begin to delineate specific taxonomies for achieving valid purpose question/passage relationships. If this is not achieved, the use of purpose questions will do little, if anything, to further the current state of the art of reading comprehension assessment.

The issue of test bias

One of the most prevalent concerns about the effect of reader background on test results is whether standardized instruments are fair to groups whose cultural experience is distinctively different from that reflected in the content of reading test passages. Data from the broad administration of standardized tests has tended to yield lower scores for urban centered and black populations and for readers for whom English is not a first language.

It is obvious that such testing can be politically self-defeating. Levine (1976) charges that this use of tests is politically motivated by controls outside the minority populations' immediate environments. Whether this is true or not, the issue of test use is as fundamental to the solution of this problem as is the attempt to control background relevance in assessing the reading ability of such populations. Tests should be selected on the basis of valid information needs that are clearly defined and related to reasonable and accessible instructional goals for a particular population.

Equally important, the issue relates to misuses of the resulting data. For example, when might a school with a high percentage of Mexican-American children want to administer a reading test designed for the mainstream school population of the country? The answer ought to be obvious (but from the proliferated misuse of such data apparently is not): Only when the educators need to know how individual students would succeed in a curriculum that adequately matches the test.

Unfortunately, many students for whom English is not a first language are forced to cope with such curricula. The test could indicate appropriate levels of difficulty from which instructional materials written in English should be selected. Conversely, the data would tell very little about the child's reading potential, and the test's overall demands might be so frustrating for individual children that any indications it gave for specific instruction would be overwhelmed by the children's inability to cope with the items.

The only possible use that can be contrived for the schoolwide use of such test results might be to convince a community that bilingual education and/or special funding ought to be installed or retained. Otherwise, the public use of such test data is as suspect as Levine (1976) contends—a self-defeating exercise insensitive to the reality of the students' situation and inviting to the simplistic idiocy of critics who may be innocently incapable of understanding what the data mean (or more importantly, do not mean).

One of the concerns about test bias relates to what has been loosely called "genre" knowledge. In responding to assessment materials in standard English, lexical and other language "grammars" or "scripts" are assumed to be less available to a reader for whom English is a second language or to a reader who communicates in a distinct dialect. In addition, all the handicaps discussed here for special populations would limit a reader's ability to build a script for tests, "test-wiseness" (Powers & Sahers, 1981).

Test tailoring is being recommended for special populations, and at face value it appears to make a great deal of sense. Special tests could be designed to assure a background fit for particular groups of examinees. But, the development of tests tailored to special populations would probably need to be subsidized, for the careful development of these tests is expensive. This problem suggests that the development of informal assessment techniques for teaching reading to specific populations is an attractive solution. Since the purpose of the tailoring would be to yield information useful to instruction, teacher made assessment, including trained observation, has a high potential for answering the need. The background relevance of informal assessment conducted in a specific setting is quite apt to be automatically tailored to the individual assessed. All teachers ought to be trained to make and use such assessment, and teachers of special populations should be given additional training on how to do that.

Tests tailored for specific populations would be something like the instruments with assured background relevance as suggested by Johnston (1981). They could also present the same potential measurement problems. Having assured a high degree of background involvement in the reading process assessed, one is more reliant than ever on yet unperfected technologies that can isolate and allow the valid diagnosis of subprocesses. Another requirement would be instructional materials that tend to match the background fit of the assessments.

There is a possible issue that would be unique to tailored tests as they related to, say, teaching urban black children using materials written in a black dialect. Johnston (1981) notes that if a test matches a particular background, it may not always match real life tasks. Certainly it will be more apt to relate to the real life reading demands of children growing up in a special culture relatively isolated from broader arenas. But assuming that the child may want to compete someday in American society at large, should we be gearing instruction more to the communication demands of the broader arena? If so, assessment will need to reflect that goal.

This is obviously a complex issue that necessitates further investigation. It generates a host of interesting questions: Does teaching bilingual children using instruction and materials in their first language tend to build a background of concepts and generic "scripts" faster than teaching the children using the second language? If so, will bilingual education then insure faster growth if the children are later taught in English, or does the relationship between vocabulary and stored concepts hamper the fluency of that switch?

Matching reading tests to reading instruction

While the preceding discussion reviews some of the more prominent issues underlying the construction, use, and interpretation of reading comprehension tests, there exists a host of more instructionally related concerns that merit consideration as well. Chief among these is the necessity for test consumers to understand thoroughly the relationship between their theories of instruction and the theory embodied in a particular assessment device; specifically, wise test consumers must decide which tests best assess the behaviors that are taught (see Chapters 3 and 4, this volume). The fact that no widely held performance based definition of reading comprehension currently exists exacerbates the necessity for every test user to carefully delineate the relationships between the specific behaviors that need to be assessed and the manner in which they should, or can, be assessed.

However, while it is the obligation of the test consumer to be certain there exists a satisfactory degree of theoretical consistency between reading instruction and reading comprehension assessment, it is ultimately the test maker's responsibility to make available to consumers a variety of instructionally valid and theoretically sound assessment devices. Since virtually no consensus exists among reading professionals about what reading comprehension really is, to what extent can either test consumers or test makers be held accountable? When one considers how new concepts and constructs have evolved (i.e., how the reading "thought collective" has changed) since Pinter's study (1913) comparing oral and silent reading comprehension, it is apparent that new directions in reading theory are pointing to new directions in reading comprehension assessment. The development of such "tests" as the Reading Miscue Inventory (Goodman & Burke, 1972), the use of purpose questions on tests, and test tailoring exemplify the extant parallels between reading theory and assessment. Yet some theoretical advances continue to hinder practical implementation in comprehension assessment.

The emerging descriptions of how reader background figures in the reading process suggest one dilemma to the test designer. If background is integral to reading comprehension, measuring the process ought to involve reader background. This is not an unwelcome determination, since factoring background out of reading assessment appears to be almost impossible. Yet background must be controlled so that it will not account for too much—or worse yet, an undeterminable amount—of the assessment results. This problem becomes paramount to the test maker concerned about passage dependence and the potential bias of particular tests.

The frustrating challenge in reading comprehension assessment may be to keep reader background in reasonable balance to new information that can be understood only if the reader can use other aspects of the reading process that background helps call into play. As suggested in preceding sections of this chapter, that is what many test designers have attempted to do, using editorial judgment in lieu of having a system validated by research. It seems worth examining whether assessment designed to diagnose particular aspects of reading comprehension can limit background in some way without producing text that lacks appeal, thus validity, to the reader. In the long run, validity to the reader is tantamount to instruction/assessment validity, especially with respect to the overall "fairness" of the total context of reading comprehension assessment.

Recommendations for test consumers

A brief list of recommendations for the consumer of reading comprehension tests synthesizes a number of considerations that must be addressed if the assessment itself is to have any theoretical, thus instructional, validity.

1. The necessity for assessment dictates the type of test chosen for use. Before any reading test is administered there should be a particular need demanding its results. Whether the need for test results is for group or individual diagnosis, for group progress evaluation within a single class-room or across an entire school district, or whether the results are to be used for determining graduation eligibility, such uses impinge upon the selection of particular instruments. Therefore, it is important that the goals for assessment are reflected in the information that test results provide, and that the interpretation of those results remain only in the context of assessment goals so that haphazard generalizing out of that context is not possible.

2. *The theory of reading assessment must coincide with the theory of reading instruction.* It is very important that every reading test consumer carefully explicate the theoretical orientation of a particular test so that a satisfactory degree of theoretical cohesion can be found between the reading behaviors that are taught and those that are assessed. The test user must review the test items to determine the theory of reading subsumed in the test, and then ascertain the extent to which that theory is reflected in the actual test items. Does the method of assessment (passage/multiple choice, oral reading, cloze) seem to parallel the test maker's definition of the comprehension process? Do the items themselves demonstrate that careful attention was paid to the development of a particular theoretical orientation, or do the items appear inconsistent with the accompanying theoretical perspective? An example of poor theoretical cohesion can be found when, in a particular classroom, the theory of instruction emphasizes a holistic model while the theory of assessment reflects a subskills-first-meaning-later approach (see Chapter 3).

3. *One measure reflects only one behavior.* It is never the case that the assessment of a particular reading behavior provides a context for understanding all reading behaviors, nor is it the case that an especially informative instrument provides an indication of how a reader performs under quite different circumstances. Thus it is crucial that adequate assessment be couched in the administration of a variety of assessments, especially informal diagnosis, close observation, and performance evaluation when reading more naturally occurring texts.

Needed research in reading comprehension assessment

The task of bringing reading assessment more closely in line with extant notions of the comprehension process does not, however, lie exclusively in the hands of the test consumer. Indeed, it is through continuing research that new directions in reading assessment can be determined, and it is the responsibility of all factions within the field of reading (researchers, teachers, theorists, and test makers) to prescribe the directions in which such research must embark. The following recommendations point to a few of these directions.

We need increased emphasis on analyses of existing instruments

Close analyses of assessment instruments are rare and should be encouraged. As the number of questions offered here suggests, there is a great deal to be learned from analyses of assessment instruments, especially when such analyses are crossed, as Haertel's were (1980), with extant score data.

- Do reading assessment instruments now in use distinguish between the subskills that they profess to measure?
- Do these instruments appear to distinguish key subprocesses now being defined for the reading process when such processes are overlaid on the instruments as Haertel (1980) did?
- How are any of these overlaid subprocesses actually labeled and defined on the instruments? What percentage of existing items can be overlaid with newly defined subprocess designations? How do current designations and definitions relate to emerging taxonomies of reasoning and inferencing?
- What inferences, if any, are now required in responding to items now classified as "literal comprehension"? How frequently do details highlighted by literal items figure in making inferences required by adjoining items? How related are the details highlighted by literal items to any reader purpose that is assigned or that can be assumed for the passage on which the items are based?
- How can items that profess to require synthesizing or evaluation be described? How do they relate to any purpose that is assigned or can be assumed for reading the passage they are based on? Can they be reclassified under any emerging subprocess taxonomies?
- How well do the instruments reflect the reading materials that the subjects they are designed for encounter in their daily lives? How are the difficulty levels of the text of the instruments determined and controlled? Is there any consistency in this across instruments?
- What reading purposes, if any, engage the examinee during assessment, and how do such purposes compare with purposes for reading identified as likely for the examinee outside the assessment environment?

- What skill or subprocess distinguishing purposes do distractors in multiple choice items serve?
- What professed or assumed subskills or subprocesses are distinguished by instruments using the cloze technique?
- How passage dependent are different item technologies? Are there wording techniques within such technologies that can assure passage dependence? For example, does beginning an item that might be answered from reader knowledge with the phrase "In this story..." assure that the examinee will have to refer to the passage?
- In terms of background engaged, submeasures professed, types of passages, reader purposes, and item types, are there existing categorizations within instruments that could be described as "domains"? If there are, how distinguished are those domains in terms of information reported?

This long list compiles just a sample of the questions that assessment analyses could attempt to answer. Such an effort could contribute greatly to the implementation of research by specifying how existing instruments do and do not reflect and distinguish aspects of emerging theory. At the same time, it should provide the criticism of such instruments with specifics that could raise the state of the critical art to a truly constructive perspective.

We need much more research that analyzes written materials

Increased emphasis on and support of analyses of various types and lifetask genres of written materials is essential to the explication of the reading act in two general ways. Foremost, it is important that the descriptions these analyses produce will impact on the work of the test makers; for not only should a definitive model of reading comprehension depict generic operations, but it also must be applicable to existing reader situations in which the test is used.

Reader purpose should, it appears, be a centralizing perspective in the analysis of written materials. If each such study defines the type of materials and/or task in terms of reader purpose as a primary obligation, reader purpose should help synthesize, structure, and direct the overall task of text analysis.

Research should also address questions such as: What describes various adult reading competencies? Can they be meaningfully synthesized and defined as a single competency? Can adult competencies be quantified in some way on continua so that reader growth can be better measured and reported?

We need a comprehensive survey of test use and misuse

Much of the criticism of standardized tests is fired by the frequent misuse of tests. The data created by tests are often misapplied by both educators and the public. The blame for this is too easily laid on the test itself, even when the test maker has clearly warned the user against it.

A thorough study of test use and misuse needs to be conducted and reported to all educators, media personnel, and the public at large. Such a study could help stop the misuse of tests resulting from political manipulation (Levine, 1976) and from ignorance. To do this, the effort must clearly explain what tests can and cannot tell us and, on this basis, recommend how they should be used. Obviously, such a study would also be able to identify assessment needs that are not met by existing instruments and techniques.

Meanwhile, an analysis of attacks on extant tests ought to enlighten test makers as to what proportion of the criticism relates directly to their determination to produce instruments that yield grade equivalents. The National Conference study group on Linguistic Communication (Miller, 1973) sighted the problem: "We believe that grade level criteria may often be more misleading than informative" (p.4).

Grade equivalents have had a long history in educational measurement, and their current prominence in reading assessment points to a continuation of their use. Even though grade equivalents are in fact a popular score used to report performance, they remain largely misunderstood and incorrectly applied. On the other hand, it has been effectively argued that a grade equivalent scale is a valid metric — as appropriate to use as is any other standardized scale score (Hoover, 1983).

We need to search for assessment strategies to measure emerging models of reading comprehension

Perhaps the most exciting outcome of research of the past several years is the promise that we may soon be able to identify specific aspects of reading comprehension with some definitive certainty. Meanwhile we need to devise methods of measuring them, using the indicative definitions we now have. As Johnston (1981) put it,

> We are approaching the stage of being able to classify items and item clusters with respect to the information they could yield. Thus we approach a position from which to select items which have a clear relationship to the structure of the text, the reader's prior knowledge, and the nature of the requisite cognitive processes. Knowing the characteristics of these item clusters, we should be able to generate tests which provide more, and more meaningful, information. (p. 69)

The response to this potential will be varied. Those who argue strongly that the cloze procedure is the technology that assures we are measuring the reading act should be experimenting with deletions controlled to reveal various levels of reasoning as well as linguistic, psychological, and psycholinguistic features of text.

Even as cloze is used to determine the suitability of specific material for specific readers, research is needed to establish percentages that indicate what is suitable for instruction and for independent reading. The percentage recommended by Koslin, Koslin, and Zeno (1979), for example, would place independent readers in material in which every tenth word is not recognized. They would use instructional materials where every fourth word is unrecognized. The potential for serious reader frustration seems highly probable in either case.

As domain referencing guides assessment experimentation (Anderson et al., 1978; Wardrop et al., 1978), various aspects of the reading act may be better isolated and categorized for diagnosis. Then different domain controls can be implemented in single assessments to test whether they yield distinctions among subprocesses.

Those who would rely on the statistically clean reporting potential of latent trait theory will probably be engaging the technology of the computer and its branching potential to channel subjects to assessments of increasingly specific subprocesses.

Test makers whose expertise is developed in constructing multiple choice items face a challenge that is yet to be enlightened by research on the potentials of distractor control. Is it possible, for example, to pinpoint the reason examinees fail to pursue a particular type of reasoning by noting that they frequently select a distractor representing the same faulty line of reasoning?

Sentence verification techniques (Royer, Hastings, & Hook, 1979) will be tested to see how they can distinguish between levels of memory, which in turn may help distinguish subprocesses. And there is, of course, the probability of the development of other, still undevised assessment techniques. It does not, for example, seem unreasonable to suppose that someday, in the not too distant future, technology may allow us to analyze openended responses as effortlessly and nearly as absolutely as we score multiple choice tests.

Future technology should allow us some way to assess reading comprehension in terms of what the reader does with what is read. From the perspective of assessing reading that values its real-life relevance, how a reader uses what is read is the ultimate gauge of how well it was understood. Would such assessment tend, however, to dissolve the distinction between product and process measurement?

We need a better understanding of the potential and limitations of criterion referenced measures

Criterion referenced testing can be highly effective in the classroom setting. Teacher made assessments based on objectives set and defined by the teacher are, in the purest sense, criterion referenced measures. The use of this general technique for broader measurement to assess grade, school, city, or statewide populations is becoming a widespread practice as an accountability system. Minimum essential exams, which have swept the country, are criterion referenced measures. A benefit of this movement is the possibility that it should require frequent defining and redefining by educators of their goals, objectives, and philosophies.

The reliability of such measures, however, is usually undetermined, thus nonexistent; and their validity is no more assured than the validity of a standardized measure. It is recommended that an extensive, nationwide study be conducted of criterion referenced tests—particularly those attempting to ensure the teaching of minimum essentials. A synthesis of numerous current studies of such measures would be a useful preliminary step in this study. The objectives of such a study could be far reaching, since we know relatively little about how they are affecting instruction. Generally, these kind of questions need answering:

What characterizes these tests? Do they measure educational achievement toward goals that are carefully defined and matched to definitions on the tests (Moore, 1980)? Are they basically fact checkers and product measures? How well do they actually match the curricula of the sites where they are used? Do they measure reading or reasoning/thinking in any recognizable way? What reading skills or processes do they profess to report? Do they tend to yield much diagnostic information? What kind of use do teachers make of them? What impact have they had on teaching?

It appears that criterion referenced measures are being used to generate data that dictate a great many educational decisions. We ought to know if they are that dependable. Moore (1980) raises serious concerns about the use of such tests in Florida, questioning how they were constructed, how criterion levels were set, their reliability and validity, and their use to fail rather than to diagnose and help children.

We need to understand the full potential of informal assessment

In light of the current high regard for individualized instruction, the general distrust of standardized measures, and new knowledge about how complex a role background plays in reading comprehension, it is surprising that so little has been done to describe and analyze the potential of informal assessment. It is highly recommended that research energies be dedicated to answering questions such as the following: How can the various kinds of informal reading assessment that educators use be described? Where do they get them? Are teachers adequately trained to design effective assessments? If so, where did they learn to do this? What kind of information do the informal assessments yield? How do teachers use them? How related are the informal techniques to instructional objectives and goals set by the teacher? How do the techniques reflect the materials the teacher uses in instruction? How frequently do such techniques tend to measure process as opposed to product? What kind of technologies do such assessments use? Are the technologies derivative or original?

Observation, the most informal and perhaps most valuable of all reading assessments, needs to be studied too: What kind of observation do teachers conduct? How systematized is it? How often are students involved in the kind of self observation recommended by Strang (1970)? Are observation data generally recorded? Are they synthesized in any systematic way? How confident are teachers in using them for instructional decision making?

The most important aspect of an extensive study of informal reading assessment would be the synthesizing and reporting of what is learned for teachers and the teachers of teachers. But theorists, too, could see how their work does, might, and could impact on informal assessment.

We need to experiment with tailored assessments

It is recommended that the schema theory explanation of how reader background facilitates comprehension (Anderson, 1977) be used as the basis for constructing reading assessment tailored for special groups. The results of recent and in process studies of test bias, the linguistic capabilities of special groups, and the role of both reader purpose and background should be analyzed and incorporated in the development of these measures.

We need to enlarge our appreciation of reading as a form of communication

Theorists of reading who are developing communication models should be encouraged to seek explanations of how factors such as reader purpose, the reader's perception of the writer's purpose, and the mood and tone of the text affect comprehension. Such concerns need to be better appreciated; and perhaps they can be controlled to some degree during assessment (Kingston, 1970).

We need to consider emerging technologies

A change with impact equal to the industrial revolution is in process. This is the age of the computer, and schools are experimenting with computer instruction. Its immediate branching access to a vast array of materials recommend its use in instruction that would serve individual learner needs; thus it can be expected to impact with surprising speed on our schools. It appears that students avidly accept computer instruction and assessment, suggesting that the format may dissolve any distinction between assessment environment and general learning environment. Industry is now putting that instructional potential to relatively sophisticated use.

This same potential can serve assessment, which is built into many instructional computer programs. The branching program, for example, can begin by identifying a potential reading problem, verify the diagnosis, and switch to more focused items to try to pin down the subprocess that instruction should attend to. This exciting potential is discussed by Frederiksen (1979). Haertel (1980) notes the relevance of such use to the latent trait theory of assessment.

References

Anderson, R.C. *Schema-directed processes in language comprehension*. Technical report no. 50. Champaign, IL: Center for the Study of Reading, University of Illinois, 1977.

Anderson, T.H. Cloze measures as indices of achievement comprehension when learning from extended prose. *Journal of Educational Measurement*, 1974, 11, 83-92.

Anderson, T.H., Wardrop, J.L., Hively, W., Muller, K.E., Anderson, R.I., Hastings, C.N., and Frederiksen, J. *Development and trial of a model for developing domain referenced tests of reading comprehension*. Technical report no. 86. Champaign, IL: Center for the Study of Reading, University of Illinois, 1978.

Axelrod, J. Getting the bloodhound off the scent. *Elementary English*, 1973, *50*, 69-70, 76-78.

Bloomer, R. *Nonovert reinforced cloze procedure*. Final report, project no. 2245. Washington, DC: U.S. Department of Health, Education and Welfare, 1966.

Bormuth, J.R. Cloze as a measure of readability. In J.A. Figurel (Ed.), *Reading as an intellectual activity*. Newark, DE: International Reading Association, 1963.

Bormuth, J.R. Comparable cloze and multiple choice comprehension test scores. *Journal of Reading*, 1967, *10*, 291-299.

Bormuth, J.R. Cloze test readability: Criterion referenced scores. *Journal of Educational Measurement*, 1968, *5*, 189-196.

Bormuth, J.R. *Development of readability analyses*. USOE technical report no. 7-0052. Chicago: University of Chicago Press, 1969.

Bormuth, J.R. *On the theory of achievement test items*. Chicago: University of Chicago Press, 1970.

Bormuth, J.R. *Development of standards of readability: Toward a rational criterion of passage performance.* Arlington, VA: ERIC Document Reproduction Service, ED 054 233, 1971.

Bormuth, J.R. Reading literacy: Its definition and assessment. *Reading Research Quarterly,* 1973, *9,* 7-66.

Brown, H.A. The measurement of the efficiency of instruction in reading. *Elementary School Teacher,* 1914, *14,* 477-490.

Buros, O.K. (Ed.). *The nineteen thirty-eight mental measurement yearbook.* New Brunswick, NJ: Rutgers University Press, 1938.

Buros, O.K. *The sixth mental measurement yearbook.* Highland Park, NJ: Gryphon Press, 1965.

Carey, R. *A psycholinguistic analysis of the effect of semantic acceptability of oral reading miscues on reading comprehension.* Unpublished doctoral dissertation, University of Connecticut, 1978.

Carroll, J.B. Defining language comprehension: Some speculations. In J.B. Carroll and R.O. Freedle (Eds.), *Language comprehension and the acquisition of knowledge.* Washington, DC: V.H. Winston and Sons, 1972.

Carver, R.P. Measuring prose difficulty using the rauding scale. *Reading Research Quarterly,* 1976, *11,* 660-685.

Coleman, E.B. Developing a technology of written instruction: Some determinants of the complexity of prose. In E. Rothkopf and P. Johnson (Eds.), *Verbal learning research and the technology of written instruction.* New York: Teachers College Press, 1971.

Coleman, E.B., and Miller, G.R. A measure of information gained during prose learning. *Reading Research Quarterly,* 1968, *3,* 369-386.

Duffelmeyer, F.A. The passage independence of factual and inferential questions. *Journal of Reading,* 1980, *24,* 131-134.

Duffelmeyer, F.A. The effect of grade level on cloze test scores. *Journal of Reading,* 1983, *26,* 436-441.

Entin, E.B., and Klare, G.B. Components of answers to multiple choice questions on a published reading comprehension test: An application of the Hanna-Oaster approach. *Reading Research Quarterly,* 1980, *15,* 228-236.

Fleck, L. *Genesis and development of a scientific fact.* Chicago: University of Chicago Press, 1979. (Originally published in 1935 by Benno Schwabe and Company, Basel, Switzerland.)

Flood, J., and Lapp, D. Inferential comprehension: A grand illusion. *Language Arts,* 1978, *55,* 188-191.

Frederiksen, N. Some emerging trends in testing. In R.W. Tyler and S.H. White, *Testing, teaching and learning.* Report of a conference on research in testing, August 1978. Washington, DC: National Institute of Education, 1979.

Ganier, A.S. The post oral reading cloze test: Does it really work? *Reading World,* 1976, *16,* 21-27.

Goodman, K.S. The psycholinguistic nature of the reading process. In K.S. Goodman (Ed.), *The psycholinguistic nature of the reading process.* Detroit: Wayne State University Press, 1968.

Goodman, K.S., and Burke, C.L. *Study of children's behavior while reading orally.* Report of project no. 5425. Washington, DC: U.S. Department of Health, Education and Welfare, 1968.

Goodman, K.S., and Burke, C.L. *Theoretically based studies of patterns of miscues in oral reading performance.* Final report, project no. 9-0375. Washington, DC: U.S. Department of Health, Education and Welfare, 1973.

Gould, S.J. *The mismeasure of man.* New York: W.W. Norton, 1981.

Haertel, E. *A study of domain heterogeneity and content acquisition.* Evanston, IL: CEMREL, 1980.

Hanna, G.S., and Oaster, T.R. Toward a unified theory of context dependence. *Reading Research Quarterly,* 1978, *14,* 226-243.

Hanna, G.S., and Oaster, T.R. Studies of the seriousness of three threats to passage dependence. *Educational and Psychological Measurement,* 1980, *40,* 405-411.

Harste, J.C., Burke, C.L., and Woodward, V.A. *Children, their language and world: Initial encounters with print.* Final report. Bloomington, IN: Language Education Department, Indiana University, 1981.

Harste, J.C., Burke, C.L., and Woodward, V.A. *The young child as writer-reader, and informant.* Final report. Bloomington, IN: Language Education Department, Indiana University, 1983.

Hoover, H.D. *The most appropriate scores for measuring educational development in the elementary schools:* GES. Invited address presented at the annual meeting of the American Educational Research Association. Montreal, April 1983.

Horton, R.J. *The construct validity of cloze procedure: An exploratory factor analysis of cloze, paragraph reading, and structure-of-intellect tests.* Unpublished doctoral dissertation, Hofstra University, 1973.

Houts. P.L. (Ed.). *The myth of measurability.* New York: Hart Publishing, 1977.

Johns, J.L. Do comprehension items really test reading? Sometimes! *Journal of Reading,* 1978, *21,* 615-619.

Johnston, P. *Prior knowledge and reading comprehension test bias.* Unpublished doctoral dissertation, University of Illinois, 1981.

Johnston, P. *Implications of basic research for the assessment of reading comprehension.* Technical report no. 206. Champaign, IL: Center for the Study of Reading, University of Illinois, 1981.

Johnston, P. Prior knowledge and reading comprehension test bias. *Reading Research Quarterly,* 1984, *19,* 219-239.

Johnston, P., and Pearson, P.D. Assessment: Responses to exposition. In A. Berger and H.A. Robinson (Eds.), *Secondary school reading.* Urbana, IL: ERIC/NIE, National Conference on Research in English, 1982.

Johnston, P., and Pearson, P.D. *Prior knowledge, connectivity, and the assessment of reading comprehension.* Technical report no. 245. Champaign, IL: Center for the Study of Reading, University of Illinois, 1982.

Kingston, A.J. The measurement of reading comprehension. In R. Farr (Ed.), *Measurement and evaluation of reading.* New York: Harcourt Brace Jovanovich, 1970.

Klare, G.R. A second look at the validity of readability formulas. *Journal of Reading Behavior,* 1976, *8,* 129-152.

Koslin, B.L., Koslin, S., and Zeno, S. Towards an effectiveness measure in reading. In R.W. Tyler and S.H. White, *Testing, teaching and learning: Report of a conference on research in testing,* August 1978. Washington, DC: National Institute of Education, 1979.

Langer, J.A. The construction of meaning and the assessment of comprehension: An analysis of reader performance on standardized test items. In R. Freedle (Ed.), *Cognitive and linguistic analyses of test performance.* New York: Ablex, 1986.

Lennon, R.T. What can be measured? In R. Farr (Ed.), *Measurement and evaluation of reading.* New York: Harcourt Brace Jovanovich, 1970.

Leu, D.J., Jr. *The effects of syntactic differences between oral and written discourse on the reading comprehension of second and fifth grade students.* Unpublished doctoral dissertation, University of California at Berkeley, 1981.

Levine, M. The academic achievement test: Its historical context and social functions. *American Psychologist,* March 1976, 228-238.

Marr, M.B., and Lyon, K.R. Passage independency and question characteristics: An analysis of three informal reading inventories. *Reading Psychology,* 1981, *2,* 97-102.

McConkie, G.W., Rayner, K., and Wilson, S.J. Experimental manipulation of reading strategies. *Journal of Reading Psychology,* 1973, *65,* 1-8.

Miller, G.A. (Ed.). *Linguistic communication: Perspectives for research.* Newark, DE: International Reading Association, 1973.

Moore, W. Florida's standardized testing program: A tool or a weapon? In C.B. Stalford (Ed.), *Testing and evaluation in schools: Practitioners' views.* Washington, DC: Office of Educational Research and Improvement, National Institute of Education, 1980.

Page, W.D. Pseudoscores, supercues, and comprehension. *Reading World,* 1976, *15,* 232-238.

Page, W.D. Comprehending and cloze performance. *Reading World,* 1977, *7,* 17-21.

Panackal, A.A., and Heft, C.S. Cloze technique and multiple choice technique: Reliability and validity. *Educational and Psychological Measurement,* 1978, *38,* 917-932.

Pintner, R. Oral and silent reading of fourth grade pupils. *Journal of Educational Psychology,* 1913, *4,* 333-337.

Popham, W.J., and Husek, T.R. Implications of criterion referenced measurement. *Journal of Educational Measurement,* 1969, *6,* 1-9.

Powell, W.R. Reappraising the criteria for interpreting informal inventories. In D. DeBoer (Ed.), *Reading diagnosis and evaluation.* Newark, DE: International Reading Association, 1969.

Powers, S., and Sahers, D. *An investigation of ethnic group differences in testwiseness at the third, fifth, and seventh grade.* Paper presented at the annual meeting of the American Educational Research Association, Los Angeles, April 1981.

Prentice, W.C., and Peterson, J. *Beyond passage dependency: A closer look at what reading comprehension tests measure.* Paper presented at the annual convention of the National Reading Conference, New Orleans, December 1977.

Pyrczak, F. A responsive note on measures of the passage dependency of reading comprehension test items. *Reading Research Quarterly, 1975, 11,* 112-117.

Rankin, E.F. Cloze procedure—A survey of research. *Fourteenth yearbook of the south west reading conference.* Milwaukee: Marquette University, 1965.

Rankin, E.F., and Culhane, J.W. Comparable cloze and multiple choice test scores. *Journal of Reading, 1969, 13,* 193-198.

Rayford, L. *Reading assessment and the thought collective: The contribution of reading research to reading tests.* Paper presented at the Tenth Southeastern Regional Conference of the International Reading Association, Lexington, Kentucky, November 1984.

Reynolds, R.E., and Anderson, R.C. *Influence of questions on the allocation of attention during reading.* Technical report no. 183. Champaign, IL: Center for the Study of Reading, University of Illinois, 1980.

Rowe, D.W., and Rayford, L. *Instantiating background knowledge in reading comprehension assessment.* Paper presented at the annual convention of the National Reading Conference, St. Petersburg, Florida, 1984.

Royer, J.M., and Cunningham, D.J. *On the theory and measurement of reading comprehension.* Technical report no. 91. Champaign, IL: Center for the Study of Reading, University of Illinois, 1978.

Royer, J.M., Hastings, C.N., and Hook, C. *A sentence verification technique for measuring reading comprehension.* Technical report no. 137. Champaign, IL: Center for the Study of Reading, University of Illinois, 1979.

Schlesinger, I.M., and Weiser, Z. A facet design for tests of reading comprehension. *Reading Research Quarterly, 1970, 5,* 566-580.

Schreiner, R., and Shannon, P. *The recall of explicit and implied propositions by good and poor readers using three types of assessment procedures.* Paper presented at the annual convention of the International Reading Association, St. Louis, 1980.

Spiro, R.J. Remembering information from text: The "state of schema" approach. In R.C. Anderson, R. Spiro, and W. Montague (Eds.), *Schooling and the acquisition of knowledge.* Hillsdale, NJ: Erlbaum, 1977.

Spiro, R.J. *Schema theory and reading comprehension: New directions.* Technical report no. 191. Champaign, IL: Center for the Study of Reading, University of Illinois, 1980.

Steffensen, M.S., and Guthrie, L.F. *Effects of situation on the verbalization of black innercity children.* Technical report no. 180. Champaign, IL: Center for the Study of Reading, University of Illinois, 1980.

Strang, R. Evaluation of development in and through reading. In R. Farr (Ed.), *Measurement and evaluation of reading.* New York: Harcourt Brace Jovanovich, 1970.

Swenson, I., and Kulhavy, R.W. Adjunct questions and the comprehension of prose by children. *Journal of Educational Psychology,* 1974, *66,* 212-215.

Tuinman, J.J. Asking reading-dependent questions. *Journal of Reading,* 1971, *14,* 289-292, 336.

Tuinman, J.J. Determining the passage dependency of comprehension questions in five major tests. *Reading Research Quarterly,* 1974, *9,* 206-223.

Tuinman, J.J. Reading is recognition—when reading is not reasoning. In J. Harste and R. Carey (Eds.), *New perspectives on comprehension.* Bloomington, IN: Indiana University, 1979.

Weaver, W.W., and Kingston, A.J. A factor analysis of the cloze procedure and other measures of reading and language ability. *Journal of Communication,* 1963, *13,* 252-261.

Wilhite, S.C. Prepassage questions: The influence of structural importance. *Journal of Educational Psychology,* 1983, *75,* 234-244.

Wardrop, J.L., Anderson, T.H., Hively, W., Anderson, R.I., Hastings, C.N., and Muller, K.E. *A framework for analyzing reading test characteristics.* Technical report no. 109. Champaign, IL: Center for the Study of Reading, University of Illinois, 1978.

Test References

Chapman Reading Comprehension Test. J.C. Chapman. Minneapolis: Educational Test Bureau, 1920.

Classroom Reading Inventory. N.J. Silvaroli. Boston: Allyn and Bacon, 1976.

Courtis Silent Reading Test. S.A. Courtis. N.p., n.d.

Degrees of Reading Power. New York: College Entrance Examination Board, 1980.

Durrell Analysis of Reading Difficulty. D.D. Durrell. Cleveland, OH: Psychological Corporation, 1978.

Gates-MacGinitie Reading Test. A.I. Gates and W.H. MacGinitie. New York: Teachers College Press, 1964.

Haggerty Reading Examination. M.E. Haggerty and M.E. Joonan. New York: World Book, 1920.

Kansas Silent Reading Test. F.J. Kelly. Emporia, KS: Bureau of Educational Measurements and Standards, 1916.

Metropolitan Achievement Test. G.A. Prescott, I.H. Balow, T.P. Hogan, and R.C. Farr. Cleveland, OH: Psychological Corporation, 1985.

Metropolitan Achievement Test: Reading Survey Tests. R.C. Farr. New York: Psychological Corporation, 1978.

Monroe's Standardized Silent Reading Test. W.S. Monroe. Indianapolis, IN: Bobbs-Merrill, 1919.

3

Assessing word recognition skills

Reading is comprehension. While so called skills of reading are taught and tested, current research emphasizes that the act of reading is thinking stimulated by printed symbols. How those symbols are recognized and how children are taught to recognize those symbols is the domain of reading subskills. Whatever subskills are vital to recognizing and using the symbol system is the subject of much debate and conjecture. There is no validated list of skills which are vital to learning to read, nor is there any hierarchy of skills. In addition, there is much debate about the relation of so-called separate skills of reading to the actual act of reading.

Despite the lack of evidence for the existence of separate reading skills, the search for the apparently elusive list of reading skills continues. The teaching of separate skills of reading continues to predominate the initial phases of reading instruction, and the inclusion of these reading skills on reading tests continues to be demanded by most reading test consumers.

This chapter and the next discuss the common skills of reading that are included in most reading tests. The danger in this discussion is that the presentation seems to endorse classifications, analyses, and emphases that have yet to be validated by research and which seem to be questioned seriously by most recent analyses of the reading process. On the other hand, if any analysis of reading measurement is to relate directly to what is taught in schools and to what is measured, it appears that it must be treated within classifications that have been effected in practice.

For this reason, the range of reading skills taught and assessed has been treated in these two chapters within a traditional classification scheme of word recognition skills, vocabulary, study skills, and reading rate. Word recognition skills are discussed in a separate chapter because word recognition is significantly different from the other three topics. The teaching of word recognition skills emphasizes the teaching of the relationships between spoken sounds and printed letters; and between sounds and letter combinations; the identification of syllables; and the use of other word parts as aids in the identification of words. This focus on word parts tends to deemphasize the focus on reading for meaning. The other three areas — vocabulary, study skills, and reading rate — focus on printed symbols at the word, sentence, and story levels and emphasize reading for meaning.

These two chapters may foster the impression that reading should be taught as a set of separate skill areas, and that reading can be divided into a set of separate skills. To balance the appearance that these two chapters suggest the existence of a separate list of reading subskills, the reader is advised to read Chapter 2, which treats "comprehension" with the high regard the process deserves. That chapter attempts to deal with the symphonic complexity of whatever skills and subskills may be operating when one reads.

Word recognition

Perhaps no other area of reading instruction produces more controversy than the teaching of word recognition, a general classification covering numerous reading skills that dominate instructional reading programs in the primary grades. This predominance has cued a concerned public to some of the issues, and even a person who is only vaguely familiar with the full scope of issues related to reading can readily articulate a stand in the classic simplification of the word recognition debate — phonics decoding versus sight word recognition.

Word recognition skills have been defined, classified, and subcategorized in far greater complexity than the phonics versus sight word debate implies. Understandably, this has promoted a greater variety of tests and procedures to measure word recognition skills than exist as measures of any other aspect of reading.

How research has defined word recognition

The proliferation of word recognition skills results mainly from the variety of definitions. At issue in defining the potentially encompassing term is determining the relevance of grapheme/phoneme association and grapheme/meaning association — individually and interrelatedly — to the reading act.

Generally, definitions of word recognition run along a continuum. At one end, word recognition is simply defined as the ability to provide a spoken representation for a printed word. Beck and McKeown (in press), for example, define decoding as "...the translation of print to speech, either overt or covert" (p.2). Interestingly, this definition tends to resolve the phonics versus sight word debate within its explicit limitations. Beck and McKeown write that this translation "...encompasses both 'sounding out' using phonic principles and instant recognition of word names"(p.2). At the other end of the continuum is the belief that vocal pronunciation of a word is not necessary in word recognition, which entails only the recognition of the meaning of printed symbols (McConkie, et al,1979).

Other researchers, however, have argued that word recognition must include both the pronunciation of a printed word and the recognition of a meaning for that word. Caldwell, Nix, and Peckham (1981) state that the reading process itself is not primarily a behavior which focuses on words or letters "...but a higher order unit determined by examining phoneme/ grapheme correspondences" (p. 127). The higher order unit they discuss is meaning; thus they view word recognition as being inexorably woven into the fabric of a total reading act. They, as do many others, view the ability to recognize words—whether to pronounce those words or to recognize meanings for them—as inseparable from the total thinking process we call reading.

An enduring debate. Research on the skills of word recognition has a long history. Cattell (1886) was among the first to recognize that skilled readers could recognize short, common words as quickly as they could recognize letters. By assessing reader response to letters and words, Cattell concluded that the primary recognition unit in reading is the word, not the letter. His early work is often cited as evidence for the appropriateness of the "sight word approach" to teaching reading.

It seemed logical for early researchers to focus on the recognition of letters and words, since these seemed to be the "stuff" of which reading was composed. But even relatively recent research has offered support to phonics proponents. Gough (1972) studied the response of subjects to longer and longer words as latency time. He concluded that reading is a letter by letter, left to right process. Strange (1979) studied the word recognition strategies of fifth and sixth graders and concluded that readers follow a left to right analysis of a word only until the word is recognized, at which time they discontinue their orthographic analysis of the word.

Smith's contention (1971) appears to have anticipated Strange's findings. Smith believes that a reader relies on letters only when unsure of the word. Thus, the orthographic process intervenes only when needed, but comprehension goes on otherwise "unmediated." Laberge and Samuels (1974) believe that skilled readers use "feedback strategies," based on the meaning of what is being read, to adjust word strategies based on the orthographic features of the individual words.

After investigating the role of speech/sound segmentation, blending, and discrimination in reading acquisition, Backman (1983) concluded that her results did not demonstrate that even early reading is facilitated "by precocity in discriminating and perceiving phonemes in words, or blending phonemes and syllables." She suggested that while "some more complex skill involving the manipulation of sounds in temporal order may be more closely related to early reading,...it is unlikely to be a prerequisite to reading but rather a facilitator and/or a consequence of learning to read" (p. 478).

Recent research has tended to emphasize that reading is more than identifying letters and words, that it is, instead, understanding ideas and concepts. Furthermore, there has been a strong argument in recent reading research and theory that the ideas and concepts which emerge from reading are matched by the reader to the same, similar, or related ideas and concepts embedded in the reader's mind. Bransford and Johnson (1973), Bransford and McCarrell (1974), and Carey, Harste, and Smith (1981) have shown that comprehension is a constructive rather than a reconstructive process which is heavily dependent on readers' background knowledge and experience. Essentially what the reader brings away from the text has to do with what the reader brought to the text, and with the relationship of the reader's background information to the text base. The embedded ideas may be transformed, enlarged, negated, or reinforced as a result of the implicit communication between writer and reader. In this perspective on the thought carried by broader text, the letter and word symbols are seen as clues the reader may use to relate the ideas of a writer to those the reader has stored from experience, including previous encounters with the printed page. Thus reading comprehension becomes "thinking guided by printed symbols." The emerging emphasis on larger meaning, then, does not usually deny the use of phonics and sight words in reading. It tends, rather, to ask how readers understand and use those clues so that the communication of ideas between reader and writer can take place.

Different views on emphasis. The answer to the question of how readers actually use word recognition clues is generally framed among reading theorists and practitioners as a debate between "bottom-up," "top-down," and "inside-out" views of the reading process. In using this approach to considering word recognition strategies we are applying the common and generally accepted usage of the terms. We caution the reader, however, that these analyses often oversimplify the reading process. Rosenblatt (1976, 1978) and Eco (1978) have provided a much more thorough analysis of the reading act that focuses on reading as a transactional activity.

Bottom-up theories are most closely associated with reading models that give priority focus to decoding and to developmental stage schemes. Briefly, their advocates insist that reading is the process of translating graphemes into phonemes and then combining (blending) the phonemes into words. Comprehension is viewed as the product of interpreting the words after they have been translated into oral language. Bottom-up theorists emphasize that the act of reading is determining what the author intended a selection to mean.

Top-down theorists assume that it is the reader who holds the key to the ultimate meaning of the text. Rather than being a product of the application of word recognition skills, comprehension occurs as the reader selects from a variety of contextual and textual clues to construct meaning that comes from the reader's background and experience and that serves the reader's purpose for reading. Since the reader's role is an active one, these theorists have given rise to the active versus passive distinction in explaining comprehension.

Interactive theorists suggest that reading is a search for meaning that combines a focus on comprehension with the use of word recognition skills. To the interactive theorist, reading is more than the process of matching letters with sounds, as bottom-up theory suggests; and it is something less than the total meaning construction process that top-down theory contends. Instead, this "compromise" view posits that particular word recognition strategies or skills are engaged because of a reader's experience with texts. So is the reader's ability to manipulate meaning.

This position, which is held by an increasing number of reading theorists and is being tested by more and more research, suggests that some degree of graphemic/phonemic association is apt to be operating in the reading act in conjunction with sight word recognition, and that such processes interact in the quest for meaning generated across and between words—a higher level activity that supports and informs the more isolated phonics and sight word skills as they all operate at once. Yet this explanation does not explicitly answer questions that have been with us for over a hundred years. For example:

- What behavior or skills are actually part of word recognition?

- How do the skills or the processes of word recognition relate to one another? More importantly, how do they relate to the total act of reading?
- Is any traditionally recognized word recognition skill separable from the total act of reading?
- Should the skills and strategies claimed to make up word recognition be taught? If so, what skills or strategies should be taught to a beginning reader? How should they be taught?

Given the continuing debate surrounding word recognition, is it any wonder that the assessment of word recognition continues to be muddled and confused? As reading tests and other reading assessment techniques continue to rely heavily on word recognition abilities as important indicators of reading achievement, the debate continues as to which subskills should be isolated, how and in what balance they should be tested, and whether isolating them for measurement is even valid given what we know about the reading process as a whole.

How word recognition is taught

It should not be surprising that the lack of agreement about how orthographic, sight word, and other word recognition skills figure in the reading act might be reflected in a variety of emphases in instruction. The difference between the two views of reading—that decoding is a separate skill of reading and that reading is a total process in which subskills are not separable—has led to significant differences in both the teaching and testing of reading.

At the lowest grade levels there is a potentially vital disagreement. Chall (1967) reviewed a large number of studies and concluded that decoding should be emphasized in the beginning stages of instruction in all reading programs. In a more recent book, Chall (1983) reiterated this position and presented a more comprehensive stage development theory of reading which supports those who believe the teaching of reading must emphasize word recognition skills (code emphasis) prior to emphasizing comprehension.

However, if one views word recognition as an interactive process, a conclusion emphasized by much research since the 1960s and particularly by research in the late 1970s and in the 1980s, the separation of reading into a decoding phase and a comprehension phase is inappropriate. Anderson et al. (1977) and Spiro (1980) have demonstrated that recognizing the function of printed symbols does not itself constitute an ability to comprehend text. On the other hand, numerous research studies have investigated the relationship between decoding and comprehension, with the recurrent finding that decoding is not void of comprehension processes. Likewise, research suggests that the comprehension process also requires the decoding of many kinds of information (not necessarily only printed symbols but also word shapes and pictures) (Anderson, Spiro, & Anderson, 1978; Baker & Anderson, 1982; Collins, Brown, & Larkin, 1980).

A study by Allington and Fleming (1978) of the misreading of high frequency words is typical of research that supports this general theoretical perspective. This study underlines the importance of sentence and broader meaning to less capable readers. By presenting a passage in its normal condition and with its words in an order that destroyed any possibility of using contextual or syntactic clues, they found that the poorer readers among their fourth grade subjects were most affected by the loss of context. They strongly recommended that remedial instruction focus on reading in context.

Four instructional approaches. The major instructional approach in the teaching of word recognition has been the analytic approach used by most basal reading programs. In addition to the analytic approach, some classroom teachers supplement the basal program with a word recognition program which utilizes a synthetic approach, generally emphasizing the teaching of phonic generalizations. In a few classrooms, teachers teach word recognition as a strategy rather than as a skill; and in still fewer classrooms, teachers do not explicitly teach word recognition skills at all, but merely have students read and develop reading strategies as a natural part of reading. A brief examination of each of these four approaches to teaching word recognition skills will provide a structure for considering the word recognition tests used in schools.

While these four approaches are described separately, it is seldom the case that teachers use only one of the approaches. It is also likely that teachers never consciously decide to use one approach rather than another. The reality of teaching is that these four approaches do not exist as separate approaches, particularly analytic and synthetic phonics. Discussing these approaches separately, however, does provide a heuristic for understanding the procedures for teaching and testing word recognition skills.

The analytic approach is based on the learning of word generalizations from words that are already known. Thus, the analytic approach necessitates that the beginning reader learn a set of words by sight before word recognition skills are taught. The analytic approach always uses known words to help children develop generalizations. For example, the teacher might write the known words *big, ball*, and *baby* on the chalkboard and then ask pupils how each of the words are alike—helping children to develop the generalization that words which begin with the letter *b* usually begin with the same sound as the words *big, ball*, and *baby*.

The synthetic approach, on the other hand, begins with teaching beginning readers the relationship between individual sounds and letters. These sounds and letters are taught to the pupils in isolation. Once the letter sounds are known, the pupils are taught to synthesize or blend these sounds into syllables and then to blend the syllables into words. The synthetic approach usually includes teaching the pupils to verbalize word recognition generalizations as well as to apply them.

In the strategies approach, the emphasis is on teaching beginning readers to use various cue systems to determine meaning. The emphasis is not on word identification but on developing understanding. Beginning readers are helped to learn word recognition strategies in somewhat the same approach used in the analytic approach. The differences are that in the strategies approach, the generalizations are taught in the context of helping a child construct meaning, and the word recognition behaviors are never assessed separately from the total act of reading.

In the "no direct instruction" approach, the assumption is that readers will develop whatever strategies they need as a natural part of reading. In this approach, learning to read is viewed in much the same way as learning to talk. Reading is considered a naturally occurring language process, and as such does not necessitate specific skill instruction. No overt attempts are made to teach pupils any specific skills or strategies; rather, they are encouraged to develop as readers through reading activities that are real and important in their lives.

The controversy over which approach is best is one that will not be resolved easily. Part of the controversy results from the confusion as to whether beginning readers use different skills and strategies than mature readers. Samuels, LaBerge, and Bremer (1978) discuss this as a shift in the kinds of information selected by readers of different ages. Downing and Leong (1982) also point out that skills or strategies change as they develop: "It is characteristic of skills that they change in the course of their development. Behavior appropriate to the beginning stage drops out later as mastery progresses. New behaviors are incorporated as attention is freed from acts that have become automatic" (p. 39).

The differences in approach to teaching reading do seem to involve primarily beginning readers. Beyond initial reading development, the dichotomy between authorities endorsing a decoding approach and others emphasizing a holistic approach seems to disappear. There is little debate centering on instructional emphasis in which mature readers are considered. For mature readers, reading is viewed by most theorists and researchers as a thoughtgetting process in which only the minimal textbound clues needed by the reader are used.

Approach-affected testing. At the primary grade levels, analytic, synthetic, and strategies approaches each give rise to the development of different types of word recognition tests. Testing following the analytic approach usually includes a sight vocabulary test, and the testing of specific word recognition units using whole words. The synthetic approach tests all of the elements of word recognition presented in isolation from words; blending tests are also included as are tests to determine if pupils are able to verbalize word recognition generalizations.

Following the strategies approach, testing usually involves determining whether a reader can use the cues of word recognition as strategies to determine meaning. Thus the assessment of word recognition necessitates selections to be read for meaning; the examiner tries to determine if the reader is able to use various word recognition strategies. Obviously, if the fourth approach is used, there would be no assessment of word recognition as such. Rather, the emphasis would be on assessing comprehension strategies to determine how well pupils are learning to read.

The impact of basals. The skills that are assessed in most published word recognition tests are those that are taught in basal reader programs. The number of specific skills and the actual skills included differ somewhat from one basal reading program to another, but generally the skills are similar. A list adapted from Harris and Sipay (1980) provides an overview of the kinds of skills included in word recognition instruction.

Grapheme/Phoneme Relationships
> beginning, ending, and medial consonants; consonant digraphs; consonant blends (beginning and ending); short vowels; long vowels; vowel digraphs; vowel dipthongs; schwa; r- controlled vowels; phonic generalizations

Consonant substitution

Context cues
> semantic cues; syntactic cues

Morphemic analysis
> inflectional endings; suffixes; prefixes; compound words; contractions

Structural analysis
> separating monosyllables into words; vowel sounds and syllables; syllable generalizations

Synthesis
> blending sounds into syllables; blending syllables into words

Accenting generalizations (p. 38)

In addition to these skills there are a number of word recognition skills that are usually classified as "reading readiness skills" and treated as a part of word recognition. These include visual and auditory discrimination, recognition of rhymed words, and knowledge of the letters of the alphabet. In addition, sight vocabulary is seen as an important part of the sequence by those who advocate an analytic approach.

In studying the print awareness of preschool children ages 3 to 5, however, Hiebert (1981) found that subjects did not achieve mastery levels on reading readiness tests, although they did have some proficiency on all measures used and they did show significant improvement with age. Hiebert argued that her findings support the contention that preschool children acquire both general and specific information about print in the world around them. She questions using readiness measures as the absolute determinant of whether children are ready to read.

Bourque (1980) attempted to determine the validity of any hierarchical development of word recognition skills by asking reading experts to arrange word recognition skills in a linear hierarchy. She found that "...the experts concur on only one aspect of hierarchical relationships, viz., sequence. That is, the experts indicate a willingness to say Skill I preceded Skill II. However, they stop short of saying that Skill I must be mastered before Skill II can be mastered; or that the mastery of Skill II will be facilitated by the prior mastery of Skill I; or that the mastery of both skills is mutually dependent, one on the other. In the final analysis, the hierarchies resulting from the judgments of experts, were, at best, weak" (p. 263-264). Despite her inability to determine a hierarchical word recognition skill sequence, Bourque did argue that "...hierarchical relationships among instructional relationships should foster the development of tailored testing programs and improve formative evaluation procedures" (p. 266).

Despite the differences in belief about how word recognition skills or strategies should be taught, or whether a specific skill hierarchy even exists, there is strong evidence that the teaching of word recognition constitutes a major part of reading instructional programs in the primary grades. In compensatory reading classes, over 80 percent of second grade teachers rated the following as major goals of teaching reading: phonic/structural analysis, visual discrimination, auditory discrimination, and using context clues (Howlett & Weintraub, 1979). Perhaps it is not surprising that teachers stated that teaching word recognition skills was an important goal of reading instruction; however, it is surprising that 87 percent of these second grade teachers reported that they spent a great deal of time on phonic/ structural analysis while only 45 percent reported that they spent a great deal of time promoting reading for enjoyment. In summarizing the data on teaching activities in compensatory reading classes, Howlett and Weintraub stated "...in particular, phonics and structural analysis skills were the first ranked activities at second grade in all approaches, and among the first three activities in fourth grade in all approaches" (p. 94).

How word recognition is tested

A large majority of reading tests used today have provisions for assessing word recognition. Because of the various types of reading ability testing (group versus individual, survey versus diagnostic, norm referenced versus criterion referenced) the method of testing also varies. With wide disagreement on theories and methods of teaching word recognition, the number of variations increases even more.

Matching tests to instructional approaches. Different types of word recognition tests have seemed to reflect three models of word recognition instruction. The analytic approach that most basal reading programs take is widely reflected in norm referenced group survey tests and group diagnostic tests. Analytic type word recognition tests usually include sight word tests and phoneme/grapheme tests which include whole words. For example, on the Iowa Tests of Basic Skills (1982), the word analysis subtest has nine objectives measuring knowledge of the phoneme/grapheme relationship. On all of these items, three picture or word choices are supplied. The teacher reads a word and the pupil locates a word with the same "sound."

The synthetic phonics approach is closely reflected in several individual diagnostic reading inventories: the Durrell Analysis of Reading Difficulty (1980), the Gates-McKillop Reading Diagnostic Tests (1962), and the Woodcock Reading Mastery Tests (1973). On the Durrell "Sounds of Letters" subtests, the teacher points to a consonant cluster and asks, "What does this say?" This demonstrates the belief that students must learn sounds in isolation, then whole words. Another example of the part to whole approach is found on the Gates-McKillop subtest entitled "Auditory Blending." The teacher pronounces the phonemes (for example, *st-or*, *uh-p*, *p-en*, *s-o*, *s-im-ply*), and the student must blend these to pronounce the word.

Nonsense words which mirror synthetic phonics are used frequently on these tests, emphasizing sounds first, meaning later. The Gates-McKillop uses nonsense words to test knowledge of vowels and syllabication. The student is asked to identify the vowel heard in the following words: *vum, keb, hote, rad, kine*, and to divide the following words into syllables: *laver* (which can be divided after the *a* or after the *v*), *indarill, aytherha*, and *nilowther*. The Woodcock entire word attack test of fifty items is made up of nonsense words such as *eldop, wunfambif*, and *bafmotbem*.

The third method of instruction, a more holistic model that dismisses the skills hierarchy and direct instruction of specific skills, assumes that readers will develop strategies for decoding naturally, much the way children learn language. This belief is demonstrated in the Reading Miscue Inventory (Goodman & Burke, 1972). Readers' miscues are judged for their grammatical acceptability, graphic similarity, sound similarity, dialect, intonation, semantic acceptability, and degree of meaning change. The test has grown out of the research of the Goodmans and their colleagues (Goodman, 1969, 1973; Goodman & Burke, 1973; Goodman & Goodman, 1977). They believe that the reader processes graphophonic, syntactic, and semantic cues simultaneously by 1) predicting meaning based on what the reader has already sampled in reading, 2) confirming that prediction, and 3) correcting as is necessary to construct meaning. Because it is believed that reading strategies can be inferred from oral reading behavior, the readers' miscues also aid in comprehension assessment.

Five popular tests. A closer examination of five popular group tests reveals that not only do the word recognition tests differ at a theoretical level, but they also lack uniformity in the number and type of subskills tested, the level at which specific skills are measured, the point at which word recognition as a separate process is no longer assessed, the method of assessment for any one skill, and the number of items presented to measure a skill.

The Reading Instructional Test of the Metropolitan Achievement Test (MAT) (1978) and the Stanford Achievement Test (SAT) (1981) measure word analysis to grades 6.9 and 7.9 respectively. While the Comprehensive Test of Basic Skills (CTBS) (1981), Iowa Test of Basic Skills (ITBS) (1982), and the California Achievement Test (CAT) (1977) all end their word analysis subtests by the end of third grade. The variance in the number of subtests relating to word analysis and word recognition is illustrated in the following table:

MAT

Visual Discrimination	K.5-1.4
Letter Recognition	K.5-1.4
Auditory Discrimination	K.5-2.4
Sight Vocabulary	K.5-4.9
Phoneme/Grapheme: Consonants	K.5-6.9
Phoneme/Grapheme: Vowels	2.5-6.9
Word Part Clues	1.5-6.9

SAT

Sounds and Letters	K.0-1.9
Word Reading	K.0-3.9
Word Study Skills	1.5-7.9

CTBS

Visual Recognition	K.0-K.9
Sound Recognition	K.0-K.9
Word Attack	K.6-3.9

ITBS

Word Analysis	K.1-3.5

CAT

Prereading	K.0-1.3
Phonic Analysis	K.5-3.9
Structural Analysis	1.5-3.9

This glance at the titles of the subtests really does not tell much about the content. The MAT Teacher's Manual lists a total of thirty-eight objectives for the subtests noted on the table above spanning levels K.5-6.9. Each grade level of sight words is listed separately, as is each of the short and long vowels. The ITBS lists only fifteen objectives. A closer examination of the actual items on these two tests shows that both cover similar content, with the Iowa actually including more "skills" than the MAT. The Iowa includes recognition of medial consonants, rhyming words, word building (adding letters to given bases), and substitution of initial, medial, and final consonants. An example of the last of these asks the test taker to take the *n* away from the word *churn,* to put *ch* in its place, and then to mark the picture of the word resulting. The MAT includes a sight word test, but the Iowa does not.

Specific skills tested. A content analysis shows the following skills tested at some level of the MAT, CTBS, ITBS, CAT, and SAT: letter recognition, auditory discrimination of initial consonants, initial and final vowels, long and short vowels, dipthongs and variants, recognition of prefixes and suffixes, recognition of compound words. The skills measured are tallied in the following table:

Skills Tested	MAT	CTBS	ITBS	CAT	SAT
Visual Discrimination of Shapes, Letters, or Words	X			X	
Sight Words	X	X			X
Consonants, Medial			X	X	X
Silent Letters	X		X		
Rhyming Words		X	X		
Syllabication			X	X	X
Root Words (recognition)			X		
Inflectional Endings	X		X	X	X
Contractions		X		X	X
Substitutions (Initial, Medial, Final Consonants)			X		
Word Building			X		

Levels at which skills are tested. The lack of consistency across the tests does not stop with these differences. Often there is variation as to when certain skills are tested. For example, short vowels are first tested in second grade on the MAT and ITBS but are tested as early as the middle of kindergarten on the CAT. Only one level of the ITBS tests vowels, while three levels of the MAT include vowel items. Silent letters are tested at the end of first grade on the ITBS but not until the middle of the third grade on the MAT.

Syllabication is tested through the second grade on the CTBS, but through the seventh grade on the SAT. Another major difference in tests is the number of items assessing each skill. On the ITBS, level 8 (grades 2.7-3.5), seventeen items measure knowledge of vowel sounds. An equivalent level of the MAT (Primary 2: grades 2.5-3.4) includes thirty-six vowel related items.

Different item technologies. The final difference noted is the method of assessment. An examination of the format of the vowel sections of the ITBS and MAT reveals that what is called "vowels" really may be testing something else. All thirty-six items on the MAT are read independently by the examinee. A key word with an underlined vowel or vowel combination is given. The student selects the word that has the same vowel sound from four choices. Some vowel generalizations used are not of high frequency or utility in the English language. For example, the examinee is to look at the sound made by the *ie* in the word *friend* and, rejecting the distractors *laid*, *quite*, and *field*, is to match it to the sound found in *said*.

In most items, the stimulus words would be recognizable by sight but a few, such as *united* and *fault*, may not be sight words at this level. It is possible that this test may be testing something other than the match of phoneme and grapheme.

On the ITBS, four formats are included. In each, the test taker selects from three—not four—options. In one, the examinee looks at pictures and marks the one that has a name that has the same vowel sound as a given word, which is read by the teacher. Another format has the test taker mark the word that has the same vowel sound as another word read by the teacher. Still another type of item asks the test taker to mark a picture whose name has, for example, "the long *a*" sound in it. The fourth type has the pupil mark the word whose name has, for example, "the short *e*" in it.

The variety of differences noted here on the vowel items of the ITBS and the MAT are merely examples of differences that can be noted across skills and between most tests. It is difficult to be sure that two tests which measure similar objectives with such different procedures are measuring the same thing. This question obviously, is closely related to the basic questions which underlie considerations of word recognition: Exactly what is it? How should it be assessed? How many items are needed for a true evaluation? A more important question is: Even if tests agreed to measure the same behaviors in the same ways, are these behaviors separable from the total reading process so that their assessment is itself a valid procedure?

It appears that major test publishers have followed the lead of major basal reading text publishers, offering a smorgasbord of skills—a bit of everything for everyone—hoping to achieve for their tests at least some instructional validity. This places the burden on the test users who must examine how well the test matches their instructional philosophies, objectives, and methods of instruction. This can be done only through careful item analysis.

How reliable and valid are word recognition measures?

The consideration of the reliability and the validity of word recognition tests raises important technical and theoretical questions, most of which have not been dealt with and most of which are related to questions about how word recognition is defined.

Reliability. Beyond the reliability data established for most tests when they are normed, research aimed at verifying or refuting such claims is virtually nonexistent. The potential replication of scores in test-retest situations, the equivalence of the alternate forms of a particular test, the equal ability of items that profess to measure a particular subskill to do that—all of these matters tend to be accepted on good faith by test users, if they are concerned about reliability.

Yet those who are interested in the reliability of reading instruments do not always find a plethora of information in the manuals of published tests on which to base their judgment. Descriptions of the subjects are sometimes scanty and are rarely as complete as the discerning test user would want them to be.

The tendency to take reliability for granted appears especially true for measures of word recognition because the general lack of consensus about what word recognition is and the great variety among tests that proclaim to measure it provoke discerning users to be distracted with a concern about the validity of an instrument. Test administrators seldom worry about an instrument's potential for producing random (as opposed to dependable or true) scores for the students tested; rather, they are more apt to evaluate the test in terms of whether it appears to measure the skills they believe should be used to recognize words during the reading act.

Validity and real reading. Many aspects of a test are related to its validity. In the case of a word recognition test, a prime validity concern is whether what it measures has any valid relationship to what readers do when they actually read. This concern focuses initially on whether the various word recognition skills measured by different tests can actually be isolated so that the test takers' responses to items have any semblance to what is happening when they read for pleasure or for learning from content materials.

There is clear evidence in research literature—and apparent general acceptance among authorities in the field of reading—that readers follow a trend away from word focused or component processing toward more holistic processing as they mature. Samuels, LaBerge, and Bremer (1978) found this when studying readers ranging from grade two through college. This suggests that the older the audience for which a reading test is designed, the less likelihood there should be of it containing items on word recognition.

Validity and component processing. There are research findings that can be cited to support the presence of some word recognition subskills in the processing of young readers (if not to explain their interrelationships and to establish their priority importance). Numerous studies have suggested that there is a relationship between beginning readers' phonographic awareness and their progress as comprehenders of text.

Zifcak (1981) found a significant correlation between the ability of subjects in one urban first grade class to segment words into their constituent phoneme units and to pronounce invented spellings with their achievement on the Wide Range Achievement Test (WRAT) (1965) and on a nonstandardized analytical reading test. Interestingly, this study did not find auditory analysis skills to have predictive value. Zifcak's findings appear to support Venezky's conclusion (1974) that the ability to synthesize or blend isolated letter sounds is a prerequisite to reading proficiency.

Day et al. (1981) tested orthographic linguistic awareness at various stages of kindergarten and first grade and found that the scores on the reading readiness measures they used correlated highly (.68 to .80 depending on when the K test was administered) to achievement scores on two standardized measures given in the first grade. Other reading readiness skills also have been found to relate to early reading performance. Ashmore and Snyder (1980) found that visual memory correlated significantly with the reading performance of first graders on the WRAT.

Whaley and Kibby (1980) reviewed the data of twenty-two studies and found a correlation between "sound blending performance" and reading achievement test scores. They noted, however, that only one of the studies used visual (as opposed to auditory) stimuli. This was just one of several serious limitations they found in the studies reviewed. Whaley and Kibby next studied the "word synthesis" of first grade readers as a kind of generic word recognition approach inclusive of any phonetic and grammatical emphases each subject used. They found that all the subjects used some phonics, but regardless of what approach a subject emphasized, "word synthesis" related significantly to reading achievement. Interestingly, word synthesis ability correlated even more strongly to knowledge of vocabulary than to comprehension (Whaley & Kibby, 1980). Whaley and Kibby's undelineated word recognition skill seems supported by Hiebert's findings (1981) that no fixed order of particular reading readiness proficiencies could be determined in the way that three, four, and five year old children developed print awareness.

These are but a few examples of research findings that appear to support the role of different word recognition skills in beginning reading. Yet no research appears to explain how the different skills interrelate and, despite the ubiquity of some degree of phonic activity, no research has established that phonographic performance is primary for every reader to other abilities that may be operating, or that such an emphasis is absolutely essential to success in developing reading ability. Most findings fully support Robinson's study (1972), which could not distinguish strength in either auditory or visual modality as primary in guaranteeing the reading success of subjects followed up through the third grade.

What can be assumed from research is that instruments which measure a variety of skills to determine the reading readiness or word recognition ability of beginning readers have some general, inclusive kind of validity for various activities related to unlocking the meaning of text. But to interpret any one of the measures as a valid representation of the reading act or of reading potential is to invalidly deny whatever way they may be interacting, and to arbitrarily ignore clear indications that individual readers balance that one skill differently against other word recognition skills for potentially equal benefits. Thus a test that emphasizes one subskill, or which omits a particular subskill, might not be valid. Even a subscore on a test which keeps in balance whatever subskills may be essential may actually be valid only for pupils who happen to employ the skills in that balance; a pupil who scores low on one subskill may be compensating effectively with high ability on some other subskill while actually reading.

The importance of context to word recognition. Having acknowledged in beginning reading the possibility of unexplicated roles for various language awarenesses and proficiencies, and of what we have come to call word recognition skills, one can turn to evidence in the research that questions the validity of testing word recognition skills in isolation—that is, without housing the target word in an adequate context. Even for beginning readers, the importance of context in unlocking word meaning should not be overlooked. Sobkov and Moody (1979) found that the presentation of target words in a context significantly facilitated their identification by first graders.

The importance of context becomes more obvious in research which has used subjects in the middle grades. In studying the reading of poor and average fourth grade readers, Allington and Fleming (1978) found that misreading visually similar words did not act as a distinct deficit to comprehension, but the failure to integrate semantic and syntactic clues did interfere. Their most interesting finding was that the inability to use context clues was a greater handicap for poorer readers than for better readers. Graham (1980) found that fourth, fifth, and sixth grade learning disabled pupils with reading problems exhibited adequate mastery of symbol-sound associations, and used the same semantic and syntactic clues as average readers in their classrooms.

Fleisher, Jenkins, and Pany (1979) found that drilling poor readers in grades four and five on both isolated words and words embedded only in phrases significantly increased their speed in decoding single words but did not improve their reading comprehension. Operating on the assumption that acquiring phonic syllabication skills is unrelated to reading comprehension, Cunningham, Cunningham, and Rystrom (1981) taught third graders a simple nonphonetic system for dividing words and found it unrelated to their subsequent reading achievement.

In the middle grades, as for beginning readers, there are indications from research that what happens when one reads varies from reader to reader, and that the skills of reading are intricately interrelated. In such a situation, any claims that measures of isolated word recognition skills are valid measures of anything close to real reading are questionable. McNeil and Donant (1980) found that children can learn multiple word recognition strategies — that they can be taught to identify words using graphophonic, structural, and contextual clues; but the researchers made no attempt to relate their findings to the ability of their subjects to comprehend text.

Kendall and Hood (1979), on the other hand, were primarily concerned about how word comprehension and higher levels of comprehension relate. They studied two groups of fifth graders, one tested as strong at higher levels of comprehension but weak on word recognition, and one as strong on word recognition but weak at higher levels of comprehension. They concluded that, between word comprehension and comprehension of larger segments of text, there are tradeoffs which indicate there is more involved in comprehending text than the ability to recognize words.

By the time one is considering adult readers, the validity of teaching or testing even syntactic word recognition skills may be in question. Manelis and Tharp (1977) found that college students process words with suffixes as one unit and not as affixed base words. More research of this nature might reveal at what general age level certain word recognition strategies give way to more holistic processing.

The validity of instruments which test isolated word recognition skills appears highly questionable in terms of how well such tests reflect the actual activity of reading. It seems increasingly clear that attempts to measure word recognition within a meaningful context are apt to reflect more closely the real reading activity, perhaps because they necessarily involve the test taker.

Validity and reader background. The words *meaningful context* automatically focus on another concern about the validity of tests. Reader background is an issue most pertinent to comprehension, but word recognition measures need to match that context to the backgrounds of those who will be asked to take the test. The lack of a match between an examinee's background and the content of a reading test is, of course, a problem that confounds the validity of any reading test. Hood (1982) has raised the question of how text variables in the Reading Miscue Inventory affect responses, but it is equally pertinent to all reading measures.

A concern for factoring background out of reading tests only promises to guarantee that the context used would be relatively void of context; that is, it would be free of meaning or equally unmeaningful to all who read it. In either case, the validity of such tests as they reflect what reading is all about would surely suffer severely. As Johnston (1981) points out, the question of whether such factors as reader background should be factored out of reading assessment is now moot since developing research and theory unequivocably show that comprehension depends on them.

At the same time, the advisability of measuring word comprehension in context suggests some kind of control of the relevance of the text to reader background so that its impact is not undetermined. Some use of schema theory to try to guarantee that all context falls within the background experience of readers who will take a test has been recommended by Royer and Cunningham (1981).

An issue closely related to a consideration of background and validity is that of how appropriate the content of a test is for a specific and atypical group of test takers. Some of the questions arising from this issue can be answered by the test administrator's needs. If, for example, an examiner wants to know how a group of students learning English as their second language would fare in real world, English speaking arenas, a test standardized on a broad national sample might be meaningful. It might also yield diagnostic instructional data. But it would probably be highly invalid as an indicator of the true language abilities of those students.

A study by Desberg et al. (1979) compared a group of second graders who spoke black dialect to a group that did not. They found that the dialect did not act as an interference to reading comprehension for those who spoke it. The only significant difference was that those who spoke black dialect outperformed the other group on items written in black dialect and appeared to be bidialectal. Such a study suggests the need for more research on how valid or invalid the content of standardized tests is for special groups.

The validity of testing procedures. Questions about the importance of testing word recognition in context and the relevance of that context to reader background are actually questions about how a test is written. They are, however, just two of the many questions related to how testing techniques and procedures affect validity. If there is a paucity of research related to the reliability of reading tests, the lack of research on the validity or invalidity of the host of testing procedures available is even more surprising. Since that variety is most evident in measures of word recognition, a discussion of the validity of those instruments is an appropriate place to note the need for such research. We have almost everything yet to learn about how such techniques as multiple choice and cloze affect responses, their resemblance to actual reading, and their ability to report on what is supposedly being measured. Many more studies like that done by Baumann, Walker, and Johnson (1981) are needed. They demonstrated that the difficulty of distractors had a significant effect on the scores of second, third, and fourth graders taking a word identification test. They noted that inconsistency in controlling the attraction (the difficulty) of distractors could lead to an instrument's actually measuring distractor difficulty and not target word difficulty. It seems possible that this may be true of the multiple choice format in general, even when the difficulty of distractors is uniformly controlled.

The potential number of issues to be examined in studies of the validity of testing techniques are as varied as the techniques themselves, and they are compounded by the many subordinate decisions test publishers must make once they have settled on a technique. Of particular interest is the fact that a single reading test may necessarily use strikingly different techniques to test different subskills within word recognition. Since research shows these skills to be functioning in some interrelated but unexplained way that varies from reader to reader, the validity considerations become quite complex. That fact, however, does not mean they should be ignored.

Some testing procedures are unique enough to have attracted some attention in regard to validity. The validity of the Reading Miscue Inventory—an instrument with direct relevance to word recognition—has been questioned by several reviewers (Harris & Sipay, 1980; Leu, 1982). Leu questioned whether an oral reading miscue given to the teacher as the audience genuinely reflects oral reading behavior under different circumstances, and whether it actually reports on silent reading behavior. Yet these challenges are applicable to all reading tests. Does a written response relate to reading? Does the test environment ever validly recreate real reading situations? Such questions need the attention of more researchers.

The instructional validity of tests. If the instructional validity of a test is the concern of a test user—as it certainly should be—then concern whether a test matches what happens in the actual reading process might be tactically ignored in order to evaluate and/or guide instructional practices to which a teacher or school is committed. Technically, if a pupil has been subjected to enough instruction formatted just like the test, the reading necessary to answer a word recognition item might well reflect a percentage of the pupil's "real" reading experience.

Allowing that such perspectives preclude, at least temporarily, the more important and encompassing question of instructional validity, making sure that one is measuring what has been taught is an educationally responsible procedure that should be followed by all test administrators. It means selecting tests after careful examination of their items, emphases, procedures, and content. In the light of the great variety with which different publishers identify, classify, and test what are generally called word recognition skills, this should be a highly interesting task. While such an examination might prompt an instructional staff to consider whether the instruction of some skill they discover is worth teaching, test selection should never dictate curriculum. The ideal direction of such a procedure is the careful philosophic discussion of what word recognition is, the designing and implementation of an instructional program, and the selection or creation of a testing instrument which can diagnose and/or evaluate it.

Instructional validity is the minimal validity that any educational program ought to tolerate. Hopefully, an increased amount of research on other validity issues will clarify whether word recognition skills ought to be taught and tested at what levels and if so, how.

Recommendations for word recognition assessment

With so much uncertainty about what word recognition is and about how, and even if, it should be measured, what can a test user who believes that word recognition is a valid reading emphasis do to insure that testing enhances instruction? In addition to suggestions that are stated and inferred in the preceding discussion, there are sensible and specific practices that can be followed.

The following recommendations are not based on a particular theoretical view of the function of word recognition in reading; nor are they pertinent to a particular teaching strategy. They are intended to cut across theoretical viewpoints and teaching approaches and thus should be considered by all who are concerned.

1. If a decision is made to assess students' word recognition skills, the test should be selected to match the approach used to teach them and the specific skills they have been taught. For example, if an analytic phonics approach is used, it would not be appropriate to use the test to determine if students can synthesize separate sounds into words. Moreover, if certain skills are not taught, they should not be tested. For example, if a particular instructional program does not include the teaching of syllables, then students should not be tested to determine if they can divide words into syllables.

2. Skills tests are always designed to inform on process and should not be used to judge whether a child can read. If specific skills are taught to

help a child learn to read better, the assessment should focus on better reading, that is, on whether the child can comprehend what is read. Skills tests may be used for diagnostic purposes, but they should not be used to determine whether a child has learned to read.

3. Related to recommendation 2, scores on word recognition subtests should not be added to scores on comprehension subtests to provide a total reading score. Comprehension *is* total reading, and combining word recognition subscores with comprehension subscores confounds the measurement of comprehension. Word recognition scores should serve as diagnostic references informing the instruction of proficiencies deemed important enough in the instructional program to be tested. As diagnostic informers, there is a question about the utility of totaling the scores of various word recognition subskills to get a single score.

4. It is necessary to determine how well students read before determining which word recognition skills tests to administer. Word recognition tests are diagnostic tests that recommend skills or strategies to be taught. However, if students can read satisfactorily at a particular level, there is no need to assess word recognition skills which supposedly allow them to read at that level. For example, if students can read fifth grade level material satisfactorily, it is not necessary to test them to determine if they can match initial consonant graphemes with phonemes. The students have already demonstrated that behavior by effectively reading fifth grade level material.

5. Word recognition skills and processes should help readers recognize words in the context of reading. Therefore, the assessment of word recognition skills should assess the skills in as much context as possible. The use of prefixes and suffixes should include the words to which affixes are to be added in the context of sentences. This recommendation does not encourage the use of nonsense words to determine word recognition skills.

6. Any word recognition test should be considered as a sample of the many word recognition behaviors that could be tested. Attention should not be focused on narrow objectives such as matching the initial consonant *b* with the phoneme /b/. The initial consonant phoneme/grapheme matching test should be interpreted as evidence about how well the examinee can use initial consonant clues to recognize words.

7. A test of any word recognition objective should be of adequate length to assure at least somewhat stable results. It is wasteful of teaching time to focus skill instruction on the results of an unreliable assessment. There has been a proliferation of word recognition tests made up of long lists of narrowly defined word recognition behaviors. These tests often in-

clude as few as three test items per objective. It is impossible to achieve stable assessment results with so few items. Any word recognition skill worthy of attention should be assessed by at least twelve items to diminish the possibility that chance and guessing will dictate instructional decisions.

8. Test administrators should be sure that examinees understand what they are supposed to do on the test. Word recognition tests often utilize unusual formats, and are usually administered to the lowest grade levels. It is not surprising that some pupils who are good readers do not perform well on word recognition skills tests. They do know the skills, but do not understand the test.

References

Allington, R.L., and Fleming, J.T. The misreading of high frequency words. *Journal of Special Education,* 1978, *12,* 417-421.

Anderson, R.C., Reynolds, R.E., Schallert, D.L., and Goetz, E.T. Frameworks for comprehending discourse. *American Educational Research Journal,* 1977, *14,* 367-381.

Anderson, R.C., Spiro, R.J., and Anderson, M.C. Schemata as scaffolding for the representation of information in connected discourse. *American Educational Research Journal,* 1978, *15,* 433-440.

Anderson, R.C., Spiro, R.J., and Montague, W. (Eds.), *Schooling and the acquisition of knowledge.* Hillsdale, NJ: Erlbaum, 1977.

Ashmore, R.J. and Snyder, R.T. Relationship of visual and auditory short-term memory to later reading achievement. *Perceptual and Motor Skills,* 1980, *15,* 15-18.

Baker, L., and Anderson, R.I. Effects of inconsistent information on text processing: Evidence for comprehension monitoring. *Reading Research Quarterly,* 1982, *17,* 281-294.

Baumann, J.F., Walker, R.N., and Johnson, D.D. Effect of distractor word variability in children's performance on a word identification test. *Reading Psychology,* 1981, *2,* 88-96.

Beck, I.L., & McKeown, M.G. Instructional research in reading: A retrospective. In J. Orasanu (Ed.), *Reading comprehension: From research to practice.* Hillsdale, NJ: Erlbaum (in press).

Bourque, M.L. Specification and validation of reading skills hierarchies. *Reading Research Quarterly,* 1980, *15,* 237-267.

Bransford, J.D., and Johnson, M.K. Consideration of some problems of comprehension. In W.G. Chase (Ed.), *Visual information processing.* New York: Academic Press, 1973.

Bransford, J.D., and McCarrell, N.S. A sketch of a cognitive approach to comprehension. In W. Weiner and D. Polermo (Eds.), *Cognition and the symbolic process.* Hillsdale, NJ: Erlbaum, 1974.

Caldwell, E.C., Nix, D.H., and Peckham, P.D. Higher order units in reading instruction. *Contemporary Educational Psychology,* 1981, *6,* 127-134.

Carey, R.F., Harste, J.C., and Smith, S.L. Contextual constraints and discourse processes: A replication study. *Reading Research Quarterly,* 1981, *16,* 201-212.

Cattell, J.M. The time it takes to see and name objects. *Mind,* 1886, *11,* 63-65.

Chall, J.S. *Learning to read: The great debate.* New York: McGraw-Hill, 1967.

Chall, J.S. *Stages of reading development.* New York: McGraw-Hill, 1983.

Collins, A., Brown, J.S., and Larkin, K. Inference in text understanding. In R.J. Spiro, B.C. Bruce, and W.F. Brewer (Eds.), *Theoretical issues in reading comprehension.* Hillsdale, NJ: Erlbaum, 1980.

Cunningham, P.M., Cunningham, J.W., and Rystrom, R.C. A new syllabication strategy and reading achievement. *Reading World,* 1981, *20,* 208-214.

Day, K.C., Day, H.D., Spicola, R., and Griffen, M. The development of orthographic linguistic awareness in kindergarten children and the relationship of this awareness to later reading achievement. *Reading Psychology,* 1981, *2,* 76-87.

Desberg, P., Marsh, G., Schneider, L.A., and Duncan-Rose, C. The effects of social dialect on auditory sound blending and word recognition. *Contemporary Educational Psychology,* 1979, *4,* 140-144.

Downing, J., and Leong, C.K. *Psychology of reading.* New York: Macmillan, 1982.

Eco, U. *The role of the reader.* Bloomington, IN: Indiana University Press, 1978.

Fleisher, L.S., Jenkins, J.R., and Pany, D. Effects on poor readers' comprehension of training in rapid decoding. *Reading Research Quarterly,* 1979, *15,* 30-48.

Goodman, K.S. Analysis of oral reading miscues: Applied psycholinguistics. *Reading Research Quarterly,* 1969, *5,* 9-30.

Goodman, K.S. Miscues: Windows on the reading process. In K.S. Goodman (Ed.), *Miscue analysis: Applications to reading instruction.* Urbana, IL: National Council of Teachers of English, 1973.

Goodman, K.S. Decoding: From what to what? In F.V. Gollasch (Ed.), *Language and literacy: The selected writings of Kenneth S. Goodman,* Volume 1. Boston: Routledge & Kegan Paul, 1982.

Goodman, K.S., and Burke, C.L. *Theoretically based studies of patterns of miscues in oral reading performance.* USOE project no. 90375. Washington, DC: U.S. Department of Health, Education and Welfare, April 1973.

Goodman, K.S., and Goodman, Y.M. Learning about psycholinguistic processes by analyzing oral reading. *Harvard Educational Review,* 1977, *47,* 317-333.

Gough, P.B. One second of reading. In J.F. Kavanagh and I.G. Mattingly (Eds.), *Basic studies on reading.* New York: Basic Books, 1972.

Graham, S. Word recognition skills of learning disabled children and average students. *Reading Psychology,* 1980, *2,* 23-33.

Harris, A.J., and Sipay, E.R. *How to increase reading ability,* seventh edition. New York: Longman, 1980.

Hiebert, E.H. Developmental patterns and interrelationships of preschool children's print awareness. *Reading Research Quarterly,* 1981, *16,* 236-260.

Hood, J. The relationship of selected text variables to miscue scores of second graders. *Journal of Reading Behavior,* 1982, *14,* 141-158.

Howlett, N., and Weintraub, S. Instructional procedures. In R.C. Calfee and P.R. Drum (Eds.), *Teaching reading in compensatory classes.* Newark, DE: International Reading Association, 1979.

Johnston, J.C. Effects of advance precuing of alternatives on the perception of letters alone and in words. *Journal of Experimental Psychology,* 1981, *7,* 560-572.

Kendall, J.R., and Hood, J. Investigating the relationship between comprehension and word recognition: Oral reading analysis of children with comprehension or word recognition disabilities. *Journal of Reading Behavior,* 1979, *11,* 41-48.

LaBerge, D., and Samuels, S.J. Toward a theory of automatic information processing in reading. *Cognitive Psychology,* 1974, *6,* 293-323.

Leu D.J., Jr. Oral reading error analysis: A critical review of research and application. *Reading Research Quarterly,* 1982, *17,* 420-437.

McConkie, G.W., Hogaboam, T.W., Wolverton, G.S., Zola, D., and Lucas, P. *Toward the use of eye movements in the study of language processing.* Technical report 134. Champaign, IL: Center for the Study of Reading, University of Illinois, 1979.

McNeil, J.D., and Donant, L. Transfer effect of word recognition strategies. *Journal of Reading Behavior,* 1980, *12,* 97-103.

Manelis, L., and Tharp, D.A. The processing of affixed words. *Memory and Cognition,* 1977, *5,* 690-695.

Robinson, H.M. Visual and auditory modalities related to methods for beginning reading. *Reading Research Quarterly,* 1972, *8,* 7-39.

Rosenblatt, L. *The reader, the text, the poem.* Carbondale, IL: Southern Illinois University Press, 1978.

Rosenblatt, L. *The role of the reader.* Bloomington, IN: Indiana University Press, 1978.

Royer, J.M., and Cunningham, D.J. On the theory and measurement of reading comprehension. *Contemporary Educational Psychology,* 1981, *6,* 187-216.

Samuels, S.J., LaBerge, D., and Bremer, C.D. Units of word recognition: Evidence for developmental changes. *Journal of Verbal Learning and Verbal Behavior,* 1978, *17,* 715-720.

Smith, F. *Understanding reading.* New York: Holt, Rinehart and Winston, 1971.

Sobkov, J., and Moody, M. Memory and reading: The effects of semantic context on word identification. *Journal of General Psychology,* 1979, *100,* 229-236.

Spiro, B.C. Bruce, and W.F. Brewer (Eds.), *Theoretical issues in reading comprehension*. Hillsdale, NJ: Erlbaum, 1980.

Strange, M. The effect of orthographic anomalies upon reading behavior. *Journal of Reading Behavior*, 1979, *11*, 154-163.

Venezky, R.L. *Testing in reading*. Urbana, IL: National Council of Teachers of English, 1974.

Whaley, J., and Kibby, M.W. Word synthesis and beginning reading achievement. *Journal of Educational Research*, 1980, *73*, 132-138.

Zifcak, M. Phonological awareness and reading acquisition. *Contemporary Educational Psychology*, 1981, *6*, 117-126.

Test References

California Achievement Test, Form C. Monterey, CA: California Test Bureau/McGraw-Hill, 1977.

Comprehensive Test of Basic Skills, Form U. Monterey, CA: California Test Bureau/McGraw-Hill, 1981.

Durell Analysis of Reading Difficulty, New Edition. D. Durrell. New York: Harcourt Brace Jovanovich, 1980.

Gates-McKillop Reading Diagnostic Tests, Form 1. New York: Teachers Press, Columbia University, revised 1962.

Iowa Tests of Basic Skills. A.N. Hieronymous, E.F. Lindquist, and H.D. Hoover. Chicago: Riverside Publishing, 1982.

Metropolitan Achievement Tests: Reading. R.C. Farr, G.A. Prescott, I.H. Balow, and T.H. Hogan. New York: Psychological Corporation, 1978.

Reading Miscue Inventory. Y. Goodman and C.L. Burke. New York: Macmillan, 1972.

Stanford Achievement Test. E.F. Gardner, H.C. Rudman, B. Karlsen, and J.C. Merwin. New York: Psychological Corporation, 1981.

Wide Range Achievement Test. J.F. Jastak and J.R. Jastak. Austin, TX: Guidance Testing Associates, 1936, revised 1965.

Woodcock Reading Mastery Tests. R.W. Woodcock. Circle Pines, MN: American Guidance Service, 1973.

4
Assessing reading vocabulary, study skills, and rate

Reading vocabulary

The extensive use of formal reading tests to measure reading vocabulary results from a strong emphasis on the teaching of reading vocabulary in most elementary classrooms. The common practice of testing words in isolation, however, is at odds with an instructional emphasis in many reading programs which teach words in a meaningful context—a practice endorsed by most reading researchers, theorists, and educators. Since assessment should reflect what is happening in and is recommended for the classroom, a brief review of instruction and of research and theory provides a relevant context within which the assessment of reading vocabulary can be examined.

Vocabulary instruction: Defining practices

The commonly held assumption of those who teach vocabulary and subsequently test its acquisition is that word knowledge is directly related to reading comprehension. In a recent review of eight studies of different types of reading programs, however, Mezynski (1983) examined the resultant correlations and could not conclude that word knowledge could be said to directly facilitate comprehension. Mezynski's conclusion should not seem very surprising in light of Goodman's view (1976) that vocabulary development (that is, learning the meaning of words) must be developed in a total language context. Goodman has stated that, "Vocabulary development outside of the context of new ideas and preexisting language is not possible" (p. 487).

A prevalent practice. Regardless of Mezynski's surprising observation, there is little doubt that vocabulary instruction is a prevalent practice in the schools. Based on the results of a national study of compensatory education classes, Howlett and Weintraub (1979) report that learning the meaning of words was a major goal of 81 percent of the fourth grade teachers, and 85 percent of the sixth grade teachers surveyed. An average of 70 percent of the second, fourth, and sixth grade teachers in this study said that they spent a great deal of time teaching word meaning; and 55 percent reported spending a great deal of time teaching sight vocabulary.

At all levels — from first through eighth grades — vocabulary instruction is a major focus of basal readers. Almost all basals introduce new words at the beginning of each story to develop pupils' familiarity with the words before they are encountered in the stories. Usually, the teacher is advised to introduce the words in an oral or written context. This introduction is followed by various instructional procedures designed to familiarize the pupils with the meanings of the new words. Next, some practice activity directs the pupils to apply their knowledge of the word meanings in context.

The emphasis of basal readers on vocabulary instruction takes on added significance in light of the findings by Howlett and Weintraub that the basal reader was the predominant instructional material used in compensatory classrooms. Since basal readers are much more likely to be used in regular classrooms than in compensatory classrooms, it becomes clear that basal readers are the predominant instructional material used in teaching reading.

A practice endorsed. Reading authorities often describe the learning of word meanings as the first step in developing reading comprehension. Brown (1982), in his book on reading diagnosis and remediation, divides comprehension into four categories, the first of which is the development of vocabulary meanings. Dechant (1981) believes that one of the causes of reading disability is a pupil's difficulty in associating meaning with particular printed words, contending that the development of reading vocabulary is the initial step in developing reading comprehension.

The procedures prescribed by basal programs also appear to reflect those recommended in instructional methodology books. A brief overview of the expert opinion in methodology texts concerned with the teaching of reading clearly supports the prevalent practice in elementary schools of teaching vocabulary as a discrete reading skill. Most of these books describe vocabulary instruction at some length. These texts recommend teaching vocabulary systematically and in a contextual setting.

The instruction strategies described in most of these books emphasize that teaching word meanings is the same as teaching concepts. Thus they encourage teachers to present words in context and to provide pupils with as much concrete experience with each of the words as possible. They also suggest that when vocabulary is taught in the primary grades, the emphasis should be on teaching those words that are already part of the pupils' listening and speaking vocabularies. This makes the focus of instruction one of attaching known concepts to known words which are perhaps not recognizable in print.

Reading methods books emphasize that, when teaching vocabulary, a teacher is helping pupils to associate known experiences with a given word. Thus the texts provide suggestions for building vocabulary based on the common backgrounds and experiences of pupils and then relating these experiences to a new context. There are few suggestions for having pupils learn words and their meanings in isolation, nor are practice exercises which have pupils matching words with meanings in isolation suggested. Rather, the emphasis in methods books as well as in recent research is on determining word meanings as the words are used in context.

At the intermediate grades, the methodology books emphasize the extensive development of reading vocabularies as pupils begin to study more extensively in a variety of subject matter areas. Heilman, Blair, and Rupley (1981), for example, discuss the importance of teaching a variety of word meanings, developing richer word meanings, and teaching more precise use of words based on their meanings.

An emphasis on sight vocabulary. Another area of vocabulary that is discussed and emphasized in reading methodology texts is that of sight vocabulary. Sight vocabulary is usually defined as that set of words which a pupil can immediately recognize and pronounce. In most discussions of sight vocabulary, there is little or no mention of attaching meaning to these words. Rather, the discussion focuses on the immediate recognition of the words, especially emphasizing that the pupil does not need to use any word recognition skills to determine the pronunciation of the word (Brown, 1982; Heilman, Blair & Rupley, 1981; Dechant, 1981). Thus sight vocabulary is most often discussed in those sections of the books concerned with the teaching of word recognition skills rather than in the sections which focus on comprehension.

As do many other authorities, Brown (1982) suggests that the teaching of sight vocabulary is the foundation for teaching word recognition. He advocates that the analytic teaching of word recognition skills necessitates that each pupil recognize immediately a set of words which can be used by the teacher to develop word recognition skills. Brown goes on to say that as readers mature, most words become part of their immediate sight vocabulary. That is, readers recognize the words immediately on seeing them with no need to apply any word recognition skills.

What the theorists say

In the past several years, researchers and theorists have attempted to develop a more complete understanding of the reading process and the relationship of knowledge of word meanings to that process (Dreher & Singer, 1981; Freebody & Anderson, 1981; Kuczaj, 1982; McKeown, et al., 1983). Kuczaj (1982) has examined the development of word meanings from the point of view of a semanticist. He concludes that vocabulary development can best be thought of as a semantic system in which there are both individual word meanings and relations that hold among these meanings. Kuczaj suggests that vocabulary development is based on the interactive development of conceptual meaning, reflected meaning, and connotative meaning.

Vocabulary and comprehension. The effect of vocabulary on reading comprehension has been examined in several studies (Freebody & Anderson, 1983; Mason, Kniseley, & Kendall, 1979; Yap, 1979). Freebody and Anderson (1983) studied the effects of increasing the difficulty of vocabulary on the reading comprehension of sixth grade students. They manipulated the difficulty of reading vocabulary by substituting an unfamiliar synonym for specific words in a passage. Comprehension was measured through free recall, summarization, and sentence verification. The researchers concluded that increasing the difficulty of the vocabulary did in fact decrease reading comprehension scores. However, they stated that, "...it takes a surprisingly high proportion of difficult vocabulary to produce reliable decrements in comprehension measures" (p. 293).

Yap (1979) generally supported the conclusions reached by Freebody and Anderson. In a study using primary grade children, Yap concluded that reading vocabulary and comprehension are "probably" related causally— with vocabulary "likely" to be the predominant causal factor.

McKeown (McKeown, et al., 1983) reported on a study which utilized an extensive program of teaching word meanings to fourth grade children. The dependent variables in the study included accuracy of word knowledge, speed of lexical access, and comprehension of stories containing taught words. The experimental treatment was an extensive and rich program of teaching word meanings in context and was related to the backgrounds and experiences of the fourth grade subjects in the study. The instructional method led to significant gains for the students on measures of all the dependent variables.

Mason, Kniseley, and Kendall (1979) studied the effect on comprehension of words containing more than one meaning. The researchers found that when words were used a second time in a passage with meanings different from the first time the words were used, comprehension declined. The researchers cautioned, however, that the poorer comprehension may not have been just because pupils did not know the multiple meanings of words, but rather because they did not adequately utilize context clues to determine word meanings. The researchers suggested that the development of vocabulary has three goals: learning single meanings, learning multiple meanings, and learning to choose the correct meaning in context.

Accounting for reader background. The importance of a reader's background and experiences in attaching meaning to words has been emphasized by reading authorities for decades. However, in the past ten to fifteen years the topic has been researched extensively. "Instantiation" is a concept related to the development of word meanings unique to each reader. Basically, the concept of instantiation is that readers develop word meanings based on their own particular experiences. Thus, instantiation appears to endorse developing meanings in context and using a pupil's background and experiences to develop word meanings.

In discussing the theory of instantiation, Anderson and Shifrin (1980) argue that words do not have fixed meanings but that a word "...can be conceived to have a 'family' of potential meanings" (p. 332). Anderson and Shifrin recommend that instruction should be devised to develop instantiation skills. While the authors do not discuss the assessment of vocabulary, one can assume they would strongly urge that the testing of vocabulary be done so the words tested are embedded in context.

Dreher and Singer (1981) provide an excellent summary of the theory of instantiation:

> Instantiation has been investigated in relation to word meaning in context. There is considerable evidence that the meaning of a word which people encode depends upon the context in which the word occurs (e.g., Anderson & McGaw, 1973; Anderson & Ortony, 1975; Anderson, et al., 1976; Barclay, et al., 1974; Halff, Ortony, & Anderson, 1976). For example, Anderson and Ortony (1975) have argued that "It is impossible that the sense of an utterance could consist solely of a concatenation of the dictionary readings of its individual words" (p. 168). Instead, Anderson and Ortony propose that a word can take on "indefinitely many fine grada-

tions in meaning" (p. 177) and that these fine gradations in meaning are constructed through an interaction of incoming information and existing knowledge. One specific hypothesis arising from the body of literature on context sensitivity is the instantiation hypothesis which holds that "If the context is rich and if the message is processed deeply, a noun may be identified with a single real or imagined thing" (Anderson, et al., 1976, p. 667). Thus, general terms in sentences are said to be encoded on the basis of an exemplar or instantiation suggested by the context of a sentence and prior knowledge. (p. 224)

Reading vocabulary tests

In light of the strong instructional emphasis on the teaching of reading vocabulary, it is not surprising that most group survey tests of reading achievement include a separate measure of reading vocabulary. The inclusion of such a measure has much face validity. However, the wide array of procedures used to measure reading vocabulary casts doubt as to whether any of the tests measure the same behaviors.

How vocabulary has been assessed

The variety of testing procedures is not a recent development. Twenty-six different approaches for measuring word meaning were identified in 1934 by Kelley and Krey who analyzed standardized vocabulary and reading tests. Their resulting list was adapted from Dolch (1927).

A host of approaches. Kelley and Krey categorized the approaches as follows (p. 103):

1. Unaided recall
   A. Checking for familiarity
   B. Using words in a sentence
   C. Explaining the meaning
   D. Giving a synonym
   E. Giving an opposite
2. Aided recall
   A. Recall aided by recognition
      1) Matching tests
      2) Classification tests

3) Multiple choice tests
   a. Choosing the opposite
   b. Choosing the best synonym
   c. Choosing the best definition
   d. Choosing the best use in sentences
4) Same-opposite tests
5) Same-opposite-neither tests
6) Same-different tests
B. Recall aided by association
   1) Completion test
   2) Analogy test
C. Recall aided by recognition and association
   1) Multiple choice completion test
   2) Multiple choice substitution test

Kelley and Krey concluded that there did not seem to be any one best technique for measuring word meaning knowledge. They added that with the instruments current in the early 1930s there was little hope of accurately determining the extent or the quality of the reading vocabulary of an individual.

Analyses of behaviors. With time, the tendency has been to generalize such classifications in an emphasis on the processes an item demands and a deemphasis on item formats and distinctions. In a much more recent examination than the Kelley and Krey study, Curtis and Glaser (1983) examined vocabulary items from several standardized reading tests and concluded that the items from test to test differed in three ways: "The extent to which they assess individual's abilities to: 1) recognize a correct meaning of a word, 2) determine which of several correct meanings is appropriate in a given context, and, in come cases 3) figure out an unknown word's meaning from context" (p. 137). Curtis and Glaser suggest that these differences are not important if the purpose of testing is only predicting future reading performance or determining overall reading ability since the measures are all very highly correlated regardless of the measurement approach taken. They do, however, believe that differences in what is measured are quite important if the purpose of the testing concerns diagnosis and instruction.

But the perspective of Curtis and Glaser has roots, too. An attempt to analyze the behavior involved in a child's knowledge of the meaning of a word was undertaken by Crobach (1942). Cronbach's categorization of such behavior can be presented as follows:

1. Generalization. Can the child define the word?
2. Application. Can the child recognize an illustration of the word if properly named by the word?
3. Breadth of meaning. Can the pupil recall different meanings of the word?
4. Precision. Can the pupil apply the term correctly in all possible situations?
5. Availability. Does the child actually use the word?

But the condensation of concerns over what constitutes vocabulary into responses that different item types demand has not clarified the central issue. A major conclusion that can be drawn from the three examples of vocabulary test analysis just discussed is that vocabulary is not a unitary behavior and that the assessment of vocabulary may take many forms. The confusion over what is meant by *vocabulary* and over how it should be assessed is yet reflected in the myriad of subtests on standardized reading tests which are labeled "vocabulary," but which seem to measure quite different behaviors.

For example, the Gates-MacGinitie Reading Tests (1978) follow a fairly traditional pattern of presenting a word in isolation and asking examinees to select an appropriate synonym from several alternatives. The Iowa Tests of Basic Skills (1982) differ from the Gates-MacGinitie in that the words to be read are presented in a short phrase. The Metropolitan Achievement Tests: Reading (1978) differ significantly from both of these. On the Metropolitan, vocabulary is assessed in two different ways. In the first, examinees are asked to select the appropriate meaning for a word as that word is used in the context of a reading selection. In the second approach, the Metropolitan uses a modified cloze procedure in which a sentence with a missing word is provided and the examinee is to choose from several alternatives the word which best fits the sentence context.

The Stanford Achievement Test (1981) has a reading vocabulary test at grades 8 to 13 in which a definition of a word is given in a word or phrase, and the examinee is to select the meaning or synonym from several alternatives. At the upper grade levels, the Stanford is most similar to the Iowa Tests of Basic Skills. However, at grades 4 to 8 the Stanford does not contain a reading vocabulary test. This seems incongruous, since at the primary grades (K to 4), the Stanford includes a kind of vocabulary test which is labeled "Word Meaning." On the Word Meaning test, the examinee is asked to match spoken words with printed words and to match printed words with pictures. It should also be pointed out that the Stanford does have a listening vocabulary test from grades 1 to 9.

The mixed bag of approaches to measuring vocabulary is obvious in the tests just cited. On each, the task is quite different. On one, the words are presented in isolation; on two of the others, a brief context is provided; and on a fourth, the words are embedded in context. On two of the tests, the correct answers are synonyms of given words. Another asks for words that are defined by phrases, and still another asks for meanings of words as the words are used in a reading selection. One of the tests includes an assessment of reading vocabulary at primary grade levels and at high school grade levels, but it excludes the testing of reading vocabulary at the intermediate grade levels.

Another approach to measuring reading vocabulary is the cloze test. In addition to being used as assessments of reading vocabulary, cloze tests have been used to determine functional reading levels as well as to assess reading comprehension. Cloze tests are usually used informally as part of reading instruction, and modified cloze tests have been included on published reading tests.

A cloze test is developed by deleting words in a passage (usually every fifth or seventh word) and then asking examinees to supply the word that has been left out. On published cloze tests, a choice of responses is provided for each blank and the examinees are to select the word that best fills the blank based on the context of the passage. A student's ability to select the best word to complete the blanks in the passage has been used as a context measure of vocabulary.

Mitigating the confusion. The confusion caused by the diversity of methods for measuring reading vocabulary poses a serious problem for the test consumer: Which reading vocabulary subtest should be selected from the many available? If one assumes that reading vocabulary is a distinct and measurable subskill of reading, the problem of test selection can be mitigated somewhat if, when choosing a test, the *purpose* for testing is carefully considered (Pyrczak & Rasmussen, 1974; Thorndike & Hagen, 1969). If, for example, the purpose is to determine how well students are performing on one of the major goals of most reading programs—the development of broader reading vocabularies—then almost any of the assessments will do, as long as the test is appropriate to the ability of the students and there is some congruence between the words taught in the program and the words to be assessed.

If the purpose of testing is to provide a general assessment of students' reading abilities, it is not necessary to even include a separate measure of reading vocabulary since the correlation of tests of reading comprehension and reading vocabulary is usually quite high. However, if the purpose of assessing is to find out if students are increasing their reading vocabulary skill in relation to the total reading process, it seems essential that the test selected assesses vocabulary knowledge in context. The test should determine the extent to which an examinee can use syntactic and semantic clues to determine a specific meaning of a word as it is used in a particular context.

Finally, if the goal of testing is the diagnosis of various reading vocabulary behaviors, such as those outlined by Cronbach (1942) or by Curtis and Glaser (1983), a test should be selected which provides an analysis based on the outlines suggested by these authors. At the present time, there are no published tests available which provide this kind of reading vocabulary diagnosis.

Validity and reading vocabulary measures

Since test designers or reading researchers have developed no method of assessing vocabulary that has had endorsement in the form of predominant use on tests, the question arises: Are standardized tests of reading vocabulary valid measures of the quality or depth of a student's vocabulary power? Researchers have dealt with this question for many years. Dolch and Leeds (1953) examined five tests of reading vocabulary in use at the time: the Thorndike, the Gates, the Durrell-Sullivan, the Stanford, and the Metropolitan. They concluded that those tests did not measure depth of word meaning because 1) they ignored all but the most common meaning of words; and 2) when they used synonyms, their items tested a very indefinite amount of knowledge. Dolch and Leeds suggested that the most serious weakness of the five tests was that they failed to recognize that words have different meanings for different people and for different contexts, and that there is no one meaning for any particular word. Instead, they claimed, each word has a variety of meanings. Such a criticism still applies to reading vocabulary test items today.

Testing words in context. The problem Dolch and Leeds noted could be disarmed by the responses of test makers to the most serious validity questions about the assessment of vocabulary. A vast number of tests attempt to assess vocabulary skills by presenting words in isolation and directing students to select the best synonym from a number of alternatives. This method does not reflect reading vocabulary skills as an individual actually applies such an ability in a practical reading situation. Yet the most highly endorsed recommendation for the teaching of reading vocabulary emphasizes the introduction of words in context. Pupils should be encouraged to develop meanings for words that relate to their backgrounds and experiences. The testing of words in isolation seems to ignore that both the most highly recommended teaching practices and research and theory emphasize that the meaning of a word depends on the context in which that word occurs. Goodman (1968) has pointed out that reading is a "psycholinguistic guessing game" and that a student relies quite heavily on the semantic and syntactic context clues of a reading passage in determining the meaning and pronunciation of a word. Smith (1971) has seriously questioned the validity of defining any word out of context. Ehri and Roberts (1979) conducted an experiment in which two groups of first graders were taught to read a set of sixteen words. One group of first graders learned the words in printed sentence contexts while the other group learned the words as they were presented individually on flash cards and in oral sentences. When the students were given the posttests it was found that context trained children learned more about the semantic identities of the printed words; however, the flash card trained children could read the sixteen words faster and learned more about orthographic forms. The researchers suggested that there is value in considering the use of a variety of approaches to teaching word recognition. They also suggested that the assessment of word recognition is highly dependent on the specific type of instruction employed.

Asking for valid responses. Some of the variety in types of items and in the behaviors these items require from examinees that were noted earlier may have resulted from another concern about the validity of vocabulary tests. Some researchers have questioned the validity of using the same type of vocabulary test at all grade levels. Feifel and Lorge (1950) examined the types of oral vocabulary responses of 900 children between the ages of six and fourteen and found: 1) older children (ages ten to fourteen) more often use a synonym type definition than younger children (ages six to nine) and 2) younger children supply and use description type definitions more than older children. If spoken vocabulary can be used as an indication of reading vocabulary development, Feifel and Lorge's study could be used as a basis for the development of differentiated procedures for measuring reading vocabulary at different age levels in an attempt to make them more valid across age levels.

In investigating the quality of reading vocabulary responses of students at various age levels, Kruglov (1953) administered a ten item, five option multiple choice test to pupils in grades three, five, seven, and eight and to a group of college graduates. For each test item, three or four options were correct but were of different qualitative levels. Kruglov found that 1) there was an increase in the choice of synonym as the correct response for older students and 2) there was a significant decrease in the percentage of repetition, illustration, and inferior explanation type responses between any of the groups tested as the groups increased in age.

The preceding studies present rather convincing arguments that there are qualitative differences in students' responses to vocabulary items: younger students tended to choose more concrete definitions (descriptions and use) while older students chose more abstract definitions (synonyms and classifications). The ability of present vocabulary tests to measure these differences in student responses has been studied by several of the preceding authors who consistently pointed out that present tests are inadequate for measuring all but the very lowest level of vocabulary ability.

Testing for quality. Russell (1954) made various suggestions for improving the validity of reading vocabulary measures. The most serious problem in testing vocabulary, according to Russell, is that of determining verbalization—whether students supply correct answers without a real understanding of the concept to which they are responding. As have many others in the field of reading (Kruglov, 1953; Dolch & Leeds, 1953; Curtis & Glaser, 1983), Russell recommended that words to be used as test items be placed in as meaningful a situation as possible and that vocabulary tests be developed which evaluate the quality of students' reading vocabulary. Such measuring devices would include items designed to assess students' 1) precision in knowledge of words (*e.g.*, the ability to discriminate between words such as *valley* and *canyon*); 2) breadth of vocabulary (indicated by the number of words recognized and knowledge of multiple meanings of words such as run and strike); and 3) ability to use vocabulary in speaking, writing, and reading. Russell's three categories are similar to those of Curtis and Glaser (1983) which include 1)accuracy—the storing of appropriate meaning in memory, 2) flexibility—the richness or depth of meaning, and 3) fluency—the speed with which meanings are accessed from memory.

Determining quantity. Another point of controversy that relates to the validity of reading vocabulary tests has centered on how useful standardized reading tests are in determining the size of the student's vocabulary. For many years, research has been concerned with how extensive the vocabularies of children are. Smith (1941) conducted a number of studies showing that the usually accepted estimates of the size of students' listening vocabularies may be vastly underestimated because the test constructors used abridged dictionaries in selecting the words included in that test. Estimates of vocabulary size based on a sampling of unabridged dictionaries by Smith indicated that the average first grader knows 24,000 different words, the average sixth grader knows 49,500 words, the average high school student knows 80,000 words, and the average university student knows 157,000 different words. Most other estimates (Buckingham & Dolch, 1936; Chall, 1973; Rinsland, 1945; Seashore & Eckerson, 1940; Thorndike, 1931) of vocabulary size, upon which instructional materials and tests were subsequently based, however, were much lower than this.

Bryan (1953), however, claimed that even Smith's estimates may be too low. To determine vocabulary size, Bryan used three vocabulary tests: a free association test, a stimulus-response test, and a multiple choice recognition test. The estimates of the number of words that children knew were larger when the following methods were used: 1) testing the children in a greater number of socioeconomic areas of the country; 2) testing children more often during the year so that various holidays, seasons, and recreational activities would serve to recall additional words; and 3) reconstructing for children a greater number of their common areas of experience.

Harris and Jacobsen (1982) published a vocabulary list developed from a review of the words used in basal readers. The first chapter of their book provides a complete and authoritative review of word lists as well. It is interesting to note that the quantity of words in basal readers at the lowest grade levels has increased significantly from the number of words included in basal readers in a similar study by Harris and Jacobsen in 1972. It appears that basal reader authors are beginning to recognize that children have far larger vocabularies than have been considered in the primary grade basal readers of the past.

Obviously, the number of items on any vocabulary test is limited in relation to the number of words that children can be expected to know. At the very least, this places heavy obligation on the test maker, and on those who select the tests, to test words that are highly significant to any instruction the examinee is experiencing. This fact also questions the practice of timing vocabulary tests, unless the object of the assessment is to determine the speed with which word meanings are identified.

Distinguishing vocabulary as a skill. The studies cited thus far cast considerable doubt on the ability of present standardized tests to measure either the qualitative or quantitative aspects of vocabulary. Perhaps a more important issue is whether standardized tests can validly measure reading vocabulary as distinct from the total reading process. Most validity studies of reading skills have used correlation techniques to point out that there is so much overlap between subskills that almost all of the variance on the standardized reading tests is accounted for by some kind of general factor.

Hughes (1953) correlated scores of 332 fifth graders on tests of word meaning and reading comprehension with scores made on tests of other aspects of language ability such as spelling, punctuation, capitalization, language usage, paragraph organization, and sentence sense. Despite the fact that the study was not designed specifically to isolate subtest variance, Hughes found that there is a very high degree of overlap between all the tests of language skills.

In a convergent-discrimination validity study of three upper level reading tests, Farr (1968) reported that none of the three subtests of reading vocabulary evidenced any discriminant validity (the validity of tests as measures of distinct skills or abilities). For example, the vocabulary test of the Nelson Reading Skills Test (1962) correlated .76 with the vocabulary subtest of the California Reading Test (1963); however, the vocabulary subtest of the Nelson correlated with the comprehension subtest of the California test also at .76; and the vocabulary subtest of the California test correlated at .73 with the comprehension subtest of the Nelson test. Certainly, the specific (discriminant) validity of the subtests of vocabulary as measured by these two tests should be seriously questioned.

All of these concerns with the validity of vocabulary assessment relate to the way in which vocabulary is assessed. They can be weighed against the fact that vocabulary instruction of some sort is a part of reading instruction in most classrooms. In that sense, vocabulary assessment of some kind has at least some face validity. Whether it has content validity is a classroom by classroom, test by test concern. Whether there is any construct validity to the testing and teaching of vocabulary as a separate skill of reading is the most important – and unanswered – question.

It should be noted also that a number of vocabulary tests are used to determine students' functional reading levels. Usually these tests merely ask the examinees to pronounce words but do not determine whether the pupils can attach meaning to the words they have pronounced. While these tests are essentially sight vocabulary tests, their validity will be reviewed in the section of this book concerned with tests that determine functional reading levels, since this is the purpose for these tests. Also, the validity of the assessment of sight vocabulary is included in Chapter 3 which deals with the assessment of word recognition skills.

Reliability and measures of reading vocabulary

Research on the reliability of reading vocabulary tests is a rarity. The reliability coefficients provided by most test publishers have been based on an internal consistency procedure. In reporting these estimates, test publishers sometimes fail to describe in detail the populations used in determining the coefficients. This kind of omission seriously limits their usefulness. Such factors as the test directions, the time limits for the test, dialect match between the examinees and the test items, the test setting, and the context dependency of items have been shown to influence the reliability of vocabulary test scores.

Guessing and reliability. Two factors which have been shown to influence the reliability of vocabulary test scores are related to directions on

Reading: What Can Be Measured?

guessing and the timing of tests. Swinefold and Miller (1953) investigated the effects of three sets of directions given to examinees on the amount of guessing on reading vocabulary tests: 1) they were told to avoid guessing, 2) they were told to guess even when they did not know the answer, or 3) they were given no directions regarding guessing. The group which was told not to guess responded to substantially fewer items than either of the other two groups. Swinefold and Miller found that too many difficult items on a test or too much guessing seriously reduces the test's reliability.

Slakter (1967) has shown that if examinees are discouraged from guessing because a penalty has been imposed for it, the test scores of the examinees reflect the risk taking of the examinees as well as their achievement. If the test maker is more concerned with validity than reliability, Slakter urged that tests be constructed in which examinees are encouraged to answer all questions. If such directions are used, it is crucial that the test be of appropriate difficulty. A test which is extremely difficult for a particular group and in which students are encouraged to guess would have low reliability.

Timing and reliability. Boag and Neild (1962) explored the effects of timing on the reliability of the vocabulary section of the Diagnostic Reading Test. They found that the relative standings of some high school students changed when they were given additional time on the vocabulary test. Thus, it was concluded that speed and power of reading scores should not be used interchangeably. One additional finding was that changes in relative standings under timed and untimed conditions occur with considerably greater frequency through the middle range of scores than they do at either extreme of the distribution.

Reading vocabulary assessment: Needed approaches

The most important research need in measuring reading vocabulary assessment is the development of tests based on sound theoretical and empirical evidence concerning the components of reading ability (Johnston, 1983; Kingston, 1965). While it has been logically argued that students can know the meanings of many words they read and, at the same time, lack the ability to weave those meanings together in reading sentences and paragraphs, this contention has no empirical basis. Until such evidence is forthcoming, any attempt to "diagnose" reading vocabulary as distinct from reading comprehension or other areas should proceed cautiously. Recent research has provided a firm basis to question the traditional isolated skill approach to assessing reading vocabulary. This research not only has strong recommendations for the testing of reading vocabulary, it also suggests a rethinking of those approaches to teaching vocabulary as though the words had meaning in isolation.

If past test developers' and researchers' attempts to measure vocabulary as a distinct subskill prove to be successful, the study of the qualitative differences in reading vocabulary should then become the focal point of future research. Studies already carried out have indicated that the usual assessment methods do not measure many aspects of reading vocabulary. Further studies using the Curtis and Glaser (1983) or the Cronbach (1942) analysis of reading vocabulary should be undertaken. Also needed is the development of new tests which attempt to assess these behaviors and to provide analyses which are useful for diagnosis and instruction.

In the meantime, the following conclusions regarding the assessment of reading vocabulary seem warranted:

1. Reading vocabulary is an integral part of reading instruction and, as such, has face validity as an area to be assessed.

2. Vocabulary is best taught in context, and researchers emphasize the importance of context in determining word meanings. Therefore, vocabulary tests should assess word meanings in context.

3. There is no evidence that tests that ask subjects to identify the meaning of words assess distinctly different reading behaviors from tests of reading comprehension.

4. Reading vocabulary tests should be essentially untimed tests. That is, examinees should have ample time to complete the test items. Most published reading vocabulary tests are essentially untimed in that they provide ample time for most examinees to complete the test easily in the time allowed. The time limits used for administering these tests are for administrative convenience and not to prevent students from finishing the test items. Therefore, teachers should be overtly cautious about considering the use of speeded vocabulary tests.

5. The selection of a particular reading vocabulary test should consider whether the test is a sample of those words that have been taught in the instructional program.

6. A reading vocabulary test is, at best, a general estimate of a pupil's reading vocabulary achievement, and it should be supplemented by ongoing diagnosis and assessment during the time a pupil is reading in class.

The most important consideration in the selection of a reading vocabulary test is validity. In his review of the 1978 Gates-MacGinitie Reading Tests, Jongsma (1980) placed the responsibility for examining validity squarely on the shoulders of the test consumer:

> The author has taken an admirable approach to the issue of test validity. Recognizing that the validity of a test is contingent upon the match between the content and the skills of the test and the instructional goals of the school, the author has challenged the potential users of the Gates-MacGinitie to judge for themselves whether the test is valid for their programs. (p. 344)

Study skills

The development of the reading techniques usually classified as "study skills" comes through the application of word recognition and comprehension skills to meet the specific needs of readers. These needs occur across a variety of activities that involve reading. Thus study skills are not actually skills that enable one to read; rather they are applications of reading skills to the process of learning with printed materials. For this reason, the broad consideration of study skills is not restricted to reading instruction. Instructional materials and curriculum guides in such areas as social studies, science, and mathematics all include objectives dealing with study skills.

What study skills include

Study skills include a potpourri of specific applications of reading that vary depending on the subject matter area in which the study skills are employed, on the resulting nature of the text, and on the sources of relevant information.

One of the most disconcerting problems regarding the area of study skills is the definition of just what they are. Instructional materials and tests include everything from reading graphs and tables to note taking to critical thinking to using a library. While the usual listing of study skills includes a number of very pragmatic behaviors, it is difficult to understand this area because there seem to be no parameters for determining what is, or is not, a study skill. It seems that the inclusion of particular study skills is based on the unique interests of the authors of instructional materials and tests.

Because of the potential of study skills to become relatively specific, sources that list them vary in their emphases. Heilman, Blair, and Rupley

(1981), for example, include an emphasis on reading rate in their description of study skills:

> Study skills, which include a study procedure, specific content reading skills, location information, organizing and evaluating material, effective use of library resources, and adjusting reading rate to purpose and material, are a most important cluster of reading skills. (p. 306)

Smith, Smith, and Mikulecky (1978) include study techniques, note-taking, and outlining. Harris and Sipay (1980) differentiate between study habits and study skills. In discussing study habits, they include such topics as organization of study time, physical conditions of the study environment, and a student's ability to concentrate. While such considerations are as clearly relevant to reading as the readability of text, for example, they tend to endorse the point that study skills are applications of reading as opposed to reading skills per se. They also underline the very pragmatic nature of study skills in general and thus endorse any instructional attention given to them.

The specificity of study skills has developed from such practical perspectives, and it has tended to lead to more logical classification of such skills. A good example of this is seen by comparing Forgan and Mangrum's general study skills list in 1981 with the 1985 list. The earlier list was unstructured and included several comprehension related activities and numerous specific types of information sources. It reflected little analysis of what study skills actually are and no understanding of how they are used. By 1985, the earlier list had been grouped into three user perspectives that could more effectively guide a teacher in planning instruction.

General Study Skills
Locate information through:
1. Card catalog
2. *Reader's Guide to Periodical Literature*
3. Dictionary, to pronounce and define words
4. Encyclopedias
5. Thesaurus
6. Aids in the front and back of textbooks
   a. Title page
   b. Copyright page
   c. Table of contents
   d. Preface
   e. Index

f. Glossary
　g. Bibliographies or References
　h. Appendixes
7. Government publications
8. Common references for your content area

Organize information by:
9. Preparing outlines
10. Writing summaries
11. Classifying topics
12. Associating whole to parts
13. Cause-effect relationships
14. Compare-contrast relationships
15. Problem-solution relationships
16. Time line

Interpreting information from:
17. Diagrams
18. Illustrations
19. Graphs
20. Charts
21. Time lines
22. Drawings
23. Cutaway patterns
24. Pictographs
25. Flowcharts
26. Pictures
27. Maps
28. Specific types of worksheets and/or balance sheets
29. Cartoons
30. Advertisements

Reprinted from *Teaching Content Area Reading Skills*, Third Edition, 1985, H.W. Forgan and C.T. Mangrum II. Copyright 1985 by Charles E. Merrill Company, Used with permission.

The thoughtful grouping of this list suggests a practical guide in teaching that would allow teachers to help readers use those skills in practical reading situations. The reading/thinking relationships among the skills on organizing information are obvious, and the skills related to reading the materials which are listed under Interpreting Information are sure to be highly inferential.

How study skills are taught

Many of the instructional textbooks in the field of reading recommend that most study skills should be introduced as a part of reading instruction, stressing that the skills need to be taught and practiced as they are applied in each subject matter area. Harris and Sipay (1980), for example, state:

> Some curriculum areas require special adaptations of general reading skills. The responsibility for teaching these adaptations should lie with the teacher of that subject. (p. 301)

Possible neglect of the study skills. Despite the fact that study skills are included in most lists of reading curriculum objectives, they may be neglected in many classrooms. Heilman, Blair, and Rupley (1981) thought that this was true:

> Although you could make a case for more than one neglected area in a school's curriculum, the area of study skills is probably at the top of the list. (p. 268)

These authors also contend that the importance of study skills to students "is not always paralleled by the effectiveness with which they are taught" (p. 306).

Reporting on the results of a national study of compensatory reading instruction in the United States, Howlett and Weintraub (1979) indicated that 80 percent of second, fourth, and sixth grade teachers listed study skills as a major goal of their reading programs. However, Howlett and Weintraub also reported that teachers at none of the three levels spent a great deal of time teaching study skills.

After the study practices of over 300 students who came to a university learning skills center were analyzed, Butcofsky (1971) reported that four out of five were experiencing problems in higher learning because of inferior study practices. Since such a population selects itself as having potential problems, its reflection of the total population of high school graduates attending college is, of course, questionable; but the study does clearly suggest both the importance of study skills and the possibility that there is room for improving such instruction.

Basal attention to study skills. Despite indications that study skill instruction may be neglected, the validity of study skills assessment rests primarily on the fact that study skills are included among the instructional objectives of basal reading programs. At the first and second grade levels, basal reading programs usually include such study skills as using the table of contents and glossary. Some also teach the reading of graphs, tables, and maps at early levels. By the later primary grades, study skills instruction in basals may include the writing of outlines and the use of the dictionary; and by the intermediate grades, skimming and scanning, the use of encyclopedias, and the use of such reference sources as an atlas and a phone book. The specific study skills and the grade levels at which they are introduced vary considerably from basal reading program to basal reading program; however, a review of all the major basal programs indicates that all of them include major emphases on study skills.

How study skills are assessed

Since the major basal reader programs comprise the primary content of most reading instruction, it is not surprising that every major standardized reading achievement test includes subtests assessing selected study skills. However, as with the basal readers, the specific objectives tested and the levels at which they are tested vary considerably from test to test.

Study skill assessment on some specific tests. On the 1978 edition of the Metropolitan Achievement Test (MAT), each level of the test from Primer through Advanced includes a subtest which assesses study skills. The lowest test levels assess the examinee's ability to classify topics and alphabetize words based on their first letters. At higher levels, the alphabetizing tasks become more complex as the examinee is asked to alphabetize words in which the first and second letters are the same. A variety of locational skills also are tested. The early levels of the Metropolitan assess locational skills related to a single text; at higher levels, the locational skills involve the use of special reference books and library skills are also tested. Those skills related to using a single text include the use of an index, a table of contents, and a glossary. The use of specialized reference books, including the atlas, the encyclopedia, the dictionary, and the almanac, are tested, as is locating books in a library through the use of the card catalog.

The 1977 edition of the California Achievement Test (CAT) does not follow the same pattern as the MAT. The CAT postpones any study skills assessment until the fourth grade level of the test. Alphabetical order and categorical analysis are not included at any level of the CAT. At the elementary levels of the test, the CAT does include more items assessing the use of library references than does the MAT.

The 1982 edition of the Iowa Test of Basic Skills (ITBS) is similar to the MAT in the manner in which it proceeds through alphabetization and categorical analysis assessment, but it differs in that items measuring the examinee's use of tables, charts, and graphs are included in a separate study skills test. On the MAT, those items are included in the science and math tests, with the assumption that it is in these subjects that students are most apt to learn and apply the skills. The teacher who wants to know only something about students' abilities to read tables, charts, and graph would have to administer the science and math tests if the MAT was the test being used.

Study skill assessment across major instruments. In general, most of the tests—often as a part of tests in science, math, and social studies—use fairly similar item formats, and assess similar skills.It behooves each test user, however, to carefully review the content of each test, noting the distinctions which do exist in order to determine if the skills that are included on the test are those that are relevant to the instructional program in which the tests are to be used.

The study skills items on standardized tests have a characteristic that seems to separate them from most of the other reading skills tests. The study skills items have very strong face validity. That is, they look like the skills they are supposed to be assessing. For example, the items that assess the use of the library card catalog actually present various types of library catalog cards as stimulus material for the test questions. In a similar manner, an excerpt from a dictionary or an index is used to assess study skills dealing with those texts. Graphs, charts, and tables similar to those found in textbooks are used to assess skills dealing with those study aids. Because such items use actual examples of the materials that students are using in class, they appear to provide a more instructionally valid assessment of the skills that are being learned.

One concern with study skills assessment is the limited number of items that can be incorporated into a standardized reading test. As has been noted, the number of study skills is potentially large, as is the number of other reading skills a test must incorporate in order to meet the assessment needs and demands of educators. Assuming that the study skills selected for assessment were somehow universally acknowledged as the most important, how informative would a score of 1 or 2 be to a teacher on a three item total covering a specific study skill? Which of these results indicates the need to reteach the skill, for example?

An aspect of study skills that seems to be neglected on standardized tests is that of determining whether students can actually gather material from reference sources or other different sources and summarize and use the information. Certainly, these are key factors in effective studying. Textbooks concerned with the teaching of study skills include such topics as notetaking, summarizing, text annotation, and study techniques. However, there is almost no assessment of these on standardized tests. This neglect may be due to the test developers' and publishers' conclusions that such skills are not often taught in schools. Such an assumption could be inferred if, in the marketing of an instrument, there did not appear to be a demand for assessment of such skills.

Another reason that such study skills as notetaking and summarizing may not appear on standardized tests relates to the difficulty of developing multiple choice test items that assess these skills. One can get a clearer idea of the problem by examining the complexity of methodologies designed for research studies. To determine how important notetaking (and inherently, summarizing) is to learning, Bretzing and Kulhavy (1979) used a 2,000 word text, incorporated an actual notetaking activity, and administered a test. For such a study, the length of the text was an ideal challenge for summarizing. If a comprehensive test of reading is to be administered in one or two sittings, however—and that is what educators prefer—not many, if any, of the skills tested can employ texts much longer than 300 words. And, of course, actual notetaking and summarizing could not be required. The examinee would have the advantage—or disadvantage—of merely selecting summary options prepared by the test writer.

One synthesis of research on study skills (Armbruster & Anderson, 1981) suggests aspects of reader activity when studying that may be assessable on standardized tests. Although the perspective of this review was not the assessment potential of study skills, the synthesis has implications for using multiple choice items—for example, to test a student's ability to select information from a short passage that would be most relevant to a stated (test prescribed) purpose for reading it. Test items also might be able to target on aspects of logical structure and organization within relatively short passages.

These researchers, however, could be cited by test makers who have elected not to make any such effort; for Armbruster and Anderson conclude that "research has failed to confirm the benefits of...specific study skill techniques or to find one technique that is superior to others" (p. 155). A few studies support notetaking as a vital study skill. Butcofsky (1971) suggests that for college students, notetaking may be a key to success. Bretzing and Kulhavy (1979) found that it improved understanding and recall of a text, but only when the notes were "meaningful."

If one concludes, however, that any study technique is helpful, how does a test maker and then a test user select the skills to be tested? As a study by Scales (1979) suggests, different approaches to teaching study skills as a reading development course may have equal impact. A test user may select assessment that closely matches emphases taught, but before that selection can be made from standardized reading tests, the test makers will have to decide with some assurance how to make their selection of the skills for which assessment is to be developed.

Informal assessment of study skills

Obviously, the most sensitive assessment of a teacher's, a school's, or a program's emphases in study skill instruction will need, at least temporarily, to be developed at those levels. It should not be surprising that informal assessment, which is being more thoughtfully recommended for all aspects of reading development, is particularly endorsed for the assessment of study skills. The several major types of informal assessment are all sensibly applicable to the assessment of study skills.

Classroom specific tests. One general method of informal assessment applied to study skills encourages the deliberate selection of texts, other materials, and tasks from the instructional program and using them to assess student progress. Thomas and Robinson (1977) suggest that informal tests of study skills should indeed be specific to the subject being taught and the textbooks being used. For example, after teaching underlining, a teacher may distribute an actual page or subsection of a textbook used in class, and ask the pupils to underline it. The textbook itself can be used in testing the students' outlining ability. Either of these testing activities should have learning validity for the students and do double duty as an effective review technique. Teachers can analyze the results of such an informal test at their leisure, and the class discussion of the results can act as effective skill reinforcement, or even as a reteach session if the test has indicated that one is needed.

Observation. The classroom specific relevance of informal assessment is absolutely guaranteed if the technique is observation. Daily observation allows the teacher to assess the way a student applies study techniques to the various tasks that are the real stuff of the student's learning experience. This process may be as simple as watching to see who is taking notes. It can incorporate the technique of asking students to check back to see how a new fact or concept relates to ones previously discussed. It can structure into actual lessons observable opportunities for students to tap all kinds of reference materials and reveal how effectively or ineffectively they do so. It can challenge the incorporation of such information into the stream of the lesson if the teacher is observing how well new information is synthesized. Many such opportunities may occur naturally; others can be deliberately planted. All that is required are teachers who know which study applications they value, have taught, and want to assess.

Projects can be structured for the class, small groups, or individual students so that they test particular study behaviors. For example, a project can lead students to the library and to special informational materials and can require information selection, notetaking, and synthesizing. A teacher structuring such informal assessment opportunities may want to observe with a checklist of skills anticipated as necessary to complete it. However the assessment is conducted, the opportunity is ongoing and the application of the skills is genuine.

Interviews and checklists. Another informal assessment technique particularly applicable to study skills is the interview in which the teacher, often operating from a checklist of skills and habits framed into questions, actually encourages students to play a major role in assessing themselves. Conducted with the appropriate cooperative, positive preparation, parent interviews incorporated into this process can be quite productive.

Obviously, it is difficult to discuss informal assessment, particularly of study skills, without the discussion beginning to sound like a methods text. Such is the highly practical nature of informal assessment and its most impressive endorsement.

Recommendations for assessing study skills

Because they stem so directly from the discussion of a seemingly practical concern, the recommendations appropriate for assessment of reading study skills serve also as an effective brief summary of the subject. It appears that there would be broad professional agreement in encouraging the following:

1. In most classrooms, there should be an increased use of informal assessment techniques, particularly of observation, in assessing pupil progress in developing study and learning skills that involve reading.

2. When informal or standardized tests of study skills are constructed, they should present very practical items which reflect, mimic, or even duplicate portions of actual classroom reading materials and contexts. This would make such tests not only valid in terms of instruction but also valid in a broader sense which recognizes study skills as the application of other, more generic, reading skills.

3. The recommendation above clearly assumes a more basic requirement for study skills assessment: that such an effort not examine knowledge of study skills but rather their application.

4. Developers of standardized tests should endeavor to find ways that various reading activities called study skills can be measured within rea-

sonable time limits. Doing this while adhering to the requirement that the test assess application intensifies this challenge.

5. Assessment of study skills should cover every skill it selects to test with enough items to make the performance score meaningfully directive to the teacher. For the developers of standardized tests, the challenge is further intensified.

6. If there is a genuinely supportable desire to increase the instruction of study skills, there needs to be an increased emphasis on the testing of these skills. This may lead to the acceptance of the possibility that comprehensive standardized tests cannot be expected to do the job adequately in one or two sittings that also include the testing of comprehension, vocabulary, and word recognition skills. This problem further recommends the teacher's development and use of informal study skill assessment, and brings these recommendations full circle.

Reading rate

The consideration of reading rate is separated here from earlier discussions, for numerous reasons. Rate is, as are the study skills, not a skill prerequisite to reading, but a concern clearly related to the application of the skills that are essential. That is, consideration of the rate at which one reads a text is clearly subsequent to acquisition of any skills that allow one to read the text in the first place. A lack of these skills will obviously prohibit reading at a faster rate, just as it would prohibit slower reading for critical or analytic purposes.

Consideration of reading rate is discretely separate from the study skills, which include the reading of peculiarly unique texts and skimming and scanning, which are to be distinguished here from reading at any feasible rate.

Attempting to define reading rate: Does it include comprehension?

An attempt to define reading rate engages not only the relationship between speed and comprehension but also the actual extent to which reading speed actually can be developed, and the relationship of rate to reader purpose.

Rate and comprehension. A key debate about reading rate incorporates the definition of reading itself: Does reading words entail the obligation that they be understood? Those in reading who would answer with an emphatic "Yes" are prone to argue that understanding is far more important than speed of accomplishment. Surely, they argue, it is not how many books you get through but, rather, how many ideas can get through to you (Adler, 1967).

The seemingly logical sense of arguing that reading is meaningless unless it results in some minimum level of comprehension has not precluded a fifty year long debate about the relationship of reading rate and comprehension. If one believes reading is comprehending, one would certainly argue that an increased rate that is not accompanied by an increase in concepts comprehended is not an increased reading rate.

Yet the issue is not quite that simple, and it invariably incorporates the more complex question of whether rate affects comprehension. (Interestingly, the potential of an inverse causal connection—whether comprehension affects rate—gets little, if any, attention.) It is sometimes argued that if reading speed and comprehension are unrelated—if rate does not impact on comprehension—then there is justification for training readers to increase reading speed without a concern for comprehension.

At the same time, some proponents of an emphasis on reading rate have complicated the debate considerably by claiming that increased speed increases comprehension. By citing early studies that supported the claim that increased speed increased comprehension, proponents of teaching (and assessing) reading speed tend to forfeit the argument that, being unrelated, speed and comprehension are legitimate isolated concerns; and they thus obligate themselves to establish the positive relationships between the two.

By citing the bulk of relevant research, which denies any direct correlation, those who focus on comprehension rate as opposed to reading rate, risk reviving the original argument that if speed is unrelated to comprehension, then in developing it, they need not be concerned with comprehension and can argue that they are at least teaching a reader to cover more material in less time. As Stroud pointed out, there is as much point in one's reading rapidly what is not understood as there is in reading it slowly.

Research evidence related to the contention that increased rate results in increased comprehension is somewhat mixed, but it has not tended to support that claim. Some earlier studies (Anderson & Tinker, 1932; Eurich, 1930) did suggest moderately high correlations between rate and comprehension. In 1942, however, Stroud pointed out how the very timing of tests producing the comprehension scores used in such studies contaminated them with a speed factor and invalidated the correlations. As can be noted in the descriptions of some extant tests which follow here, that concern has not deterred the development of rate scores derived from rigidly timed comprehension tests.

A study of Flanagan (1937) anticipated Stroud's point. Flanagan collected two scores for subjects on a literary comprehension test: a level of comprehension score and a rate of comprehension score. The level of comprehension score was based on the average number of comprehension items answered correctly on four 20 item scales. The rate of comprehension score was the total number of items answered correctly on all 80 items minus a correction for guessing. Flanagan computed a positive correlation of .77 between these two scores, thus indicating a great deal of trait similarity. However, when he correlated a rate of reading score (determined by the total number of items completed within a time limit) with the level of comprehension score, the correlation was only .17.

In summarizing work by Letson (1958) and Shores and Husbands (1950), Rankin (1962) further discounts the early correlations:

> In conclusion, it appears that the confounding of rate and comprehension in measurements is, at least in part, responsible for some of the earlier findings that "fast readers are good readers." Other studies of the relationship between rate and "power of comprehension," find only a slight relationship. When the material is more difficult, when more critical thought processes are involved, and when the reader's purpose is more exacting, the relationship between reading rate and comprehension is minimal. (pp. 4-5)

One relatively recent study does tend to support the claim that speed improves comprehension. Jackson and McClelland (1975, 1979) conducted research which suggests that fast readers appear to pick up more information on each eye fixation and that they are able to encode more of the content of each fixation.

But the bulk of the research over the years does not support a claim that increased speed increases comprehension. Himelstein and Greenberg (1974) contrasted the effects of manipulating the rate at which subjects read to determine any consequent effect on the reading comprehension of twenty subjects. They concluded:

> It has been demonstrated that reading rate can be easily manipulated by various reinforcement and motivational techniques. Do these techniques affect comprehension? The answer as presented in this study, as well as others that have adequately measured comprehension, is no. (p. 258)

Anyone with sufficient classroom or measurement experience should verify that there are good and poor comprehenders among both slow and fast readers. The research tends to suggest that the range of reading speed across individual readers does not directly affect the resulting comprehension. Smith (1971), however, has argued that "fluent reading is relatively fast reading." He suggests that visual information has to be quickly absorbed or it will be lost. Slow word by word and letter by letter reading, according to Smith, interferes with the objective of reading comprehension. He suggests that about 200 words per minute is a minimal rate of reading if a reader is to comprehend.

In a summary of research on reading rate, Witty (1969) wrote:

> Investigators reported that fast readers are good readers of some kinds of materials read for certain purposes. But with other kinds of materials read for other purposes, there was no relationship between reading speed and comprehension. Thus it became clear that reading rate and comprehension are not always closely related. (p. 160)

How fast is speed reading? There appears to be an accepted belief that most people can learn to read faster. Increasing one's reading speed is an alluring concept to students, business persons, professionals, and anyone who has large amounts of printed material to assimilate. Thus, these people are the targets for speed reading courses and mechanical gadgets that promise to substantially increase reading speed and to help readers get through the stacks of materials that they feel must be read in order to succeed.

The development of faster reading speed was until recently an important, if not central, goal of many high school and college reading programs. This resulted from the belief that students have large volumes of reading material which must be read and that students needed to learn to read faster to handle these materials. A second reason for the popularity of such programs was the belief that many high school and college students read at a rate below their potential and that reading speeds can be easily increased.

Speed reading courses, like some tests which assess reading speed, provide as a measure of accomplishment the number of words read per minute. The emphasis is on words read and not on ideas or concepts assimilated; it is on speed of accomplishment and not on the quality or depth of understanding. Speed reading programs still exist, and some schools currently use tests that report words per minute read.

The emphasis on reading speed has diminished considerably in the past decade, however. Its decline may have, at least in part, resulted from research which tends to question the very existence of high reading rates and to define reading to exclude the selective study skill applications of skimming and scanning.

Speed reading as skimming. In a 1963 study, Stevens and Orem reported on their experiences with teaching speed reading. They stated that none of the rapid readers in their course could read rapidly in unfamiliar materials for which they lacked a conceptual background. They also noted that, as these students reported on their reading at very fast rates (above 2,000 words per minute), they stated that their word perception became one of selecting words to be read. It seems that these readers had begun skimming rather than reading.

McLaughlin (1969) and Carver (1972) have argued that speed readers skim rather than read. Such researchers tend to claim that the maximum reading speed is approximately 900 words per minute or less. Carver (1972) wrote, "Most reading researchers agree that reading rates above 800 to 1,000 words per minute are physiologically impossible" (p. 23). He cited a study by Stanford Taylor that found no difference between the eye movements of a group that had finished a speed reading program and "regular" readers or between the speed readers and untrained readers instructed to skim.

In a more recent article, Carver (1982) reported on a study of college students that suggests that the optimal reading rate for most effective reading comprehension of materials spanning a wide range of difficulty is about 300 words per minute.

Witty (1969) summarized the current thinking of many reading specialists in a review of the research on rate:

> Again and again, reading authorities concluded that silent reading rates above 800 words per minute were largely manifestations of various kinds of skimming. Moreover, the assumption that there exists a "general" rate of reading which can be greatly accelerated by practice was questioned. Studies show that good readers learn to read different kinds of materials at different rates according to their needs and purposes. (p. 159)

Rate and reader purpose. The research on reading rate does not preclude that reading rate — as opposed to speed reading — is a reading application to be developed among readers who read, say, less than 300 words per minute and who are old enough to achieve that speed while comprehending most texts. Nor are the reading applications of skimming or scanning disdained when they are distinguished from reading per se.

This fact should point up the clear relationship between reader purpose and rate. If time is of such essence that much text needs to be covered in a considerably short period, skimming is a technique that may serve the reader well. But what is served by deluding oneself into believing one is reading and not skimming? If a reader knows a text is replete with information that will not serve a purpose established for reading it, then scanning — not reading — will serve that purpose. But teaching such techniques as "speed reading" or "developing a fast reading rate" leads to confusion about the nature of reading in general. Close, critical reading of a text's concepts, logic, style, mood, artistic techniques, or even details is unlikely to be served by a fast reading rate, suggesting that it is flexibility matched to reader purpose that may be the reasonable emphasis in instruction and thus in measurement.

Examples of reading rate tests

Although the emphasis on speed reading has declined in the past decade, there continue to exist tests which measure reading speed as a words per minute variable with no concomitant assessment of whether the reader understands what is read. Some examples include:

- The Nelson-Denny Reading Test (1981), a screening device to predict success at high school and college levels, which reports rate as merely words per minute by having the student mark the number of words read in the first minute of a timed comprehension test.
- The Nelson Reading Skills Test (1977), which includes a rate subtest as "optional," beginning at the middle of grade four. A raw word per minute score is acquired by having the students mark where they are after one minute of reading. The raw score can be converted into percentiles, stanines, and grade equivalents.

Some tests have been developed and others modified to attempt to answer the argument that reading is comprehending. Until the 1978 edition, when it dropped its reading rate test, the Gates-MacGinitie Reading Tests: Survey (1965) measured a combination of the two. Other such tests and a brief description of how rate is reported include the following examples:

- The Davis Reading Test (1962), which purports to measure "speed of comprehension." A pupil has a time limit to respond to eighty multiple choice completion items about paragraphs read.
- The Durrell Analysis of Reading Difficulty (third edition), (1980), in which the speed with which a child read paragraphs orally is used

in combination with the child's responses to literal comprehension questions to get an instructional reading level. Timing is combined with oral recall of text read silently to get an independent reading level.

- The Brown Level of the Stanford Diagnostic Reading Scales (1976), which is designed for grades five to eight and for low achieving high school students, reports rate as the number of items answered correctly in three minutes after reading a passage.
- The Blue Level of the Stanford Diagnostic Reading Scales (1974), which was designed for grade nine through the second year of college, combines the number of items answered correctly after a timed (2 minute) reading of a passage and its items with other subtest scores to yield student rank.
- The Gilmore Oral Reading Test (1968), which after timing the reader in seconds, first reports reading rate as words per minute and then combines that rate with a student's grade equivalent from subtests on accuracy and comprehension to rate the student as slow, average, or fast.
- The Iowa Silent Reading Tests (1972) and the Metropolitan Achievement Tests (1978), both of which used modified cloze as items following timed passages to get a comprehension score that is combined with a rate score (the number of items attempted). The Iowa reports a "reading efficiency" score, and the MAT yields a "rate of comprehension" score.
- The Gray Oral Reading Test (1963), which combines the time lapsed (including 5 second maximum pauses before prompts) while reading passages with the number of errors made in reading aloud to get a grade equivalent.

The validity and reliability of reading rate tests

The key validity question in considering tests that report speed of reading without any regard for comprehension is the previously discussed argument about whether reading itself means comprehending. The attempt to create measures of rate or speed of comprehension—as opposed to speed of reading—has been a response to the argument that pure word per minute scores are meaningless. Yet, ironically, the combination of comprehension and rate measures has complicated the consideration of their validity.

Scoring problems. It is questionable whether the various methods of combining comprehension and rate scores leaves one with a truly valid indication of rate. Comprehension scores have been used on many reading rate tests as if they formed a perfect ratio scale, that is, as if there were an absolute zero point on the test. On one such test, an individual's score is determined by multiplying the reading rate with the percent of comprehension. The reason for this, according to the test developer, is that the reading speed score should be reduced by the reader's level of comprehension.

The invalidity of this approach is easily illustrated through the following hypothetical situation. Suppose an examinee reads 300 words per minute and scores 85 percent on comprehension. Multiplying the two would result in a reading speed score of 255 words per minute.

If the examinee merely reads the title of the selection and then reports that he or she has read the material, his or her speed would be taken as approximately 20,000 words per minute. A subsequent comprehension score of 55 percent would result in a rate of reading score of 11,000 words per minute. Such a comprehension score without reading would not be unreasonable, since examinees can usually answer several questions correctly on the basis of their prior knowledge and several other items can be guessed correctly. The main point here is that combining comprehension with measures of reading rate detracts from the validity of measuring speed of reading.

A Hawthorne effect. Another problem affecting the validity of reading speed scores is the apparent "slack" that most readers seem to have in normal reading speeds. Laycock (1955) investigated the effect of giving students a mental set to try to read faster without decreasing their comprehension. Under that condition, subjects increased reading speed by as much as 40 percent. These results suggest the possibility that supposed gains in reading speed, following a session of reading improvement classes, may be due to the new "mental set" students have established. And if such a course has emphasized purposes for reading fast, it is possible that the students learned to engage speeds they already had to match those purposes.

The impact of difficulty and interest levels of text. The difficulty level and interest appeal of the reading selections included on a particular test are always considerations in judging the validity of the reading measurement instrument. However, because of the susceptibility of reading speed tests to the Hawthorne effect, it is more of a problem in measuring reading rate than in measuring other aspects of reading.

The effects of the reading level of materials on the measurement of reading rate is a problem which is often overlooked. If seventh grade students, for example, are unable to read seventh grade material, the speed that they "read" texts at that level of difficulty is probably not a valid measure of their reading speed. Should subjects' reading speed be determined on material of relatively easy reading? Or should several reading speeds be reported on texts of varying difficulty and interest appeal?

Research suggests that such questions, which are generally ignored by most constructors of reading rate tests, need to be answered. Carlson (1951) found significant differences in reading speed for varying difficulty levels of reading material. The primary statistical procedure used in this study was a Pearson Product-Moment correlation. As would be expected, all of the correlations between reading rate and level of difficulty were significant, but they were not large enough for any predictive use. Carlson's study also pointed out the limitation of measuring reading speed when the difficulty level of the reading material is not controlled.

One attempt to investigate the relationship between reading rate and the interest appeal of reading selections was undertaken by Bryant and Barry (1961). They concluded that interest did not significantly influence reading rate in the case of relatively simple, narrative articles. The procedure used by Bryant and Barry involved asking subjects which of two articles they found more interesting. From a sample of 100, two groups of 17 were selected: One group had favored the first selection, while the other had favored the second. This procedure does not seem valid for selecting materials with much positive or negative attraction; the small number of students choosing selections as "most interesting" would seem to support this contention. Thus, the mildly positive or negative attitudes which Bryant and Barry found are not surprising; neither is the lack of significant differences in reading speed.

Reliability of reading rate measures. Few studies focus on the reliability of tests of reading rate. Traxler (1938), for one, studied the relationship between the length and the reliability of one test. Seventy-eight high school juniors were given two forms of a 177 line reading rate test in alternate order. The students were asked to mark the line they were reading at the end of each 100 seconds.

Traxler then correlated the number of lines read at each 100 seconds. The correlations were significantly higher (.86) for 400 seconds than for 100 seconds (.62). Traxler concluded that the time allowed for most tests of reading rate (one minute to five minutes) is too short for high reliability. He called for the development of tests two or three times the length of those then in existence.

In a more recent study, Chang and Hanna (1980) studied the reliability of rate measures when the subjects were given warmup passages before the rate tests were administered. They also attempted to determine if one minute, rather than two minute, reading rate passages were more reliable. Subjects included eighth grade and eleventh grade students. The effects of the warmup passages were inconsistent; they provided greater measurement accuracy at some grades but not at others.

The effects of the increased length of passages were also inconsistent, showing a positive effect at the eleventh grade level but not at the eighth grade. Chang and Hanna concluded that their study provided little guidance for test constructors regarding the means to increase the reliability of reading rate measures.

It should be noted that Chang and Hanna used the number of words read as the dependent variable in their study. While comprehension questions were included, the researchers stated that these were included only to keep the examinees "honest" and were not the focus for analysis. It would be interesting to find out if the accuracy of the comprehension scores was affected by the experimental manipulations.

A special consideration in reading rate measurement

If the measure of words per minute reading rate tests is continued, both test developers and consumers should be familiar with the research on the effects of typography on reading speed. In Hvistendahl's study (1965), subjects were presented the same magazine page in four different formats: one with paragraph heads, another with boldface lead ins, another with boldface paragraphs, and a final one containing no typographical aids. Each of these variations was also presented in two and three column formats. Rate of reading was determined by asking the subjects which page they thought they could read fastest. The results were statistically significant in favor of all the pages containing typographical aids, but there were no significant differences in the use of a two versus a three column format. These findings are limited, however, because of the criteria used to determine rate of reading.

The effect of print size on the reading speed of first, second, and third graders was examined by McNamara, Patterson, and Tinker (1953). The print used ranged in size from 8 to 24 points (one-ninth to one-third of an inch). Little difference in the rate of words read for any of the type sizes were found at the first two grade levels. In grade three, there was a definite trend indicating students read material set in 10, 12, and 14 point type faster. McNamara, Patterson, and Tinker's conclusion that the type size of reading material should not be a consideration in selecting materials in the first two grades is subject to the notation that it is based solely on rate, which is not an important factor in reading instruction in these grades.

Recommendations that suggest the need for research

The many questions regarding reading rate suggest the obvious need for more research in the area. With more knowledge, the implications for measurement of rate should become clearer.

Emphasizing skimming. The question of whether speed reading is even attainable beyond several hundred words per minute appears to recommend breaking away from the concept of assessing and developing reading speed and attending more to the process of skimming. The phenomenal reading rates reported in some rate improvement programs should be considered skimming rates rather than reading rates, especially since some of the rates reported have exceeded the physiological limits of the normal progression of eye movements across and down a page.

The assessment of skimming should be based on further study of the difficulty and interest appeal of selections used in assessment. Probably the best approach for such research would be through a series of studies combining purposes for reading, difficulty of selections, and interest level of selections in a three-way analysis of variance. Such an investigation could help to determine the effects of each of these factors individually as well as the unique interaction effects among all three factors. Replication could then be conducted with a number of different age groups.

Understanding rate as reading flexibility. The concept of rate of comprehension is very closely related to that of reading flexibility. In measuring rate of comprehension, what the teacher needs to know is how fast readers achieve their purpose, that is, how quickly they understand the selection (McDonald, 1965; Sheldon & Carrillo, 1952). The teacher does not have to know that a reader can pass over words at 300, 800, or 1200 words per minute; what the teacher needs to know is how long it takes the reader to comprehend the material for a given purpose.

If students were asked to determine the general content of a selection, they would be expected to read at a rate different from that which they would use if asked to read to determine the specific cause leading up to a certain event. Whenever a test utilizes specific purposes for reading, the examiner should be aware that the test's purpose is always modified by the reader's purpose.

According to McDonald (1958), most research has failed to reveal that readers tend to change their reading rate to satisfy particular purposes unless special instruction is provided to effect this flexibility. This implies that the most meaningful measures of reading flexibility should establish a clear purpose for reading the text used that would validly call for fast reading – but not skimming.

Reader purpose, in general, is an area that needs the illumination of more research; but it seems of special potential significance to measurement of reading rate. There is actually little evidence that most students have any ability to adjust their reading rate to suit specific purposes. McDonald (1966), in an overview of research studies, concluded that the vast majority of readers are untrained in reading flexibility and, therefore, do not change their reading rate to any great extent even when instructed to read for different purposes.

In a study of fourth graders, Gifford and Marson (1966) supported McDonald's conclusion. The subjects in their study did not vary their reading speed to suit the specific purposes for reading for main ideas and details. Hill (1964) found that purpose for reading had little influence on reading rate and comprehension when college students were asked to read for one of three different purposes: 1) as a course assignment over which the reader was to be tested the following day, 2) to identify its main ideas, and 3) to analyze critically the motives and attitudes of the author. The selections dealt with relatively complex concepts. They were written for the well educated adult and their organizational patterns and author attitudes were identifiable but presented subtly. It seems possible that the complexity of the reading material prevented any reader flexibility.

The fact that readers do not adjust their speed in different situations should not be taken as an indictment of reading tests; if anything, it points out the shortcomings of reading programs which develop such inflexible readers. If reading tests were to include more specific directions about purposes for reading, however, and would vary these purposes, more reading programs might begin to teach flexibility.

Consideration of text difficulty. More research is needed on the relationship between reader purpose, text difficulty, reading rate, and comprehension. The difficulty level of the material to be read appears to be a limiting factor in measuring rate of comprehension, but the actual interrelationships of all these factors are not yet very clear.

Sheldon (1955) found that college students who had been identified as good readers varied their reading speed considerably, depending on the type of material read. Their comprehension scores were also uniformly high. The poor readers, on the other hand, had a very uniform (about 300 words per minute) reading rate regardless of the type of material read or of the purposes given for reading. Yet their comprehension varied greatly.

A somewhat contradictory finding was reported by Letson (1958) on the relationship of reading speed and comprehension on easy and difficult reading material for college freshmen. Letson's results indicated that: 1) the relationship between speed scores on difficult and easy materials was high; 2) the relationship between comprehension scores on difficult and easy materials was moderate; and 3) the relationship between speed and comprehension scores was high for easy material, but decreased as the difficulty of the material increased. However, the readers in the study tended to maintain a reading rate independent of the difficulty of the materials.

Other rate measurement problems that need attention

Measures of reading rate are bound to be confounded by artifacts resulting from the measurement procedures followed. In addition, peculiarities imposed on tests that combine rate with other measures, particularly comprehension, appear to have effects on the related measure as well. Letson (1958) noted that when speed and comprehension are measured simultaneously, the resulting score includes the time taken to read the selection, to read the question, and to look back and reread the text. Letson suggested that such a measure would be a speed of working, rather than a speed of reading, score.

Fricke (1957) studied the results of the Cooperative English Test: Reading Comprehension to determine if speed of reading scores and level of reading scores could be replaced by two new scores: rate and accuracy. Both the speed and accuracy scores were rate of comprehension scores; however, the speed score suggested by the manual was the number of correct answers less one quarter of the wrong answers. Fricke stated that this score does not validly measure the rate of comprehension of the fast but careless reader. He suggested that the rate score (speed of comprehension) should be simply the number of correct responses.

The possible effects of interruption. A related measurement problem is the undetermined effect of interrupting students during their reading in order to get the indication of rate. When the test administrator interrupts but once to have the test taker mark the text for a simple word per minute score, the effect would be on other aspects of reading that the test measures. If one of those is a comprehension score that will be figured in some rate report, rate might be affected.

The modified cloze procedure used on some rate tests interrupts the student's reading to the extent that the correct alternative to fill a blank in the reading text must be considered. In effect, the student is the reader/writer, and there is some evidence that this interruption could affect any attempts to measure rate of reading comprehension.

McDonald (1960) studied the reading rate and comprehension of 177 college students under four timing procedures involving various amounts of interruption. Reading performance was significantly hampered by periodic interruptions; reading rate was not affected, but significant reduction in reading comprehension was noted. McDonald concluded: "Timing procedures which produce periodic interruptions during the reading process should be avoided. Methods of timing reading which minimally interrupt the students should be selected" (p. 33).

Differential effects on reading comprehension scores as the result of an interruption have been found for slow and fast readers. Cook (1957) attempted to discover if time announcements during the administration of reading tests given to all entering students at a major university affected comprehension scores. The loss of comprehension was more significant for slower readers than for faster readers.

Determining the Hawthorne effect. Research ought to attempt to reveal what being instructed to read for speed does to the validity of a rate test. Can the instruction to read for speed be justifiably housed in instructions that set a valid purpose?

Research has already indicated that students can increase their reading speed without any loss in comprehension under a set of instructions to read faster. Maxwell (1965) supported this hypothesis in a study involving 104 college students, concluding that the "...study has shown that instructing students to read faster on a standardized test results in signficantly faster reading rate, and further suggests that reading test speed increases as a function of a warmup period" (p. 186).

A final challenge to researchers. Research on the measurement of rate of reading comprehension must first focus on the utility of such a measure. Can research produce evidence that will relate this score to the objectives of reading instructional programs? How does reader purpose figure in such a rationalization? How can a reading rate score be utilized by teachers? What kind of a rate score is most useful and meaningful?

Specific research in measuring rate of comprehension should investigate more carefully the effects of the difficulty of material, the interest level of the selections, readers' purposes, and the effects of certain timing and scoring procedures.

Almost all of the studies which have begun to examine these variables have used college students. Much work needs to be done at younger age levels if flexible reading patterns are important for elementary and high school students.

Perhaps future research will conclude that there is no general rate of reading comprehension; instead, it might well prove that for each reader there are a number of reading rates dependent on variables like purpose and difficulty of materials. If this should be the case and if there is general agreement that improvement in rate of comprehension is an important objective of the reading program, a variety of tests for use in differing class situations needs to be developed and/or teachers need to be trained to assess this skill informally in each learning situation.

Recommendations for educators concerning reading rate measurement

Amid the uncertainties surrounding the measurement of reading rate, there are a number of recommendations that can be offered to those determined to assess students' reading rates.

1. The most important of these is that there is no evidence that reading rate should be part of reading instruction before a child is able to read at least at a sixth grade level. Prior to that time, the child is learning to use a variety of reading skills to determine the meaning of printed materials. Therefore, there should be no assessment of reading rate before a child achieves sixth grade reading level. After that time, if reading rate is of concern, the succeeding recommendations should be followed.

2. The assessment of reading rate should include some measure of reading comprehension. There seems to be no reason to determine a reader's word per minute rate if there is no accompanying evidence of the reader's comprehension of what is read. While the assessment of reading rate and comprehension provides a combination of two skill areas, it is impossible to believe that anyone is interested in a reader's reading rate if there is no comprehension of what is read.

3. The assessment of reading rate will vary considerably depending on the reading difficulty of the selection to be read. While there is perhaps an optimal reading rate for each reader, that rate will depend on whether the reader has the background and experiences to read the material. Therefore, the assessment of reading rate will be strongly influenced by the difficulty of the reading material, the reader's interest in the passage to be read, and the reader's purpose for reading.

4. In most cases, slow reading rate is a symptom and not a cause. That is, slow reading is often the result of limited background knowledge in the topic of the text that is being read, poorly developed general reading ability, lack of purpose for reading, or anxiety due to the highly structured testing situation.

5. The assessment of reading rate using artificial devices such as pacers or other mechanical devices is not recommended. The testing situation is an atypical reading situation as it is, and any validity of a test is further reduced by the introduction of more artificiality.

References

Adler, M.J. *How to read a book*. New York: Simon and Schuster, 1967.

Anderson, R.C., and Shifrin, Z. The meaning of words in context. In R.J. Spiro, B.C. Bruce, and W.F. Brewer (Eds.), *Theoretical issues in reading comprehension*. Hillsdale, NJ: Erlbaum, 1980.

Anderson, R.C., Spiro, R.J., and Montague, W. (Eds.). *Schooling and the acquisition of knowledge*. Hillsdale, NJ: Erlbaum, 1977.

Anderson, V.L., and Tinker, M.A. The speed factor in reading performance. *Journal of Educational Psychology*, 1932, *27*, 621-624.

Armbruster, B.B., and Anderson, T.H. Research synthesis on study skills. *Educational Leadership*, 1981, *39*, 154-156.

Boag, A.K., and Neild, M. The influence of the time factor on the scores of the Triggs Diagnostic Reading Test as reflected in the performance of secondary school pupils grouped according to ability. *Journal of Educational Research*, 1962, *55*, 181-183.

Bretzing, B.B., and Kulhavy, R.W. Notetaking and depth of processing. *Contemporary Educational Psychology*, 1979, *4*, 145-153.

Brown, D.A. *Reading diagnosis and remediation*. Englewood Cliffs, NJ: Prentice-Hall, 1982.

Bryan, F.E. How large are children's vocabularies? *Elementary School Journal*, 1953, *53*, 210-216.

Bryant, N.D., and Barry, N.E. The relationships between interest and reading rate and between interest and reading comprehension. In E.P. Bliesmer and A.J. Kingston (Eds.), *Phases of college and other adult reading programs*. Yearbook of the National Reading Conference, 1961, *10*, 127-130.

Buckingham, B.R., and Dolch, E.W. *A combined word list*. Boston: Ginn, 1936.

Butcofsky, D. Any learning skills taught in high school? *Journal of Reading*, 1971, *15*, 195-198.

Carlson, T.R. Effect of certain test factors in measurement of speed of reading. *Journal of Educational Research*, 1951, *44*, 543-549.

Carver, R.P. Speed readers don't read; they skim. *Psychology Today*, August 1972, 22-30.

Carver, R.P. Optimal rate of reading prose. *Reading Research Quarterly*, 1982, *18*, 56-88.

Chall, J.S. Learning to read. In G.A. Miller (Ed.), *Communication, language, and meaning*. New York: Basic Books, 1973.

Chang, S.S., and Hanna, G.S. Reliability of reading rate tests as a function of warmup passage and time limit. *Reading World*, 1980, *19*, 232-238.

Cook, D.L. A comparison of reading comprehension scores obtained before and after a time announcement. *Journal of Educational Psychology*, 1957, *48*, 440-446.

Cronbach, L.J. Analysis of techniques for diagnostic vocabularly testing. *Journal of Educational Research*, 1942, *36*, 206-217.

Curtis, M.E., and Glaser R. Reading theory and the assessment of reading achievement. *Journal of Educational Measurement*, 1983, *20*, 133-147.

Dechant, E. *Diagnosis and remediation of reading disabilities*. Englewood Cliffs, NJ: Prentice-Hall, 1981.

Dolch, E.W. *Reading and word meaning*. Boston: Ginn, 1927.

Dolch, E.W., and Leeds, D. Vocabulary tests and depth of meaning. *Journal of Educational Research*, 1953, *47*, 181-189.

Dreher, M.J., and Singer, H. The validity of the instantiation hypothesis. *Journal of Reading Behavior*, 1981, *13*, 223-228.

Ehri, L.C., and Roberts, K.T. Do beginners learn printed words better in context or in isolation? *Child Development*, 1979, *50*, 675-685.

Eurich, A.C. The relation of speed of reading to comprehension. *School and Society*, 1930, *32*, 404.

Farr, R.C. The convergent and discriminant validity of several upper level reading tests. In G.B. Schick and M.M. May (Eds.), *Multidisciplinary aspects of college-adult reading*. Yearbook of the National Reading Conference, 1968, *17*, 181-191.

Feifel, H., and Lorge, I. Qualitative differences in the vocabulary responses of children. *Journal of Educational Psychology*, 1950, 41, 1-18.

Flanagan, J.C. A proposed procedure for increasing the efficiency of objective tests. *Journal of Educational Psychology*, 1937, *28*, 17-21.

Forgan, H.W., and Mangrum, C.T. II. *Teaching content area reading skills*, third edition. Columbus, OH: Charles E. Merrill, 1985. See also second edition, 1981.

Freebody, P., and Anderson, R.C. *Effects of differing proportions and locations of difficult vocabulary on text comprehension*. Technical Report #212. Champaign, IL: Center for the Study of Reading, University of Illinois, 1981.

Freebody, P., and Anderson, R.C. Effects of vocabulary difficulty, text cohesion, and schema availability on reading comprehension. *Reading Research Quarterly*, 1983, *18*, 277-294.

Fricke, B.G. Speed and level versus rate and accuracy of reading. In E. M. Huddleston (Ed.), *Measurements used in education*. Yearbook of the National Council of Measurement in Education, 1957, *14*, 73-77.

Gifford, E.M., and Marson, A.R. Test anxiety, reading rate, and task experience. *Journal of Educational Research*, 1966, *59*, 303-306.

Goodman, K.S. The psycholinguistic nature of the reading process. In K.S. Goodman (Ed.), *The psycholinguistic nature of the reading process*. Detroit: Wayne State University Press, 1968.

Goodman, K.S. Behind the eye: What happens in reading. In H. Singer and R.B. Ruddell (Eds.), *Theoretical models and processes of reading*, second edition. Newark, DE: International Reading Association, 1976.

Harris, A.J., and Jacobsen, M. *Basic reading vocabularies*. New York: Macmillan, 1982.

Harris, A.J., and Sipay, E.R. *How to increase reading ability*, seventh edition. New York: Longman, 1980.

Heilman, A.W., Blair, T.R., and Rupley, W.H. *Principles and practices of teaching reading*. Columbus, OH: Charles E. Merrill, 1981.

Hill, W. R. Influences of directions upon the flexibility of advanced college readers. In E.L. Thurston and L.E. Hafner (Eds.), *New concepts in college-adult reading*. Yearbook of the National Reading Conference, 1964, *13*, 119-125.

Himelstein, H.C., and Greenberg, G. The effect of increasing reading rate on comprehension. *Journal of Psychology*, 1974, *86*, 251-259.

Howlett, N., and Weintraub, S. Instructional procedures. In R.C. Calfee and P.R. Drum (Eds.), *Teaching reading in compensatory classes*. Newark, DE: International Reading Association, 1979.

Hughes, V.H. A study of the relationships among selected language abilities. *Journal of Educational Research*, 1953, *47*, 97-106.

Hvistendahl, J.K. The effect of typographic variants on reader estimates of attractiveness and reading speed of magazine pages. *Communications Research Report*. Brookings, SD: Printing and Journalism Department, South Dakota State University, 1965.

Jackson, M.D., and McClelland, J.L. Sensory and cognitive determinants of reading speed. *Journal of Verbal Learning and Verbal Behavior*, 1975, *14*, 565-574.

Jackson, M.D., and McClelland, J.L. Processing determinants of reading speed. *Journal of Experimental Psychology: General*, 1979, *108*, 151-181.

Johnston, P.H. *Reading comprehension assessment: A cognitive basis*. Newark, DE: International Reading Association, 1983.

Jongsma, E.A. Test review: Gates-MacGinitie reading test (second edition). *Journal of Reading*, 1980, *23*, 340-345.

Kelley, T.L., and Krey, A.C. *Tests and measurements in the social sciences*. New York: Scribner, 1934.

Kingston, A. Is reading what the reading tests test? In E.L. Thurston and L.E. Hafner (Eds.), *The philosophical and sociological bases of reading*. Yearbook of the National Reading Conference, 1965, *14*, 106-109.

Kruglov, L.P. Qualitative differences in the vocabulary choices of children as revealed in a multiple choice test. *Journal of Educational Psychology*, 1953, *44*, 229-243.

Kuczaj, S.A. II. Acquisition of word meaning in the context of the development of the semantic system. In C.J. Brainerd and M. Pressley (Eds.), *Verbal processes in children*. New York: Springer-Verlag, 1982.

Laycock, F. Significant characteristics of college students with varying flexibility in reading rate. *Journal of Experimental Education*, 1955, *23*, 311-330.

Letson, C.T. Speed and comprehension in reading. *Journal of Educational Research*, 1958, *52*, 49-53.

McDonald, A.S. A reading versatility inventory. In O.S. Causey (Ed.), *Significant elements in college and adult reading improvement.* Yearbook of the National Reading Conference, 1958, *7*, 48-53.

McDonald, A.S. Factors affecting reading test performance. In O.S. Causey and E.P. Bliesmer (Eds.), *Research and evaluation in college reading.* Yearbook of the National Reading Conference, 1960, *9*, 28-35.

McDonald, A.S. Research for the classroom: Rate and flexibility. *Journal of Reading*, 1965, *8*, 187-191.

McDonald, A.S. Flexibility in reading approaches: Measurement and development. In J.A. Figurel (Ed.), *Combining research results and good practices.* Newark, DE: International Reading Association, 1966.

McKeown, M.G., Beck, I.L., Omanson, R.C., and Perfetti, C.A. The effects of long term vocabulary instruction on reading comprehension: A replication. *Journal of Reading Behavior*, 1983, *15*, 3-18.

McLaughlin, G.H. Reading at impossible speeds. *Journal of Reading*, 1969, *13*, 449-457.

McNamara, W.J., Patterson, D.G., and Tinker, M.A. The influence of size of type on speed of reading in the primary grades. *Sight Saving Review*, 1953, *23*, 28-33.

Mason, J.M., Kniseley, E., and Kendall, J. Effects of polysemous words on sentence comprehension. *Reading Research Quarterly*, 1979, *15*, 49-65.

Maxwell, M.J. An experimental investigation of the effect of instructional set and information on reading rate. In. E.L. Thurstone and L.E. Hafner (Eds.), *The philosophical and sociological bases of reading.* Yearbook of the National Reading Conference, 1965, *14*, 181-187.

Mezynski, K. Issues concerning the acquisition of knowledge: Effects of vocabulary training on reading comprehension. *Review of Educational Research*, 1983, *53*, 253-279.

Pyrczak, F., and Rasmussen, M. Skills measured by selected reading tests designed for high school use. *Reading Improvement*, 1974, *11*, 5-8.

Rankin, E.F. The relation between reading rate and comprehension. In E.P. Bliesmer and R.C. Staiger (Eds.), *Problems, programs and projects in college-adult reading.* Yearbook of the National Reading Conference, 1962, *11*, 1-5.

Rinsland, H.D. *A basic vocabulary of elementary school children.* New York: Macmillan, 1945.

Russell, D.H. The dimensions of children's meaning vocabulary in grades four through twelve. *University of California Publications in Education*, 1954, *11*, 315-414.

Scales, A.M. *An analysis of reading and study skills elements.* (ED 225 127)

Seashore, R.H., and Eckerson, L.D. The measurement of individual differences in general English vocabularies. *Journal of Educational Psychology*, 1940, *31*, 14-38.

Sheldon, W.D. Diagnostic techniques and tools: The flexibility of reading rate. In O. S. Causey (Ed.), *Exploring the goals of college reading programs.* Yearbook of the Southwest Reading Conference for Colleges and Universities, 1955, *5,* 116-117.

Sheldon, W.D., and Carrillo, L.W. The flexibility of reading rate. *Journal of Educational Psychology,* 1952, *43,* 37-45.

Shores, J.H., and Husbands, K.L. Are fast readers the best readers? *Elementary English,* 1950, *24,* 52-57.

Slakter, M.J. *The measurement and effect of risk taking on objective examinations.* Final Report, Project No. 5-8428. Washington, DC: U.S. Office of Education, 1967.

Smith, C.B., Smith, S., and Mikulecky, L. *Teaching reading in secondary school subjects: A bookthinking process.* New York: Holt, Rinehart and Winston, 1978.

Smith, F. *Understanding reading.* New York: Holt, Rinehart and Winston, 1971.

Smith, M.K. Measurement of the size of general English vocabulary through the elementary grades and high school. *Genetic Psychology Monographs,* 1941, *24,* 311-345.

Stevens, G.L., and Orem, R.C. Characteristic reading techniques of rapid readers. *Reading Teacher,* 1963, *17,* 102-108.

Stroud, J.B. A critical note on reading: Rate and comprehension. *Psychological Bulletin,* 1942, *39,* 173-178.

Swineford, F., and Miller, P.M. Effects of directions regarding guessing on item statistics of a multiple choice vocabulary test. *Journal of Educational Psychology,* 1953, *44,* 129-139.

Thomas, E.L., and Robinson, H.A. *Improving reading in every class.* Boston: Allyn and Bacon, 1977.

Thorndike, E.L. *A teacher's word book of the twenty thousand words found most frequently and widely in general reading for children and young people.* New York: Bureau of Publications, Teachers College, Columbia University, 1931.

Thorndike, R.L., and Hagen, E. *Measurement and evaluation in psychology and evaluation,* third edition. New York: Wiley, 1969.

Thurstone, L.L. *A factorial study of perception.* Chicago: University of Chicago Press, 1944.

Traxler, A.E. The relationship between the length and the reliability of a test of rate of reading. *Journal of Educational Research,* 1938, *32,* 1-2.

Witty, P.A. Rate of reading—a crucial issue. *Journal of Reading,* 1969, *13,* 102-106.

Yap, K.O. Vocabulary—building blocks of comprehension? *Journal of Reading Behavior,* 1979, *11,* 50-61.

Test References

California Achievement Test, Form C. Monterey, CA: California Test Bureau/ McGraw-Hill, 1977.

California Reading Test. E.W. Tiegs and W.W. Clark. Monterey, CA: California Test Bureau, 1957, revised, 1963.

Davis Reading Test. F.B. Davis and C.C. Davis. New York: Psychological Corporation, 1958, revised, 1962.

Durrell Analysis of Reading Difficulty, new edition. D. Durrell. New York: Harcourt Brace Jovanovich, 1980.

Gates-MacGinitie Reading Tests: Survey A. A.I. Gates and W. MacGinitie. New York: Teachers College Press, Columbia University, 1926; revised, 1965.

Gates-MacGinitie Reading Tests. A.I. Gates and W.H. MacGinitie. Boston: Houghton Mifflin, 1926; revised, 1978.

Gilmore Oral Reading Test. J. Gilmore and V. Gilmore. New York: Harcourt Brace Jovanovich, 1951; revised, 1968.

Gray Oral Reading Test. W.S. Gray. Austin, TX: Pro-Ed. Publishing, 1963.

Iowa Silent Reading Tests. R. Farr. New York: Psychological Corporation, 1972.

Iowa Tests of Basic Skills. A.N. Hieronymous, E.F. Lindquist, and H.D. Hoover. Chicago: Riverside Publishing, 1982.

Metropolitan Achievement Tests: Reading. R.C. Farr, G.A. Prescott, I.H. Balow, and T.H. Hogan. New York: Psychological Corporation, 1978.

Nelson-Denny Reading Test: Vocabulary-comprehension-rate. M. Nelson, E. Denny, and J. Brown. Lombard, IL: Riverside Publishing, 1931; revised, 1981.

Nelson Reading Skills Test. M.J. Nelson. Boston: Houghton Mifflin, 1931; revised, 1977.

Stanford Achievement Test. E.F. Gardner, H.C. Rudman, B. Karlsen, and J.C. Merwin. New York: Psychological Corporation, 1981.

Stanford Diagnostic Reading Scales. B. Karlsen, R. Madden, and E.F. Gardner. New York: Psychological Corporation, 1976.

5

Validity and reliability in reading assessment

Validity as the term relates to tests is defined in *A Dictionary of Reading and Related Terms* (1981) as "the characteristic of a test that determines that the test measures what it is supposed to measure and/or that it can predict performance on other measures" (p. 343). Validity is the most important characteristic of a test, but the search for validity evidence is much more elusive than this definition suggests. Indeed, the search for validity is a search for the true behavior being measured. Since there is still much to be learned about reading, it is reasonable to accept the notion that a totally valid reading test does not exist. Considered from this perspective, it is best to think of a test in terms of degrees of validity. A test may measure some aspect of reading and, along with other observations of performance, may provide some insight into a person's reading ability.

Reliability is defined by *A Dictionary of Reading and Related Terms* as "consistency in measurements and tests" (p. 276). The term has taken on a more general concept: the amount of faith that can be placed in the results from a particular test. A test user's concern with reliability is whether the results from one test given at one time will be generally the same as the results of the same test given at a slightly different time. The answer is that they will not. This means that the information provided by any test is only an estimate of the information one is attempting to gather.

Previous chapters of this monograph have been concerned with the validity, and to some extent the reliability, of the assessment of reading comprehension as well as separate skills of reading. This chapter will consider the validity and reliability of various types of reading tests. Validity and reliabilty are concerned primarily with why tests are used and with whom they are used. Since the major uses of tests can be related to types of tests, this chapter begins with a review of test classification.

Classifications of reading tests

It is obvious to anyone who has attempted to select a reading test that the myriad of tests available is overwhelming and that attempts to categorize those tests into particular types present significant problems. Reading tests do not fall into neat, nonoverlapping categories because test authors and publishers often attempt to develop tests to serve a wide range of educational uses. In addition, test users have tried to use single tests for many different purposes, often including purposes for which the tests were not developed. Distinctions are also blurred because there are no clear definitions for such test terms as *diagnostic, survey, instructional, criterion* or *objective referenced*.

These factors have contributed to reading tests being categorized in a variety of ways, not only by those who use and evaluate them, but by test publishers as well. It is axiomatic that the successful seller of reading tests would like to have a particular test included in as many different categories as possible. In that way, the chances are increased for having a test being considered and selected for use.

The aim of the numerous test classification systems has been to assist the test consumer in locating and evaluating a particular test to serve particular needs. However, most systems poorly serve this basic aim. A major reason for this failure is that the categories in most systems are not determined by uses that will be made on the tests' results. Whatever determines them, the categories often are not effectively defined and frequently overlap. These shortcomings in classification systems cause tests that provide results which can be used in significantly similar ways to be placed in separate categories. The end result is that the categorization is not especially helpful to the user. A consumer with a specific testing need might overlook tests that will serve that need by using this inadequate system.

A typical approach to categorizing tests is to determine whether they are *survey* or *diagnostic*. The survey category includes tests which attempt to provide information about an examinee's general reading development. A diagnostic test attempts to provide more indepth information about specific reading behaviors. The usual format for survey tests provides fewer subtests. Diagnostic tests include subtests of a variety of reading skills. This means that survey tests are usually shorter than diagnostic tests, both in testing time and the number of test items.

In addition, it is typical for survey tests to emphasize normative information, while diagnostic tests emphasize criterion referenced information. Normative information relates an examinee's test performance to a sample of examinees on whom the test was normed; criterion referenced information relates an examinee's test performance to the accomplishment of a specific task such as success on a set of test items that supposedly indicates mastery of a particular learning objective.

Despite the supposed distinctions between these two categories, one quite often finds the same test categorized as a survey test in one classification system and as a diagnostic test in another. More commonly, one often finds two very similar tests in different categories within the same classification system.

Another test classification system is based on the examinee's *response mode*. That is, tests are categorized as to whether they are oral or silent reading tests. While this system seems to be an effective means to distinguish tests, such is not the case. Many reading tests include both oral and silent reading response modes. Moreover, the typical test user is not interested in assessing oral reading as an end in itself but rather as a means of evaluating an examinee's reading development, or the use of particular reading strategies.

Still another classification system is based on the *age level* or *reading level* of the examinees who are expected to take the tests. For this classification, tests are categorized as: reading readiness, primary grade reading, elementary grade reading, high school reading, and adult reading. The specific grade level breakdowns in such a classification system are, of course, arbitrary and can cause problems when the grade level classification system does not match the grade level span in which the consumer is interested. Also, the grade level classifications are sometimes confusing because the grade levels can refer either to the reading level of the examinees for whom the tests are intended or to the actual grade placement of the examinees. There are many reading tests that do not seem to fit any of the classification systems listed, including tests that accompany certain instructional reading programs. Basal reader tests are a prime example. Another category is reading tests that are used with special populations, such as learning disabled students.

The best advice for the test consumer is to first determine the specific use or uses for the test results and to make sure appropriate test uses are clearly stated. Then the search for potential tests can begin within the most obvious categories. However, useful tests will be overlooked if the search does not include examining other categories for tests that also meet the specified testing need.

Three types of reading assessment

The most useful test classification would categorize tests according to the uses to be made of the test results. This would mean that many tests would be classified in several categories because tests can be developed to serve more than one purpose. Perhaps the reason a classification system based on test use has not been developed is that many tests would be classified in multiple categories and this might bother those who believe classification systems should result in discrete categories. In any event, one classification system that relates to test usage and that also generally results in a single classification for each test includes norm referenced, criterion referenced, and informal tests.

These three types may include similar test item types, they may be used to gather similar kinds of information, and they may even produce similar kinds of test scores. The primary intent for the use of each test type is, however, quite different. The interpretation and use of test performance is the major difference among norm referenced, criterion referenced, and informal tests rather than any substantive differences in the test items or the organization of the test.

Norm referenced tests are generally used to determine an examinee's status in reading development. The use of norm referenced test results is to compare students' scores with the scores of the population of examinees on whom the test was normed. Norm referenced test developers emphasize content that one could reasonably expect to be familiar to any student who is administered the test. Test development also includes selecting material to cover a fairly broad range of ability levels—broad enough so that more able examinees will have challenging material and the less able will have material with which they can be successful. Also, these tests are developed with easy, average, and difficult test items. In this way, test developers hope to spread out the performance of students to allow for comparisons. Subtests usually are included within the test attempts to assess such things as reading comprehension, reading vocabulary, and word recognition skills.

Norm referenced tests are designed to be administered according to a specific set of directions. Because of these specific (or *standard*) directions, the test is often referred to as a *standardized test*. Standardized directions include such factors as controlled testing conditions, specified time limits, and particular response modes. The standard directions must be followed if the norm referenced interpretations are to be used. Norms are developed by administering the test to a sample representative of the population of interest. Thus, the norm referenced scores are descriptive scores that indicate how a particular student or group of students compares to the population used to norm the test.

A student's score on a norm referenced test is reported in stanines, percentiles, grade equivalents, deciles, normal curve equivalents, or other standard scores which compare an examinee's test performance to the norming population. Presumably, the scores are useful because they reveal how the performance of an individual, or group, compares to that of some reference group such as age or grade groups. The percentile score, for example, tells what percent of the norming sample scored below and above a particular score.

Despite the fact that norm referenced tests are developed primarily to compare students, the items on the tests are based on the reading objectives and curriculum of school districts and state education departments, and on instructional reading materials used throughout the country. Consequently, some norm referenced tests are also criterion referenced. That is, they can be used to compare an examinee's performance to the objectives being assessed on the test as well as to the sample of students used to norm the test. Glaser (1964) demonstrated that the information generated by a norm referenced and a criterion referenced assessment can be quite different. Glaser compared the instructional reading levels of retarded seventh grade and advanced third grade students as determined by an informal reading inventory to their score on the Gates Reading Survey (a norm referenced test). The IRI, as it is commonly referred to, is a criterion referenced test. All of the students in both groups scored between 5.0 and 5.9 on the Gates Survey. The findings of Glaser's study indicated:

1. The instructional reading levels of the advanced and retarded readers as determined by the IRI's were consistently lower than the levels of their standardized reading test scores, with a slightly larger spread evident for retarded readers.

2. About half (52 percent) of the retarded seventh grade readers reached frustration level on the IRI on passages of fifth grade difficulty; 57 percent of the third grade pupils met the criteria for frustration on the IRI at this level.

3. The instructional reading levels on the IRI were consistently below the standardized reading test scores for the two groups.

4. Providing reading instruction and materials for students on the basis of standardized reading test scores could hinder their progress and possibly affect their attitude toward reading.

The main point of Glaser's study is that the norm referenced and criterion referenced test scores provide different information; however, the tests themselves may actually be similar and the test scores may appear to provide the same information.

Criterion referenced tests are generally regarded as tests that relate more specifically to instructional decision making. The focus is on how well a student can perform on a particular test objective rather than how well the student performs in relation to other students. Criterion referenced tests are used to determine which examinees have mastered a particular set of instructional objectives. Thus the goal of criterion referenced tests is to determine how well examinees perform on specific test items which are supposed to reflect specific test objectives, rather than to attempt to generalize to the reading curriculum in a wide variety of school districts.

Presumably the items on a criterion referenced test are carefully selected to reflect the values that have predicated the development and administration of the test. If its purpose is assessing the acquisition of minimum essentials in reading, for example, the items can be expected to reflect some predetermined judgment about which reading behaviors are considered minimally essential to living, to learning, to satisfying taxpayers and educational critics, or to some behavior that ought to be specified but all too often is not.

The standard for a criterion referenced test, as Glass (1978) effectively argues, is invariably set arbitrarily and is, therefore, as meaningful as the judgment used to arrive at it is fallible. More often than not, it establishes some cutoff score that dictates dichotomous decision making, such as whether a student will pass or fail, be graduated or be reinstructed or exposed to more advanced educational material. In situations where the criterion referenced test determines decisions such a pass/fail or graduate/not graduate, the judgment involved in constructing the test's content is very serious business, and certainly incorporates a moral responsibility on the part of the test maker.

The norm referenced test developer's goal is not to determine who can accomplish a specific task. Rather, the test maker is interested in how much of a particular ability (such as reading) each examinee has achieved. On the other hand, criterion referenced test developers are interested in whether the potential examinees have "mastered" specific sets of objectives. They assume each student should be able to answer each of the items correctly if the objectives of instruction have been achieved. Thus, the criterion referenced test developer is not interested in how much of a specific behavior the examinees possess. Rather, the test maker is interested in whether they can demonstrate proficiency on the specific objectives included on the test.

Informal measures include a wide variety of information collection procedures that are used as part of instruction. Informal reading tests are used to gather information as part of ongoing classroom instruction. The use of informal measures is perhaps one of the most neglected aspects of reading instruction. Informal measures include a teacher's discussion with a student to determine how well that student has understood something that has been read. They might also include the teacher's review of the student's workbook page in a reading program.

Informal measures include such procedures as observation, participation charts, checklists, rating scales, anecdotal records, peer appraisal, and self report techniques (Mehrens & Lehmann, 1984). Each of these approaches has significant importance in planning instruction. According to Mehrens and Lehmann, "The primary way that teachers obtain data concerning their pupils' achievements and attainments is by their daily contacts with students" (p. 203).

Among the most commonly used informal tests are informal reading inventories (IRIS) developed by classroom teachers. These are based on the materials used for reading instruction. Commercially developed IRIS or those that are prepared with materials other than those used as part of instruction are not informal tests at all; they should be classified as criterion referenced tests. The essence of an informal reading test is that it is used concomitantly with instruction and is administered in an informal manner determined by the circumstances. A commercially developed informal reading inventory, on the other hand, is administered following a specific set of directions and is used to determine whether a child can read a particular set of materials. Thus it is criterion referenced to the particular materials read by the examinee.

How clearly different are reading assessment types?

These three types of tests are not simplistically exclusive, and issues which focus on their strengths and weaknesses tend to blur their differences. The norm referenced test is distinguished by the fact that its primary goal is to report a student's performance in comparison to the performance of some sample of students on whom the test has been normed. Since in a norm referenced test an individual's performance is interpreted in relation to others who have taken the test, the more score variation an item creates, the more possible are the comparisons. This fact, perhaps more than any other, often distinguishes the construction of norm referenced test items from those of criterion referenced tests, which are developed with a single focus on how well they reflect what they purport to measure.

As already pointed out, a particular test can be both norm referenced and criterion referenced. Indeed, the argument has often been made that the criterion levels established to determine success on a criterion referenced test are determined by the expectations that are held for average performing students. Considered in this way, criterion referenced tests are norm referenced. In addition, the items included on a norm referenced test are based on the curricula used in schools; thus norm referenced tests are in a very real sense criterion referenced to those materials.

A criterion referenced test that has a criterion determined by how well a norm population performed on the test is the General Educational Development test (GED) administered by the American Council on Education. This test is administered each year to approximately 800,000 people who would like to receive a high school diploma. They are usually people who have dropped out of school or who are immigrants to the United States. The interesting aspect of the GED test is the way in which the cutoff (*criterion*) score is established. The criterion score is the test score one would have to achieve to be awarded a high school diploma. The specific score varies from state to state and is actually determined by the education department of each state. The basic procedure is to administer the GED test to a sample of high school seniors who are expected to graduate that year. The criterion is then set as the score above which a certain percentage of the seniors score. Thus, the criterion interpretation is based on the norming population of high school students to whom the test is administered.

In studying the Iowa Test of Basic Skills, Hambleton and Novick (1973) pointed out how a test could be norm referenced as well as criterion referenced. They noted that the purposes which dictate a test's use may be a key distinction between the two types of tests—criterion referencing tends to look on testing "as a decision-theoretic process" (p. 162) and, as Cronbach and Glesser (1965) said, to be used in selection problems that are not dictated by quotas in which the comparison reports of norm referencing would be more applicable.

Royer and Lynch (1982), on the other hand, expressed a prevailing criticism of the norm referenced test that contends it is as limited as a criterion reference. They argued that the topics on norm referenced tests do not reflect what is taught in schools and the items are not adequately criterion referenced to any individual student's educational environment. They would not have educators use norm referenced tests in making instructional decisions. They also contended that most norm referenced tests are aptitude—not achievement—tests and are insensitive to learning gains. Their charge against the instructional usefulness of norm referenced tests, however, is based on the least meaningful of the translations given to such tests, the grade equivalent scores (GE) produced by such tests. They rightfully argue that placing students in an instructional program based on their GE is a blatant misuse of such scores. The GE is a norm referenced score which provides one means to compare a student's performance with that of the norm group. It is not a criterion referenced score which relates a student's reading performance to ability to read a specific level of instructional material.

However, Royer and Lynch did not consider other scores and interpretations possible from norm referenced tests. Some norm referenced reading tests provide extensive criterion referenced interpretations that are intended to help teachers plan instruction.

Royer and Lynch also charge that the number of items used to assess individual skills on norm referenced tests is far too small to allow for dependable judgments about instruction. The small size of the sample of behaviors observed is, of course, one of the most serious shortcomings of all tests—norm referenced, criterion referenced, and informal alike. To make instructional judgments based on just a few test items or a few samples of behaviors is only slightly better than relying on chance.

A clearer distinction between the assessment types is that a criterion referenced and an informal test can be developed to focus just on the reading behaviors that are taught in a specific school system, school, or classroom. Ideally, each teacher should be a master at observing student behavior and assessing each child's reading development. A teacher can provide extensive information about the progress each child has made on the specific objectives that comprise the local reading curriculum. Also, the teacher can gather a broad sample of reading behaviors, thus insuring a more valid and reliable assessment.

The major problem usually encountered with all three test types is that they each try to assess too broad a range of reading behaviors; in doing this they try to cover a myriad of reading subskills with too few items. They also provide artificial testing situations and attempt to relate these "indices" of reading to all reading behaviors. If tests were seen for what they are, samples of behaviors gathered under artificial conditions, then they might be used more cautiously and helpfully in planning instruction.

Problems in test design are inherent across types

Much of the discussion and research on reading assessment and the value of information produced by assessment emphasize traditional problems that for decades have been the focus of test developers and researchers. Although these problems are sometimes couched in attacks and criticisms that make them appear to be recently discovered problems, they include such traditional measurement issues as validity, reliability, passage dependence (a special test item validity problem), test administration techniques, and threats to validity because of bias against a specific cultural group. These are not new problems; they are the same ones that have always vexed test developers eager to develop tests that provide more useful information to educators.

Test criticism has usually focused on norm referenced tests; however, the problems are just as real for criterion referenced tests and informal tests as they are for norm referenced tests. Simply because methods of determining the reliability of criterion referenced tests have not been promoted by a reporting scheme that compares students' scores does not mean that such tests should not be reliable across forms and populations, especially when they are used for making important educational decisions.

Other questions which focus on norm referenced tests also have relevance across all three test types. Whether a student can answer a test item correctly without reading the passage on which it is based is just as serious a concern for criterion referenced and informal tests as for norm referenced tests. Passage dependence issues invoke debate based on the desire to eliminate the influence of reader background on test results and the emerging acceptance of a definition of reading that makes this undesirable, if not impossible. Distinguishing valid comprehension from guessing is another general test problem faced by any assessment that uses an item format where multiple answer choices are provided.

Validity: Does a test measure what it claims to measure?

There is, as Nitko (1983) points out, no single validity question, index, or coefficient for tests. Rather, there are a variety of validity questions. Nitko clearly states the most important of validity concerns: "The answer to the general question, 'Is this test valid?' depends on the purpose for which the test is being used and the context in which it is used. A test may be valid for some specific purposes and may not be valid for others. It is important, therefore, to clearly specify the decisions you want to make before searching for validity information about them" (p. 440).

Nitko* provides several examples of the kinds of validity questions which might be asked, depending on the testing purpose:

Content validity

- To what extent are the items a representative sample of content (behavior) from the test publisher's domain?
- To what extent are the psychological processes required by the test items representative of the processes required by the test developer's domain?

Curricular relevance

- To what extent are the test items and their required psychological processes representative of the domain as we define it (e.g., our school curriculum, our view of intelligence, and/or our view of a certain personality trait)?

Construct validity

- To what extent can the test scores be interpreted as meaningful beyond the mere level of items to the level of construct interpretations which are believed to underlie observed performance on the test items?

Criterion oriented validity

- To what extent can scores on the test be used to infer a person's standing on a second measure (criterion)?
  a. To what extent can the scores be used to select persons for jobs, schools, etc.? What is the magnitude of the error?
  b. To what extent can the test be used to assign pupils to different levels of instruction? (Nitko, 1983, p. 438)

The specific validity questions Nitko raises provide direction for examining test validity and demonstrate that the most important validity question is whether a particular test meets a user's specific information needs. Any study of test validity must be based on the purpose for which the test is being used. It is true that a test does not have validity; test validity relates to how valid a test may be for a given purpose. A particular test may be valid for one purpose but not for another.

* Paraphrased from *Educational Tests and Measurement* by A.J. Nitko. Copyright 1983 by Harcourt Brace Jovanovich, Inc. Used with permission.

The most common use of norm referenced and criterion referenced tests tends to highlight their differences. Singer (1977) succinctly stated the primary rationale for the use of most norm referenced tests:

> Unlike criterion referenced tests, use of standardized tests will enable schools to make a relative, quantitative interpretation of an individual's progress in learning how to read through reference to the norms for the test (p. 147).

Singer suggested that schools could use a norm referenced test as a kind of criterion measure by setting up the 90 to 95 percentile as the criterion and, after a period of instruction, repeating the administration of the same level of a test that was given before the instruction. Schultz (1971) reported that the use of norm referenced tests should be based on the development of improved tests as well as improvement of the use of tests by educators, who often use norm referenced tests for the wrong reasons.

Content and construct validity: Of basic importance

In addition to the important consideration of user validity, the content and construct validity of tests need to be carefully considered. *Content* validity refers to the match between the items on the test and the curriculum that has been taught. *Construct* validity refers to whether the test items actually measure the construct (or behavior) that is supposedly being measured. A test may have content validity for a particular reading curriculum, but there may be some question whether the construct being assessed is actual reading behavior. Thus the question of construct validity can raise questions about the curriculum being taught as much as about the test being used to assess that curriculum.

To determine content validity one must examine the items on each subtest to see if they fall within the boundaries of the domain of that particular subtest. Then one must judge if the items included on the subtest are representative. In the case of affixes, for example, one must ask if the words tested are proportionately representative of words with affixes which appear in the vocabularies of the instructional program or in the reading texts the students are most likely to encounter. It is difficult to imagine answering "yes" to this question or determining validity for any subtest of limited length, without extensive analysis of the vocabularies in the texts that students encounter.

One approach to determining the relevance of each norm referenced test item regarding its relationship to a particular curriculum has been suggested by Cox and Sterrett (1970). Their approach also may have use in determining the content validity of any type of assessment.

Cox and Sterrett suggested that a precise description of curriculum objectives should be developed (if they are not already available) to help educators fully understand the extent to which a test reflects a particular curriculum. Next, the test items should be coded to indicate their relation to the curriculum. Finally, each student's test should be scored in two ways. The first scoring should be for test items that reflect curriculum the student has been taught, and the second for test items that reflect curriculum the student has not been taught. Cox and Sterrett believe this analysis will show the true match of test items to the curriculum.

The process seems tedious and detailed, and the construct validity of a test that passes such a review will still be open to question; but such a test is sure to have some content relevance to the student's classroom reading experience. The more distant the test development is from the individual classroom, the less likely it is to match this perspective on content validity. Viewed in this way, the norm referenced test is at a considerable disadvantage, as is a published criterion referenced test, a statewide criterion referenced test, and a commercially developed informal reading test. The teacher's ongoing informal testing stands the best chance of meeting this validity criterion.

The primary evidence for content validity is, of course, the match of the test objectives to the curriculum objectives. This is true for norm referenced, criterion referenced, and informal tests alike. However, criterion referenced tests are most apt to have content validity since the use of such tests to ascertain accomplishment of specific curriculum goals is their main focus. Presumably, criterion referenced tests are derived from the existing educational goals in an educational arena of some size. One designed for a particular school district should reflect the stated broad goals of instruction, as well as the specific instructional objectives for that school district. When criterion referenced tests are designed to report on, and even enforce, educational accountability, the goals and objectives measured are apt to become the major, or perhaps the only, goals and objectives emphasized in individual classrooms. While this would assure content validity, it would almost surely reduce the emphasis on individual learning objectives for each student, and subsequently drive out the use of informal testing based on the objectives of instruction for individual students.

Linn (1979) and Hambleton and Novick (1973) argue that the content validity of criterion referenced tests is often assumed because the test includes items that supposedly measure the specific objectives of instruction.

However, merely matching test items or objectives to curriculum objectives is not the essence of determining test validity.

The key validity question is whether the test items actually measure what they purport to measure. The most important issue should not be content validity (the curriculum/test objective match) but the construct validity of the test items as a measure of the reading process. An analysis of test validity at this level will certainly question the validity of the curriculum objectives as well as those of the test.

Kirsch and Guthrie (1980) attempted to assess the construct validity of a published adult functional reading measure (a criterion referenced test) by analyzing how readers actually processed the test items. They found that the salience of test item information contributed more than any other variable to the overall difficulty examinees had in extracting relevant information. Kirsch and Guthrie conclude from their analysis of processing demands that assessment of construct validity requires the statement of a test's purpose, in terms of cognitive processes, and a description of the relationship between performance and its demands on these processes.

Examination of a test's construct validity incorporates the consideration of whether subtests which purport to measure specific subskills actually do measure those subskills so that the score results are not contaminated by a host of other comprehension facilitating features that we now understand interact in very complex ways. One of the most persistent criticisms of the construct validity of reading tests which purport to measure distinct skills is that they do not convincingly distinguish subskills.

Most research on discriminant validity has been either too limited or too equivocal to support the contention that specific subskills can be validly measured (Chall, 1958; Murray & Karlsen, 1960). It has been pointed out, however, that there exists a significant lack of consistency across test publishers with regard to the specific subskills included on the various tests. Farr and Roelke (1971) found only limited convergent validity for assessments of three subskills among teacher judgment, reading specialist judgment, and norm referenced tests. Their results indicated there was no discriminant validity for the three subskills. Drahozal and Hanna (1978) examined items on the Nelson-Denny test identified as testing three subskills and found that they did "not reflect corresponding attributes...at grades three through nine" (p. 419).

This lack of evidence for discriminant validity has led researchers such as Hunt (1957) and Farr (1968) to question the validity of using subskill scores for diagnosis that would direct instruction; and Goodman's charge (1968) that any assumption of discriminant validity could be attributed to a lack of understanding of the reading process has gathered numerous supporters as the reading process is examined more closely.

One California school district's response to such criticism has been atypical (Agra, 1978). In devising a minimum competency test that high school graduates must pass, the district tested only the general comprehension of passages presented in a newspaper format while avoiding subskill identification altogether. Like most norm referenced tests, however, almost all criterion referenced tests boldly factor reading into selected subskills.

Closely related to the discriminant validity of subskill assessment is consideration of whether a test's items measure the aspects of reading they claim to measure, given that the skill has been distinguished somehow. If, for example, a subtest professes to measure an assumed reading subskill, such as a student's ability to recognize prefixes and suffixes, how well is that domain (which potentially includes every affix/root combination students might reasonably encounter in their reading materials) represented by the particular choice of test items? Obviously, tests which attempt to cover this aspect of word recognition with from three to twelve items—as do many norm referenced and criterion referenced tests—are open to serious question regarding validity.

In the case of reading tests and subtests which assess reading comprehension as a single composite skill, determining content or construct validity must be based on the test user's theory of reading comprehension. The item types, choice of text to be read, and the combination and weighting of items all need to be considered.

Informal tests, which can focus on different aspects of a given reading behavior at different times, have the greatest potential to be valid for three important reasons. First, the samples of behaviors can be gathered at different times and under differing conditions; second, informal tests can sample a much larger set of behaviors using a variety of item types; and third, the tests are almost certain to be useful for instructional decision making since they are based on actual classroom activities.

A test consumer can evaluate construct validity only by examining the operational definition of reading embodied in the test itself, and then the validity evidence the test publisher provides to indicate that the test items actually measure what the publisher states they measure. Norm referenced reading tests are often criticized because they do not provide information about *why* examinees read as they do. They only provide information about *how well* the examinees read. That is, most reading tests only assess the construct of the *product* of reading. From these *products*, test users assume certain conclusions about the reading *process*. Reading tests are valid measures to describe, rather than explain, reading behavior; therefore, the information they make available for classroom instruction has its limitations. Criterion referenced and informal tests are subject to the same limitations. They all describe how well students perform on specific tasks and on specific objectives, but they do not tell why students perform as they do.

Norming sample validity: In need of more attention

One important validity question often overlooked in the selection of a norm referenced test is the validity of the norming sample. This is neither a content nor a construct validity issue, but it is important if the test norms are to be used. The major norm referenced tests seem to be much alike in the scores they provide. Linn (1975) noted that the Anchor Test study, which equated the scores across eight norm referenced tests, found high intercorrelations among the tests. This result did not mean that the tests were each measuring the same things, or even that the norms of the eight tests were comparable. It merely emphasized examinees who got high scores on one of the tests were very likely to get high scores on the other tests.

Generally, the more information a test publisher supplies about the norming sample and procedures, the better judgment the user can make as to whether the test is appropriate for the intended use. An interesting study by Baglin (1981) makes it clear why the user needs to pursue complete norming information with some determination. Baglin examined the norming procedures of three major norm referenced reading tests in use today, petitioning the publishers for specific information and data not published with the tests. Two of the three publishers were cooperative, and reasonable approaches were devised for estimating the needed data for the third.

Baglin discovered that, while the school systems invited to participate in the norming of the tests were drawn to fill a scientifically constructed stratified random sample grid, a low percentage (from 13 to 32 percent) of the schools invited to participate in the norming agreed to do so. This meant that the publishers had to seek specific types of schools in specific types of communities to fill the cells in their norming designs. Some of the cells went unfilled; but in their eagerness to fill as many as possible, the publishers frequently petitioned school systems using a previous edition of the test and/or schools using instructional materials published by their firm or sister firms. Thus schools with similar characteristics tended to be over-represented in the norming samples. Baglin argued that school systems in the norming samples were, in a way, "self selected." "The actual norming samples," Baglin reported, "which claim to be random, are in reality highly selected" (p. 104). This potential intensifies the need for a test user to understand as thoroughly as possible how the norming sample of a test matches the students who will be tested and whose scores will be interpreted in comparison to the norming sample.

Baglin's study has been critiqued by Beck (n.d.) who commented that the study provided no evidence that the self selection of schools had any effect on the validity of the norms. Beck states, "More importantly, Baglin presents *no* data in support of his assumption. Absent this, the sense of alarm voiced by the author is at best premature."

The relationship of the time of testing in a school and the time of year the normed data were collected has been pointed out as a potential problem by Beggs and Hieronymous (1968). They suggested that, if the norm referenced scores are to be used, the test should be administered as close as possible to the time of the year the test was normed. Further, they pointed out that the problems of interpretation become more serious in lower grade levels. Similar findings were also reported by Tallmadge and Wood (1976) with a population of students in Chapter I programs.

Grade equivalent scores: Often misinterpreted

Another validity criticism of norm referenced tests concerns the misuse of grade equivalent (GE) scores. GES seem to promote their own misuse by connoting that they have meaning in regard to the curriculum at a particular grade level. Some test manuals seem to suggest this interpretation to be a valid use of GES. The fallacy of the GE as an indication of the level of instructional material an examinee has mastered is exposed by noting that an examinee who is administered a reading comprehension test which includes passages written, say, between a second and sixth grade difficulty level may achieve a score that translates to a GE of perhaps 8.3. It is, of course, sheer nonsense to assume that a student who gets such a score can actually read grade 8 material, particularly when there was no grade 8 reading material included on the test.

In a discussion of how GES do not produce a pupil/material match, MacGinitie (n.d.) wrote:

> A student's GE is not an estimate of [his/her] instructional level. It is not intended to be. It is not a frustration level, either. It is just a test score.

With that, the total usefulness of the GE is described; it exists as a descriptive number that relates an examinee's test performance to those in the norming population. Unfortunately, its presence invites applications that reflect unfavorably on the norm referenced measures that produce it. The problems of interpreting GEs have been well documented (Anderhalter, 1960; Horst, 1976).

The International Reading Association took note of the misuse of grade equivalents in a resolution adopted by the Delegates Assembly in 1981. The resolution notes that "...one of the most serious misuses of tests is the reliance on a grade equivalent as an indicator of absolute performance." The resolution concludes: "Resolved that the International Reading Association strongly advocates that those who administer standardized reading tests abandon the practice of using grade equivalents to report performance of either individuals or groups of test takers..." (International Reading Association, 1981).

Out-of-level testing: When to use it

Another validity issue in the use of norm referenced tests that has received widespread attention is whether it is appropriate to use out-of-level testing for students whose instructional reading levels are lower than their actual grade placements. This concern asks whether the on-grade level tests that special education students encounter as they are mainstreamed in regular education classes are appropriate for them. Yoshida (1976) contended that such children were not included in the norming population for the tests and giving teachers the freedom to pick out-of-level tests that matched the reading levels of these students resulted in more reliable test results. The increased reliability occurred because there was less guessing by the examinees who were more familiar with the content of the test.

Smith et al. (1983) found that grade level testing of special education students resulted in misleadingly high grade equivalents. Gunning (1982) argued that out-of-level testing is appropriate if individualized instructional materials (out-of-level materials) are appropriate for special education students. Gunning contended that:

> Grade level testing for most classes is a pervasive but indefensible practice. [It]...yields erroneous information, can be frustrating to children for whom the test is a mismatch, may mask achievement gains, and, worst of all, may prevent some children from getting the help they need by falsely minimizing or even hiding the severity of their reading problems. (p. 905)

Gunning cautioned, however, that norm referenced scores for students taking tests intended for grade levels lower than their actual grade placements should be compared to scores achieved by children at their own grade levels, when such comparisons are possible from the norm data provided with the test.

Other studies tend to support out-of-level testing, at least for children at lower grade levels. Long, Schaffran, and Kellog (1977) found that testing slow readers in grades one and two with on-level tests yielded lower scores than using tests designed for their instructional reading levels; however, at grades three and four, the opposite was true. Ayrer and McNamara (1973) studied out-of-level testing given to several thousand Philadelphia students and found that the out-of-level test results were more reliable than those produced by grade level testing; however, they also found that beginning at about grade three, the advantage for out-of-level testing was much less significant than in the first three grades.

Pelavin and Barker (1976) studied the effects of out-of-level testing with the Metropolitan Achievement Test. They concluded that the level of the MAT administered to a student can have a substantial effect on the student's score. They found the effects to be particularly pronounced with fifth grade students who were given the elementary level of the test. They concluded that, if these fifth grade students had been given the Intermediate Level of the test, their mean score would probably have been higher.

A very useful guide for test users who need to decide when to use on-level or out-of-level testing was provided by Arter (1982). Her guidelines follow:

In-level testing should occur when:
1. Out-of-level (OOL) testing is not allowed or is not practical.
2. The test series has been selected to have a content coverage that is generally appropriate across grades, *and*
   the only use to which scores will be put is program evaluation involving group averages and a comparison group.
3. The specific test content is important for diagnostic or other reasons, *and*
   the in-level test content is adequate, *and*
   the in-level test scores are valid, even if low.

Out-of-level testing should occur when OOL testing is a practical alternative, and:
1. The specific test content is important for diagnostic or other reasons, *and*
   the specific in-level content is not adequate, *and*
   the difficuly of the lower level is likely to be appropriate, *and*
   the content of the lower level is adequate.

2. The specific test content is important for diagnostic or other reasons, *and*
   the scores on the in-level test are not valid because the test is too difficult, *and*
   the content of the lower level of the test is adequate.
3. Test scores will be used for diagnostic purposes as well as for program evaluation involving groups, *and*
   the specific in-level content is not adequate *and*
   the difficulty of the lower level is likely to be appropriate, *and*
   the content of the lower level is adequate, *and*
   the vertical equating is adequate.
4. Test scores will be used for diagnostic purposes as well as for program evaluation involving groups, *and*
   the scores on the in-level test are not valid because the test is too difficult, *and*
   the vertical equating is adequate.

Another test or test series should be chosen when:
1. The specific test content is important for diagnostic or other reasons, *and*
   the content of neither the in-level nor the OOL test is adequate.
2. The specific test content is important for diagnostic or other reasons, *and*
   the test level with the appropriate content does not have the appropriate difficulty.
3. Test scores will be used for diagnostic purposes as well as for program evaluation involving groups *and*
   the test series either does not have a VSS or the vertical equating is inadequate. (pp. 36-37)

The cut score: An essential issue in criterion referenced testing

While the development of norms and out-of-level testing are factors that relate to the validity of norm referenced tests, the most important validity concern with criterion referenced tests is determining the criteria or "cut" score. The cut score is the score that is used to separate those who pass from those who fail. The establishment of the cut score is the most important issue because criterion referenced tests are motivated by the need for decision making information. As already noted, the prevalence of the criteria in instruction constitutes content validity.

An example of a school district which almost guaranteed an invalid estimate of a criterion level was reported by Western (1978). The school district decided to use a norm referenced test to measure the minimal essential requirements in reading for high school graduation. The raw scores of the grade twelve test takers were translated to percentiles using a scale designed for eighth graders.

Another example of a peculiar, if not suspect, approach to criterion setting was reported by Anders (1981). This particular school district correlated the content of its specially developed criterion referenced test to that of other tests, two of which were norm referenced; it offered no rationale for this particular method of selecting skills and emphases for its test. There was, for example, no argument made that the content of the selected tests matched the curriculum of the schools. Such test development procedures lead to a kind of "circular" validity in which one test is validated against another, and that test against a third, and the third against the first.

Sheehan and Marcus (1977) suggested that the uses made of criterion referenced tests are often a detriment to their validity and reliability. Yet, there is circular frustration for the user in the contention that the accuracy of decisions based on such tests constitutes their reliability. Can valid and consistent decisions be based on passages and items that are not content or construct valid, or that do not measure reading behaviors consistently?

Although grade equivalents, for example, are a concern unique to norm referenced measures, and decision/performance relationships are most commonly related to criterion referenced measures, validity questions in general are relevant to both types of tests and to many types of informal tests. All validity problems can potentially impact on a student's performance during assessment, thus raising questions about whether it is valid to interpret a score as a truly meaningful piece of information about how much a student's reading ability has progressed, how well the student actually performs on some reading curriculum objective, what kind of instruction he ought to receive, or how well he will actually succeed in comprehending various texts encountered in various situations.

Passage dependency: A special validity question

A persistent issue for the past ten years has been whether a student actually has to read a passage in order to answer test items. That is, how much of the score resulting from a test is actually the consequence of the student having read something on the test? After all, that is a major part of what a reading comprehension test purports to measure. The issue has been a matter of considerable discussion by such researchers as Tuinman

(1971, 1972), Farr and Smith (1970), Preston (1964), and Pyrczak and Axlerod (1976).

The question of passage dependence relates to a number of interesting questions for which researchers have not determined answers. Passage dependency certainly relies on the background knowledge a reader possesses. If a reader reads a passage describing George Washington's career as the first president of the United States and is then given a question which asks who was the first president of the United States, most people would suggest that the test item is passage *independent* since that fact is considered common knowledge. On the other hand, if the passage concerns Steve Wozniak, the founder of the Apple Computer Company, and is followed by a question which asks the name of the first president of the Apple Computer Company, most people would consider the question to be passage *dependent* since it is not considered common knowledge—or is it? The point is that background knowledge makes one a better reader of material about which one is better informed.

Since reader background is emerging as a key factor in reading comprehension, is it possible to develop test items that are entirely passage dependent? Can the impact of reader background be controlled, especially to eliminate the possibility that tests are biased toward certain examinee populations, without affecting the validity of the tests?

The answers to both questions are negative. It is certainly not possible to assess reading comprehension with test items that are totally passage dependent. A definition of reading based on such a set of test items would deny the fact that reading is a constructive process. And to deny the importance of reader background would seriously limit the definition and resulting assessment of reading. Yet it is important that some degree of passage dependency be maintained so that a reading comprehension test score will reflect a reader's interaction with passage content, and not merely represent an index of existing background knowledge for that content.

Reliability: How consistent are a test's results?

Reliability concerns the consistency of the results obtained with a particular test. It is useless to assess a child's reading behavior if the results obtained at one time are significantly different than the results obtained at a different time. Perhaps the most important point to remember about it is that reliability is not a characteristic of a test but of the results of a test given to a particular student or group of students at a particular time. Just as validity is specific to a particular test use, so is reliability specific to a particular test situation. Therefore, reliability should not be thought of as something a test possesses, but rather as a characteristic of the test results.

Mehrens and Lehmann (1984) contrasted the relative reliability of physical measures with those of behavioral measures by identifying three basic reasons for this difference.

1. Physical characteristics can usually be measured directly rather than indirectly.
2. The instruments used to obtain the measures are quite precise.
3. The traits or characteristics being measured are relatively stable. (p. 267)

These three reasons provide the basis for understanding why reading test results are not very reliable. All reading tests—standardized, criterion, and informal—are only indicators of reading behaviors. Reading tests only indirectly measure reading behavior. All reading measures use the products of reading behavior as a means of trying to assess the reading process. Even our assessment of reading products is an indirect measurement because we can really assess the true product of reading only by realizing changes in understanding and/or beliefs that have resulted from reading.

The precision of reading tests is limited because we lack understanding of the reading process and agreement about the kinds of test items and approaches that should be used to measure reading behavior. If there were more agreement about the reading process, greater precision of reading tests would be possible.

Reading behaviors are not stable because they are so akin to thinking. Thinking is a human behavior which varies considerably depending on the particular circumstances. Being tired, confused, scared, or motivated can influence people's thinking and, therefore, their reading. Physical circumstances also influence the way people think and read at a particular time.

Reliability is certainly a useful criterion for a measurement when much is understood about the behavior being measured. However, we should also understand that reliability may not only be impossible when we assess a child's reading performance; it may, in fact, be undesirable. If reading behaviors vary from situation to situation and are determined to a great extent by a person's affective disposition, it is likely that different test results will be produced as the conditions and circumstances vary. This is the primary reason that a single assessment should not be used as the sole criterion for making any instructional decision.

The reliability of the results from a single test are influenced by a number of factors in addition to the natural variability in reading behaviors. These include test directions, test length, whether time is a factor in test performance, item difficulty, the homogeneity of the group to which the test was administered, and the examinees' test taking sophistication.

Test directions can affect test results

Test publishers assume that test administration directions affect test scores. That is why they carefully describe the directions and procedures for administering tests. Because the administration of criterion referenced tests and informal tests are often used to determine a child's reading development, the directions used to administer the test should be consistent across time so that confidence can be placed in any revealed behavior changes that result, and so that the results are not due to differences in the way the test was administered.

Several studies have shown that differences in test administration influence test results. Taylor and White's study (1982) found that training teachers in test administration affected the scores of students who took the tests. Ferris and Nichols (1969) found that special test administration techniques produced some score differences for third and seventh graders on certain types of questions, but not on multiple choice items. Interestingly, they also found that scores were higher when the tests were administered to groups of students than when they were administered individually. The possibility that too much attention in the form of standardized administration may make the testing environment significantly indelible needs further study.

Tuinman, Farr, and Blanton (1972) found that giving material rewards as reinforcement to junior high students had a significant impact on both the number of test items attempted and the number answered correctly. In effect, special reinforcement contrived outside the standardized administration appears to have resulted in an immediate, but real, purpose to read. This suggests that reading test designers might consider presenting passages within convincing reading purposes as another way to standardize the measures.

The impact of the way in which test takers are required to respond also affects scores. Solomon (1971) found an indication that students who mark their answers on the test booklet will score higher than those who must mark special answer sheets. Beck's study (1974) also examined this issue. He used the Metropolitan Achievement Test with 4,000 third and fourth graders, and found that those examinees who marked on the booklets scored higher than those who used special answer forms; however, the reliability of scores of the former did not vary significantly from comparative norming reliabilities for the test. Muller, Calhoun, and Orling (1972) discovered that middle school students using separate answer sheets made three times the marking errors of those who marked on the booklets. They noted that the answer sheet in their study was similar to that used in gathering most normative data for tests.

Test length affects reliability

Generally speaking, the longer a test is the more reliable it will be. Greater test length provides an opportunity for positive and negative errors to cancel each other out. A positive error is one in which an examinee answers a question correctly even though he does not know the answer. A negative error is one in which an examinee answers a question incorrectly even though she knows the correct answer. Positive and negative errors occur on all tests.

There is, of course, a point of diminishing returns in lengthening a test to increase its reliability. After a certain length, the addition of more test items will provide only marginal increases in reliability. Guidelines for adequate test length to achieve minimally acceptable reliability depend on a number of factors. However, criterion referenced tests with less than fifteen items for each test objective should be interpreted very cautiously. Most test developers include twenty-five to thirty test items as minimal numbers when the test results are to be used to make educational decisions.

Speeded tests result in misleading reliabilities

A test is considered a speed test if most of the examinees are unable to finish the test in the time provided. Merely providing time limits for the test's administration does not make it a speed test. The time limits allowed on most standardized and criterion referenced tests are merely convenience times. They are developed so that most of the examinees will be able to finish the test in the time provided. The time limits are established so that some examinees will not continue pondering test items beyond a reasonable period.

On tests in which time is a factor, some examinees are able to attempt all, or most, of the test items while others may have time to attempt only a few. Most internal consistency estimates of test reliability are spuriously high if some items are answered by some examinees but not by others. According to Meherns and Lehmann (1984), "If a test is speeded, reliability should be computed by one of the methods that requires two administrations of the test" (p.280).

As would be expected, the arrangement of test items affects the speed with which the test can be completed. Sax and Cromack (1966) studied the effects of ordering items according to their difficulty. He contrasted performance differences with and without time constraints. The results indicated that arranging items from easy to hard produced higher mean scores. This was especially apparent when the test was timed.

Speed tests, except for the assessment of reading rate, have generally fallen out of favor primarily because serious questions have been raised about the validity and reliability of such tests. Reidy's review (1978) of standardized achievement testing for the National School Boards Association was critical of tests designed so that many pupils were unable to finish; however, relatively few such tests were cited in the report.

Item difficulty affects reliability

If examinees are unable to answer large numbers of test items on a reading test, it is likely that the amount of guessing will increase; an increase in guessing necessarily decreases the reliability of the results. On the other hand, if the test items are easy for examinees and most of the test items can be answered correctly, the amount of variability in test performance across examinees will be minimal. When there is little variability in test performance, the internal consistency methods of computing test reliability are affected.

Guessing is a factor which affects both the validity and the reliability of reading test results. If an examinee guesses a correct response, the final score is a reflection of both the behavior being assessed and some amount of guessing. Also, because a guess represents a chance response, it is unlikely that an examinee will provide the same guess on a second test administration. Thus, the reliability of the test results is affected.

It is impossible to determine what percentage of test results can be attributed to chance or guessing, and what percentage can be guaranteed as a thoughtful response to an item. Slakter (1968) found that guessing, especially when it was not penalized by the test scoring system, did raise test scores. Donlon (1981), however, noted that there is little professional agreement on what to do about chance scores, despite the agreed upon influence of guessing.

Two major suggestions are to penalize examinees for guessing and to provide test directions that suggest examinees avoid guessing. Penalizing examinees is a procedure followed in scoring the Scholastic Aptitude Test (SAT). On this test, an examinee's score is determined by subtracting one-fourth of the number of items answered incorrectly from the items answered correctly. Examinees are given this scoring information prior to the test administration. The belief is that such directions will reduce guessing. Slakter suggests that these procedures will differentially assess examinees, and that when such procedures are used, test results will depend on the particular ability being measured as well as on the examinee's "risk taking" behavior.

A second strategy suggested to reduce guessing is directing examinees that they are to avoid guessing, without including any penalty for incorrect responses. Arguments regarding such directions have usually questioned what examinees understand as guessing.

Assuming that a significant proportion of students taking tests sometimes mark responses in a purely random fashion, it is probable, as Tuinman (1971) points out, that six correct answers on a thirty item test with five multiple choice options might result from guessing. But research does not confirm that students actually do this. MacRae and Green (1971) found that true chance distributions do not occur in a theoretically random fashion and are therefore not random. Donlon (1981) also noted that chance scores do not appear to be random. If the so-called chance scores are not random, it is probably because each response involves a different amount of guessing and a different amount of "true" score.

Yet the potential for guessing and its influence on the validity and reliability of test results is an important issue. In pointing out that pure guessing on the major standardized norm referenced tests would place test takers at grade levels ranging from 1.2 to 7.0, depending on the particular level of the test, Fry (1971) urged that only student scores above chance levels should be interpreted, and those at or below chance levels should be disregarded.

The homogeneity of the test taking group can influence reliability estimates

When all of the examinees have similar abilities, it is assumed that they will perform in similar ways on tests. When test performance is similar, there is little variance in test performance; thus, the standard reliability estimates tend to be low. This is an important factor in examining the reported reliability for a particular test. If, for example, the published reliability for a reading test was based on the administration of the test to students in grades 7 to 9, it is likely that the reliability will not be as high if the test is administered only to ninth grade students.

Test bias is a factor closely related to the homogenity of examinees. The considerable national concern about whether tests are biased to favor the performance of mainstream American culture and thus to handicap special and minority cultures has been the subject of much research. The search for the elusive "culture fair" test has not been successful. In fact, research emphasizing the importance of background knowledge in reading comprehension has resulted in the generally accepted conclusion that, in a sense, all reading assessment is culturally biased, and that such bias is impossible to eliminate. Indeed, without such bias the assessment of reading comprehension as it is currently defined would be impossible.

Publishers of reading tests have responded in various ways to the concern about bias against specific populations. Most publishers have their tests reviewed by groups representing various cultural and racial groups to identify specific reading passages and test items which may be biased. Additionally, the tests are tried out with various cultural and racial groups and the results are analyzed to determine if bias can be detected.

Davis and Personke (1968) administered both Spanish and English versions of the Metropolitan Reading Readiness Test (MRT) to bilingual children. They found no significant differences in performance across versions. A study by Mitchell (1967) reported no validity differences on readiness tests between black and white students; and Reynolds (1980) found no significant sex or race interaction biases in the predictive validity of five reading readiness tests. Reynolds contrasted the predictive validity of each of the five readiness tests against the subjects' performance on a norm referenced reading test administered in grade one. If, however, both the readiness and the followup test were biased, the same results would have been obtained.

The issue of test bias is particularly significant to reading tests which rely on passage content selected as being representative of materials students may encounter and may interest them. It may be complicated considerably, however, by factoring content validity into considerations of how well a test's content matches children's total reading experiences and their learning and school experience. The latter consideration broadens the question to the potential bias of all instructional materials and raises questions like the following: Should test makers forge the way in rigid efforts to eliminate potential content biases, even if doing so creates a mismatch with instructional materials that may, even purposefully, expose all students to a kind of mainstream experience?

Test taking skills may affect reliability

Examinees' test taking skills are threats to both the reliability and validity of reading tests. Research has not yet clarified the impact of testwiseness on reading test scores. While Taylor and White (1982) found no differences for subjects trained in test taking, Rowley (1974) found that a multiple choice format on a vocabulary test favored ninth grade testwise students who were risk takers. In a study by Callenbach (1973), the scores of test naive second graders improved on posttests given one week and four months after they received test taking training.

Erickson (1972) cited the research of Wahlstrom and Boersma (1968) and McMillan (1967) and recommended that all students be given sensible test taking training based on different item types. They would be taught, for example, to read the items first, looking for those that focus on details, and then to scan the passage for the answer or answers. In effect, test takers so trained would be skimming. It seems reasonable that having identified a question that calls for getting the main idea of a passage, the test taker could also be trained to scan the passage. These are perfectly legitimate reading skills that have lifelong usefulness, even if they may not be what the test purports to measure.

Erikson's recommendation relates testwiseness to reader purpose, which usually goes unspecified on reading tests. In this case, any reader purpose that may have rationalized the test maker's decision to include a passage and a particular accompanying item is superseded by a real, if contrived, immediate reader purpose—getting as many answers correct as possible. Students reasonably adopt such a purpose every time they are tested, but the validity of this purpose is questionable in relation to the full scope of reader purposes.

Training all students to employ skimming and scanning techniques on all reading tests would theoretically even out the impact of potentially major testwiseness factors. But its impact on the interpretation of scores that profess to measure reading skills other than skimming and scanning is the real issue. Such training, universally effected, would certainly force a close analysis of how reading test passages and their respective items are constructed, what reading behavior responses they are most apt to produce, what the scores they produce actually tell us, and how they can and ought to be interpreted.

Standard reliability estimates: Generally not valid for criterion referenced tests

A norm referenced test is developed to maximize individual differences; thus the statistical analyses of reliability depend on differences among students' performances. On the other hand, criterion referenced tests, especially those that are considered mastery tests, are developed so that all students who have learned the particular curriculum content will achieve maximum scores. Thus, the results of many criterion referenced tests produce little variation between students' performances.

Since criterion referenced tests are often used for making specific instructional decisions, such as whether a student has mastered the particular curriculum or whether a student is to be promoted from one grade to the next, the reliability of the decision for which the test is used should become the focus of reliability considerations.

Popham and Husek (1969) have argued that the methods used to establish reliability on a norm referenced test should not be applied to criterion referenced tests because doing so would contaminate what they believe is the criterion referenced test's potential to reflect reading behavior. Norm referenced items, they charged, have been deliberately constructed to include "spurious factors" that create score variation to enhance the score comparison. "Those who write criterion referenced items are usually far more attentive to defining the domain of relevant test responses and the situations in which they should be required," they argue (p. 4). In criterion referencing, Popham and Husek contended, the content validity, even of distractors in multiple choice items, is more important than score variation that helps establish reliability.

The advice offered by Meherns and Lehmann (1984) regarding the interpretation of reliability estimates for criterion referenced tests seems to be the general position taken by most testing specialists:

> Much work needs to be done in the conceptual and operational definitions of reliability where norm referencing is not used. For both criterion referenced and gain score measurements, where we may not be interested in maximizing the differences between individuals, classical reliability estimates may yield values that present a pessimistic picture of the precision of the scores or categorization decisions. Excessive emphasis should not be placed on them in judging the technical adequacy of such scores. (p. 284)

Informal tests present unique validity and reliability issues

Because informal assessment tends to be relatively exempt from many of the issues surrounding reading assessment, it has not been discussed in the preceding sections as thoroughly as its importance merits. Informal assessment includes a wide range of methods, such as informal reading inventories, student self evaluation, teacher judgment, determining students' reading habits both in school and out of school, using teacher made checklists of reading skills, and parent interviews. Relatively few studies have investigated the validity and reliability of most of these approaches.

Research on informal reading inventories has been, perhaps, the most prevalent in this area. These studies have investigated the validity of IRIS by comparing their results to norm referenced test results (Patty, 1965; Sipay, 1964; Williams, 1963). Studies have been conducted to validate students' self evaluations (Purcell, 1963: Spaights, 1965) and others have compared teacher judgments of students' reading with performance on norm referenced reading tests (Henig, 1949; Hitchcock & Alfred, 1955; Kermonian, 1962).

Because informal tests use a wide variety of procedures to assess reading performance over a number of different occasions, it is not surprising that they can be more reliable and valid measures than criterion or norm referenced tests which cannot be used as often and are more divorced from daily classroom instruction.

When they are used to plan instruction, informal tests are generally considered to be more valid than formal testing approaches. McCracken (1964) studied the validity of a published informal reading inventory for determining functional reading levels. McCracken's results indicated not only that the informal reading inventory was valid for determining functional reading levels, but that the reliability between alternate forms of the test suggested they could be used interchangeably.

By using informal reading assessments in daily classroom situations, the teacher can evaluate students' abilities to apply their reading skills to various learning tasks. The teacher can learn not only about the development of the students' basic reading skills, but also about student attitudes toward reading tasks, about their reading interests, and about their ability to apply their reading skills.

Johnson (1960) suggested that classroom teachers should determine appropriate levels for independent and instructional reading solely through the use of informal reading inventories. The use of IRIS for determining students' functional reading levels and diagnosing skills is a fairly well established practice (Johnson & Kress, 1966).

The IRI is composed of a series of graded paragraphs which are usually read aloud by the student to the teacher; comprehension questions follow each paragraph. As the student reads, the teacher keeps track of errors such as mispronunciation of words, unknown words, reversals, repetitions, substitutions, word by word reading, and other word call errors. On the basis of these readings, the teacher determines the functional reading level. One limitation of this approach is that since the paragraphs are read orally, a relation to silent reading must be assumed. Some IRIS include paragraphs to be read silently so that this weakness can be alleviated. IRIS range from the truly informal reading a teacher may ask a student to do in the classroom, to published standardized inventories which should more correctly be considered criterion referenced tests.

Despite the accepted worth of informal reading inventories, several problems limit their use. First, the criteria for evaluating IRI performance are subjective and arbitrary (Betts, 1940; Sipay, 1964). Second, selecting passages for an IRI, even from a graded reader, will not accurately guarantee a progressing range of reading difficulty. Gerke (1980) even questions the readability of difficulty levels on several commercially developed IRIS. Though the levels seemed to be comparable, Gerke found that they did not correlate with the Spache readability formula, and the publishers of these tests did not specify that any readability analysis was done with the passages.

Gerke's study raises many questions about the nature of reading text and the factors that make some reading selections more difficult to read than others. Because of the extensive influence of background information in reading, there may be little generalizability of the results of IRIS. Despite the fact that various reading texts may be written at similar reading levels according to readability analyses, they may pose quite different reading tasks for a reader who has extensive background knowledge on the topic of one text but not another. A third problem in using IRIS is the need for the examiner to have considerable knowledge about reading in order to record errors and make judgments about a student's performance.

Some research has concentrated on comparing the information derived from norm referenced tests and IRIS. While this research is interesting, it is based on the false assumption that both types of tests are supposed to provide the same kind of information. However, the research has probably been worthwhile since norm referenced test scores such as grade equivalents are often misused as indications of instructional reading levels.

Research results indicate that any comparisons between IRI performance and norm referenced test performance are entirely dependent on: 1) the standardized test used, 2) the materials used to construct the IRI, 3) the criteria used to evaluate performance on the IRI, and 4) the ability and skill of the examiner in recording errors and judging performance on the IRI.

Finally, it seems that IRIS are not as useful at the upper grade levels as they are at lower grade levels, for several reasons. First, the difference between reading materials at the upper grade levels is more difficult to determine than at the lower grade levels. It is far easier to determine the difference between first and second grade reading materials than to determine the difference between tenth and eleventh grade reading materials. Also, at the upper grade levels, background information takes on even greater importance than it does at the lower reading levels. Second, as Wells (1950) found, it seems that at the upper grade levels, oral and silent reading levels may be more unlike than they are at the lower grade levels. Killgallon's observation (1942) is worth noting:

> Above the sixth grade level, certain limitations inherent in available reading textbooks render the estimates of grade placement based upon them probably less refined than those of the standardized tests at corresponding levels. Prominent among the limitations referred to is the lack of carefully graded vocabulary and the absence of any satisfactory control of comprehension difficulties arising from sources other than vocabulary difficulty such as sentence length, sentence structure, extent of reference to subjects foreign to the experiential background of the pupils, and unrestricted use of fiction, or words for which concrete referents are unavailable. (p. 180)

Compared to that of norm referenced tests, the validity of IRIs to determine functional reading levels appears to hold up consistently in studies conducted over a long period of time. Betts (1940) compared the accuracy of determining grade placement with five silent reading norm referenced tests and an IRI; he found that the norm referenced tests were inaccurate by comparison. Another early study (Killgallon, 1942) compared the performance of fourth graders on the Gates Reading Survey with that on an IRI. The IRI yielded independent, instructional, and frustration reading levels that were lower than the Gates. However, the range of possible reading levels on the IRI was not as high as that of the norm referenced test. An example of Killgallon's findings included a pupil who scored at a grade equivalent level of 2.8 on the Gates but could not read the preprimer material on the IRI. Killgallon concluded that the pupil's Gates score was the result of guessing. Killgallon's study indicated that pupils generally scored about one year higher on the standardized reading test than the instructional reading level determined by the IRI.

Sipay (1964) compared the functional reading levels for fourth graders yielded by three norm referenced tests to those yielded by an IRI. All three norm referenced tests tended to overestimate the instructional level by one or more grade levels; the instructional and frustration levels they produced varied considerably from test to test. Other such comparisons also found standardized tests to yield higher instructional levels (Glaser, 1964; McCracken, 1964). Williams (1963), however, found that a text based IRI and three norm referenced tests yielded similar instructional reading levels for normal, but not for disabled, middle grade readers. Differences Liebert (1965) found for second grade readers were attributed to the wider range of skills tested by the norm referenced test used in the comparison to an IRI.

In a more recent study, Bristow, Pikulski, and Pelosi (1983) compared the estimates of reading levels for five different approaches, including a teacher made IRI, a commercial IRI, the Metropolitan Achievement Test (MAT), the Wide Range Achievement Test (WRAT), and a classroom teacher's actual placement of a child in instructional reading materials. The WRAT and the MAT are published reading tests that provide criterion referenced scores which can be used to assign pupils to instructional reading levels. These researchers found that the teacher made IRI, the commercial IRI, and the MAT results produced reading level estimates that were within one grade level of one another; however, the WRAT substantially overestimated the pupils' instructional reading level.

The validity of the Instructional Reading Level score produced by the Metropolitan Achievement Test (MAT) was examined in a series of studies by Farr and Beck (1984). They concluded:

> The Metropolitan IRLS are an alternative to traditional means of determining instructional reading levels. As a group administered assessment procedure, the IRLS compare favorably with the traditional methods and, in addition, provide consistent information across time and examiners. They are also economical to administer from the standpoint of time and personnel.
>   No single measure should be used as the criterion for instructional decision making. The IRLS should be considered as one facet of the evaluation program. Teacher observations and analysis of student performance on an ongoing basis, as well as teacher judgment of pupil progress, and information from test scores should be the sources for the decisions which are made. The Metropolitan IRLS provide data useful both as a starting point for student placement in appropriate materials and as a confirmation of teacher judgment. (p. 64)

Several factors must be carefully considered in interpreting these comparison studies. First, the grade equivalents produced by the norm referenced tests are not recommended—nor were they developed—for determining functional reading levels. The prevalent practice of using grade equivalent scores from norm referenced tests as indicators of instructional reading levels is, as already noted, a misuse of those scores. Also, IRIs based on the texts that students are reading on a daily basis tap content more familiar to students than that on standardized tests. Estimates of student performance on immediate classroom instructional materials are probably of greatest value to teachers, however.

Another informal testing procedure sometimes used is student self evaluation. While self evaluation is a well accepted practice in psychological analysis, it has been used only moderately (and researched even less) in reading instruction. Purcell (1963) polled college and adult students in reading improvement classes to determine the relative importance the students assigned to factors which could have been causing them to read slowly. The factors rated by the students as most important were backtracking, daydreaming, word by word reading, vocalizing, and monotonous plodding.

Spaights (1965) compared the self evaluations of eighty junior high students in four ability tracks with their performance on the California Achievement Tests and found that the less able the reader, the more self assessment correlated with the test results. In an investigation by Darby (1966), self referred students and formally referred students did not differ in the amount of reading growth they experienced during a reading improvement program. However, at the conclusion of the program, the self referred students scored higher on a survey of study habits and attitudes.

Most self assessment studies have failed to relate self analysis to development in the areas of identified weaknesses. If students are able to identify their own reading deficiencies, they should be expected to make greater improvements in the areas so identified. The mere comparison of students' self evaluations with test results does not seem to be a useful approach to studying this validity of self evaluation. Even if perfect correlations are established between the two, it would not indicate whether the self evaluation or the test score is the more valid assessment. Rather, it would indicate that, at a general level, one measurement procedure might be substituted for the other.

One of the important values of self evaluation is that it causes the student to think about his reading ability and to consider strategies for improvement. As a result, students become responsible for their own learning. Additionally, self evaluations are revealing as to how students perceive what others view as their reading abilities. A common response when asked to evaluate one's own reading ability is to report what one believes others think, usually teachers and parents. While self evaluation may not be valid as an indication of reading ability, it does provide the teacher with information for planning instruction that may enhance a pupil's self concept as a reader.

Comparisons of teachers' ratings of students with norm referenced test scores has been done on occasion. Both Kermonian (1962) and Harris (1948) found that subjective teacher ratings of reading readiness were as valid as results obtained by norm referenced tests. Kermonian also found that teachers with more than ten years of experience predicted reading success with greater accuracy than those with less experience. Ebbesen (1968) followed up on pupils' first grade performance on a standardized test to determine that kindergarten teachers had significantly predicted the degree of pupil success without the use of any tests.

Contrary evidence to these studies regarding the predictive validity of teachers' ratings was provided by Kapelis (1972). Her study was designed to contrast two screening tests and teacher ratings for predicting end of year reading performance of first grade pupils. The results indicated that both the tests and the teacher ratings significantly predicted end of year reading achievement for the 100 first grade pupils in the study. However, the two screening tests had higher predictive validity than the teacher ratings.

For older readers, Coleman and Harmer (1982) found there were significant differences between tutors' judgments of students and students' scores on three norm referenced tests which reported that the students could read materials the tutors judged too difficult for them.

Teachers' ability to make diagnostic evaluations of students' reading performance apparently is related to the amount of training the teachers have had in reading courses, amount of teaching experience, and type of college attended (Burnett, 1963). Studies in which teacher judgments were compared to norm referenced reading tests seem to be most dependent on the type of test to which the teacher ratings were being compared, and the amount of teacher knowledge of reading education. Hitchcock and Alfred (1955) found a strong relationship between teacher evaluation and performance on such tests. But both Preston (1953) and Emans (1964) found that the more experience teachers have with making diagnostic evaluations, the less agreement their ratings have with diagnostic tests. Preston found that elementary teachers tended to classify students as retarded readers when they were actually reading up to or near capacity. From 43 to 60 percent of the normal readers in two schools were, according to an index developed by Preston, incorrectly classified as retarded by the teachers.

Emans' study (1964) compared remedial reading teachers' rankings of the reading skills with which they thought their students needed help and the skills weaknesses indicated by the individually administered Gates Diagnostic Reading Tests. Emans found that teachers did not perceive the same needs indicated by the test results. Perhaps the best criterion for determining the usefulness of diagnostic evaluations would be to compare the amount of improvement made by students selected for a remedial program on the basis of teacher ratings with the gain of those selected by norm referenced test scores. A study of this type was conducted in Scotland by Lytton

(1961). Lytton found it made no difference whether children were selected for remedial reading instruction by teachers' judgments or by test scores when the criterion was norm referenced test score improvement in reading.

MacGinitie has stated that the best way to achieve a student/material match is for the teacher to make a sound judgment based on student interest. This suggests that such a match can increase the range of the instructional reading level by increasing student tolerance to frustration levels. MacGinitie advised that teachers should do this while regarding all other assessments as tentative. One of the best ways for a teacher to learn about a student's interests is through careful observation, a process which incorporates and overlaps the techniques of interview. The student interview is a useful way to learn more about a student and has been recommended by Reidy (1978).

Recommendations

This chapter has attempted to delineate some of the more important issues related to the validity and reliability of norm referenced, criterion referenced, and informal tests. There are many serious concerns about both the validity and reliability of the various types of reading tests that are used to make important instructional decisions about children. The approaches that are generally used to determine a test's validity and reliability present serious problems as well. However, it is clear that the use of tests is not going to cease. It is also clear that tests can provide useful information for planning instruction as long as the information is used with an understanding of test limitations. Test consumers hold the most promise for significant improvements in how tests are used.

The following recommendations are based on the major points in this chapter, and are provided as a kind of checklist for test consumers to consider when attempting to determine whether a particular test is valid and reliable.

1. The purpose for which the test results are needed should be the most important consideration in examining the validity of a test. The major validity question is whether a particular test will provide the information needed for a particular educational decision.

In considering the three major types of reading assessments described in this chapter, the following tests are most appropriate for the following purposes:

- *Norm referenced* tests are primarily useful for comparing students to a norm group in relation to the behaviors measured by the particular test.
- *Criterion referenced* tests are useful for determining students' accomplishments or ability to succeed on certain specific curricular objectives.
- *Informal tests* are used to provide a variety of information about reading behaviors and reading development within the instructional context.

2. *Norm referenced* and *criterion referenced* refer to the interpretation of the results produced by a test. It is especially important to remember that the same published test may provide both norm referenced and criterion referenced information.

3. When an instructional decision is to be made, the most valid and reliable information should be used. There is no single measure that provides a valid assessment of reading ability. A variety of assessment measures are needed to truly understand reading ability. This does not mean that a large number of formal reading tests should be given. Rather, a constant variety of informal measures should be used. The more formal tests should be used less often, probably no more than twice a year, and most likely no more than once a year. This admonition includes such tests as district or schoolwide standardized tests, state mandated criterion referenced tests, instructional tests which accompany a reading program, and special program tests mandated by a funding agency. Far too many formal tests are administered to most students in a single academic year. This vast amount of testing confuses instruction and wastes valuable teaching time.

4. Extremely brief samples of reading behavior tend to be less reliable than longer samples. The more a behavior is observed, the more faith can be put in the reliability of the observation. This concern becomes especially important when one examines the brief three item samples of behaviors on criterion referenced tests. The reliability of the mastery/no-mastery decisions based on such brief samples is very low.

5. Validity and reliability are not characteristics of tests. It is misleading to state that a particular test is valid or reliable. A test is valid or not valid for a particular decision. The validity relates to the reason test results are needed. Just as important, it is wrong to think of a test as being totally valid. Rather, a particular test provides one aspect of the behavior one is attempting to understand. Other information must be added to the test information for a more thorough and, subsequently, more valid understanding.

Reading: What Can Be Measured?

Similarly, reliability is the consistency of the results that are obtained with a particular test with a particular group of students. A test may provide somewhat reliable results with one group of students but very unreliable results with another group.

6. The criterion levels, or cutoff scores, provided on criterion referenced tests are arbitrary scores. They should be examined critically to see if they make sense in the particular circumstances in which the test is to be used. More importantly, because of the limited reliability of any test, criterion scores should also be considered as unreliable. Thus, no important decision should be made on the basis of criterion scores alone.

7. The norms on norm referenced tests are not criterion levels to be achieved. This is especially true for grade equivalent scores which are often misinterpreted by both educators and the lay public. Too frequently one hears even sophisticated educators state that the goal is to "get all the students reading up to grade level" on a norm referenced reading test.

Normed scores merely provide a description of how a particular group of children compare to a norm population. They can help to determine instructional groupings, to provide information about progress on the behaviors measured by the test, and to make comparisons with children who may have similar backgrounds and experiences. But such scores are not goals to be achieved.

8. Educators should spend much more time developing and refining informal measures that seem to provide some of the best information for planning instruction. Education courses and instructional materials do not provide adequate assistance for teachers to engage in informal reading assessment. Informal testing information must be accepted by school administrators and the lay public as providing important information about students' reading development. Informal testing should not be thought of as "second class" information that is useful only when more formal information is not available. Indeed, informal testing holds the greatest promise for increasing the validity and reliability of information used for instructional planning.

References

Algra, C. Meeting the challenge of a minimum reading graduation requirement. *Journal of Reading*, 1978, *25*, 392-397.

Anders, P.L. Test review: Tests of functional literacy. *Journal of Reading*, 1981, *24*, 612-619.

Anderhalter, O.F. *Major misconceptions about "grade equivalent" scores.* Bensinville, IL: Scholastic Testing Service, 1960.

Arter, J.A. *Out-of-level versus in-level testing: When should we recommend each?* Paper presented at the annual meeting of the American Educational Research Association, New York, 1982.

Ayrer, J., and McNamara, T. Survey testing on an out-of-level basis. *Journal of Educational Measurement*, 1973, *10*, 79-83.

Baglin, R.F. Does "nationally" normed really mean nationally? *Journal of Educational Measurement*, 1981, *18*, 97-107.

Beck, M. Critique of "does 'nationally' normed really mean nationally?" New York: Psychological Corporation (mimeo, n.d.).

Beck, M. Achievement test reliability as a function of pupil response procedures. *Journal of Educational Measurement*, 1974, *11*, 109-114.

Beggs, D.L., and Hieronymus, A.N. Uniformity of growth in the basic skills throughout the school year and during the summer. *Journal of Educational Measurement*, 1968, *5*, 91-97.

Betts, E.A. Reading problems at the intermediate grade level. *Elementary School Journal*, 1940, *15*, 737-746.

Bristow, P.S., Pikulski, J.J., and Pelosi, P.L. A comparison of five estimates of reading instructional level. *Reading Teacher*, 1983, *37*, 273-279.

Burnett, R.W. The diagnostic proficiency of teachers of reading. *Reading Teacher*, 1963, *16*, 229-234.

Callenbach, C. The effects of instruction and practice in content independent test taking techniques upon the standardized reading test scores of selected second grade students. *Journal of Educational Measurement*, 1973, *10*, 25-29.

Chall, J.S. Readability: An appraisal of research and application. *Bureau of Educational Research Monographs*, No. 34. Columbus, OH: Ohio State University, 1958.

Coleman, M., and Harmer, W.R. A comparison of standardized reading tests and informal placement procedures. *Journal of Learning Disabilities*, 1982, *15*, 396-398.

Cox, R.C., and Sterrett, B.G. A model for increasing the meaning of standardized test scores. *Journal of Educational Measurement*, 1970, *7*, 227-228.

Cronbach, L.J., and Glesser, G.C. *Psychological tests and personnel decisions*. Urbana, IL: University of Illinois Press, 1965.

Darby, C.A. Referred and self initiated students in a reading-study program. *Journal of Reading*, 1966, *9*, 186-192.

Davis, O.L., Jr., and Personke, C.R., Jr. Effects of administering the Metropolitan Readiness Test in English and Spanish to Spanish speaking school entrants. *Journal of Educational Measurement*, 1968, *5*, 231-234.

Donlon, T.F. Uninterpretable scores: Their implications for testing practice. *Journal of Educational Measurement*, 1981, *18*, 213-219.

Drahozal, E.C., and Hanna, G.S. Reading comprehension subscores: Pretty bottles for ordinary wine. *Journal of Reading*, 1978, *21*, 416-420.

Duffelmeyer, F.A. A comparison of reading results in grades nine and twelve. *Journal of Reading*, 1980, *23*, 606-608.

Ebbesen, J.A. Kindergarten teacher rankings as predictors of academic achievement in the primary grades. *Journal of Educational Measurement,* 1968, *5,* 259-262.

Emans, R. Teacher evaluations of reading skills and individualized reading. *Elementary English,* 1964, *42,* 258-260.

Erickson, M.E. Test sophistication: An important consideration. *Journal of Reading,* 1972, *16,* 140-144.

Farr, R. The convergent and discriminant validity of several upper level reading tests. In G.B. Schick and M.M. May (Eds.), *Multidisciplinary aspects of college-adult reading.* Yearbook of the National Reading Conference, 1968, *17,* 181-191.

Farr, R. The evaluation of reading behavior. In J.D. Walden (Ed.), *Bulletin of the School of Education,* 1969, *45,* 101-111.

Farr, R., and Beck, M. Validating the "instructional reading level" of the Metropolitan Achievement Tests. *Journal of Research and Development in Education,* 1984, *17,* 55-64.

Farr, R., and Smith, C.B. The effects of test item validity on total test reliability and validity. In G. Schick and M.M. May (Eds.), *Reading: Progress and pedagogy,* Nineteenth Yearbook of the National Reading Conference. Milwaukee, WI: National Reading Conference, 1973.

Farr, R., and Roelke, P. Measuring subskills of reading: Intercorrelations among standardized reading tests, teachers' ratings, and reading specialists' ratings. *Journal of Educational Measurement,* 1971, *8,* 27-32.

Ferris, J.M., and Nichols, D.G. The effects of four methods of administration on test achievement. *Journal of Educational Measurement,* 1969, *6,* 85-91.

Fry, E. The orangoutang score (with comments by Walter N. Durost, Walter H. MacGinitie, Douglas J. MacRae, and Donald Ross Green). *Reading Teacher,* 1971, *24,* 360-365.

Glaser, N.A. *A comparison of specific reading skills of advanced and retarded readers of fifth grade reading achievement.* Unpublished doctoral dissertation, University of Oregon, 1964.

Glaser, R., and Nitko, A.J. Measurement in learning and instruction. In R.L. Thorndike (Ed.), *Educational measurement,* second edition. Washington, DC: American Council on Education, 1971.

Glass, G.V. Standards and criteria. *Journal of Educational Measurement,* 1978, *15,* 237-261.

Goodman, K.S. The psycholinguistic nature of the reading process. In K.S. Goodman (Ed.), *The psycholinguistic nature of the reading process.* Detroit: Wayne State University Press, 1968.

Gunning, T.G. Wrong level test: Wrong information. *Reading Teacher,* 1982, *35,* 902-905.

Hambleton, R.K., and Novick, M.R. Toward an integration of theory and method for criterion referenced tests. *Journal of Educational Measurement,* 1973, *10,* 159-170.

Harris, C.W. Measurement of comprehension in literature: II. Studies of measures of comprehension. *School Review,* 1948, *56,* 332-342.

Harris, T.L., and Hodges, R.E. (Eds.). *A dictionary of reading and related terms.* Newark, DE: International Reading Association, 1981.

Henig, M.S. Predictive value of a reading readiness test and of teachers' forecasts. *Elementary School Journal,* 1949, *50,* 41-46.

Hitchcock, A.A., and Alfred, C. Can teachers make accurate estimates of reading ability? *Clearinghouse,* 1955, *54,* 422-424.

Hoover, H.D. *The most appropriate scores for measuring educational development in the elementary schools: GEs.* Paper presented at the Annual Meeting of the American Educational Research Association, Montreal, 1983.

Horst, D.P. *What's bad about grade equivalent scores.* Technical paper no. 1. Mountain View, CA: RMC Research Corporation, 1976.

Hunt. L.C. *A further study of certain factors associated with reading comprehension.* Unpublished doctoral dissertation, Syracuse University, 1952.

Johnson, M.S. Reading inventories for classroom use. *Reading Teacher,* 1960, *14,* 9-14.

Johnson, M.S., and Kress, R. *Informal reading inventories.* Newark, DE: International Reading Association, 1965.

Kapelis, L. *Early identification of reading failure: A comparison of two screening tests with teacher ratings.* Unpublished doctoral dissertation, University of Pittsburgh, 1972.

Kermonian, S.B. Teacher appraisal of first grade readiness. *Elementary English,* 1962, *39,* 196-201.

Killgallon, P.A. *A study of relationships among certain pupil adjustments in language situations.* Unpublished doctoral dissertation, Pennsylvania State University, 1942.

Kirsch, I.S., and Guthrie, J.T. Construct validity of functional reading tests. *Journal of Educational Measurement,* 1980, *17,* 81-93.

Klare, G.R. A second look at the validity of readability formulas. *Journal of Reading Behavior,* 1976, *8,* 129-152.

Lindvall, C.M., and Nitko, A.J. *Measuring pupil achievement and aptitude,* second edition. New York: Harcourt Brace Jovanovich, 1975.

Linn, R.L. Anchor Test Study: The long and the short of it. *Journal of Educational Measurement,* 1975, *12,* 201-213.

Linn, R.L. Issues of validity in measurement for competency based programs. In M.S. Bunda and J.R. Sanders (Eds.), *Practices and problems in competency based education.* Washington, DC: National Council on Measurement in Education, 1979.

Long, J.V., Schaffran, J.A., and Kellogg, T.M. Effects of out-of-level survey testing on reading achievement scores of Title I, ESEA students. *Journal of Educational Measurement,* 1977, *14,* 203-213.

Lytton, H. An experiment in selection for remedial education. *British Journal of Educational Psychology,* 1961, *31,* 79-84.

McCracken, R.A. The development and validation of the Standard Reading Inventory for the individual appraisal of reading performance. In J.A. Figurel (Ed.), *Improvement of reading through classroom practice*. Newark, DE: International Reading Association, 1964.

MacGinitie, W.H. *Predicting instructional levels*. Mimeograph, 1983.

MacRae, D.J., and Green, D.R. Comment. *Reading Teacher*, 1971, *24*, 364.

McMillan, G. Help for pupils who take achievement tests. *Grade Teacher*, 1967, *84*, 48-49.

Mager, R.F. *Preparing instructional objectives*. Palo Alto, CA: Feardon, 1962.

Mehrens, W.A., and Lehmann, I.J. *Measurement and evaluation in education and psychology*. New York: Holt, Rinehart and Winston, 1984.

Mitchell, R.W. *A comparison of children's responses to an original and experimental form of subtests GS and ND of the Gates Basic Reading Tests*. Unpublished doctoral dissertation, University of Minnesota, 1967.

Muller, D., Calhoun, E., and Orling, R. Test reliability as a function of answer sheet mode. *Journal of Educational Measurement*, 1972, *9*, 321-324.

Murray, C.F., and Karlsen, B. A concurrent validity study of the Silent Reading Tests and the Gates Reading Diagnostic Tests. *Reading Teacher*, 1960, *13*, 293-294, 296.

Nitko, A.J. *Educational tests and measurement: An introduction*. New York: Harcourt Brace Jovanovich, 1983.

Patty, D.L. *A comparison of standardized oral reading test scores and informal reading inventory scores*. Unpublished doctoral dissertation, Ball State University, 1965.

Pelavin, S.H., and Barker, P. *A study of the generalizability of the results of a standardized achievement test*. Paper presented at the annual convention of the American Educational Research Association, San Francisco, 1976.

Popham, W.J., and Husek, T.R. Implications of criterion-referenced measurement. *Journal of Educational Measurement*, 1969, *6*, 1-9.

Preston, R.C. The reading status of children classified by teachers as retarded readers. *Elementary English*, 1953, *30*, 225-227.

Preston, R.C. Ability of students to identify correct responses before reading. *Journal of Educational Research*, 1964, *58*, 181-183.

Purcell, J.W. Poor reading habits: Their rank and order. *Reading Teacher*, 1963, *16*, 353-358.

Pyrczak, F., and Axelrod, J. Determining the passage dependence of reading comprehension exercises: A call for replications. *Journal of Reading*, 1976, *19*, 279-283.

Reidy, E.F., Jr. Book review. *Journal of Educational Measurement*, 1978, *15*, 229-231.

Reynolds, C.R. An examination for bias in a preschool test battery across race and sex. *Journal of Educational Measurement*, 1980, *17*, 137-146.

Rowley, G.L. Which examinees are most favored by the use of multiple choice tests? *Journal of Educational Measurement*, 1974, *11*, 15-22.

Royer, J.M., and Lynch, D.J. The misuses and appropriate uses of norm-referenced tests of reading comprehension. *Reading Psychology*, 1982, *3*, 131-142.

Sax, G., and Cromack, T.R. The effects of various forms of item arrangements on test performance. *Journal of Educational Measurement*, 1966, *3*, 309-311.

Schultz, R.E. The role of measurement in education: Servant, soulmate, stool pigeon, statesman, scapegoat, all of the above, and/or none of the above. *Journal of Educational Measurement*, 1971, *8*, 141-146.

Sheehan, D.S., and Marcus, M. Validating criterion-referenced reading tests. *Journal of Reading Behavior*, 1977, *9*, 129-135.

Singer, H. Measurement of early reading ability. *Contemporary Education*, 1977, *48*, 145-150.

Sipay, E.R. A comparison of standardized reading scores and functional reading levels. *Reading Teacher*, 1964, *17*, 265-268.

Slakter, M.J. The effect of guessing strategy on objective test scores. *Journal of Educational Measurement*, 1968, *5*, 217-221.

Smith, L.L., Johns, J.L., Ganschow, L., and Masztal, N.B. Using grade level vs. out-of-level reading tests with remedial students. *Reading Teacher*, 1983, *36*, 550-553.

Solomon, A. The effect of answer sheet format on test performance by culturally disadvantaged fourth grade elementary school pupils. *Journal of Educational Measurement*, 1971, *8*, 289-290.

Spaights, E. Accuracy of self-estimation of junior high school students. *Journal of Educational Research*, 1965, *58*, 416-419.

Tallmadge, G., and Wood, C.T. *User's guide: ESEA Title I evaluation and reporting system*. Mountain View, CA: RMC Research Corporation, 1976.

Taylor, C., and White, K.R. The effect of reinforcement and training on group standardized test behavior. *Journal of Educational Measurement*, 1982, *19*, 199-208.

Tuinman, J.J. Asking reading dependent questions. *Journal of Reading*, 1971, *14*, 289-292, 336.

Tuinman, J.J. Children's willingness to skip reading passages when taking reading comprehension tests. *Southern Journal of Educational Research*, 1972, *6*, 1-13.

Tuinman, J.J., Farr, R., and Blanton, W.E. Increases in test scores as a function of material rewards. *Journal of Educational Measurement*, 1972, *9*, 215-223.

Wahlstrom, M., and Boersma, F.J. The influence of testwiseness upon achievement. *Educational and Psychological Measurement*, 1968, *28*, 413-420.

Wells, C.A. The value of an oral reading test for diagnosis of the reading difficulties of college freshmen of low academic performance. *Psychological Monographs*, 1950, *64*, 1-35.

Western, R.D. The basics movement and testing in reading: A representative anecdote. *English Education*, 1978, *4*, 232-235.

Williams, J.L. *A comparison of standardized reading test scores and informal reading inventory scores.* Unpublished doctoral dissertation, Southern Illinois University, 1963.

Yoshida, R.K. Out-of-level testing of special education students with a standardized achievement battery. *Journal of Educational Measurement,* 1976, *13,* 215-221.

Test References

Degrees of Reading Power. New York: College Entrance Examination Board, 1980.

General Educational Development Test. Washington, DC: American Council on Education, 1979.

Metropolitan Achievement Test. Cleveland, OH: Psychological Corporation, 1985.

6

Issues in accountability and reading measurement

A t a recent workshop on testing for principals and reading specialists, the publisher's representative who was leading the group began the session with the following remarks: "It is wholly appropriate to apply accountability in education. It is imperative that we treat schools as we treat businesses: They must be judged on their productivity."

This statement is important not because it is an anomaly, or because it expresses a view contrary to that of many educators and those who make decisions about the effectiveness of education (legislators, board of education members, the general public), but because it represents an assumption prevalent in contemporary education. The issue is not just that tests are often misused in accountability programs, or even that tests are usually used too extensively. Rather, the issue is the metaphor through which we characterize education. Is it appropriate, for example, to compare implicitly American public education and General Motors? Do we really want to use the same sort of language, replete with its connotative baggage, to discuss the effectiveness of schools and businesses?

The possibility exists that "accountability," as part of the corporate metaphor, represents an important, unexamined assumption which guides our perception of schools, clouds our judgment of what should (and does) happen in schools, and implicitly requires us to apply criteria for excellence that are simplistic, misinformed, or both. Ours is clearly the corporate era. We live in a period characterized by huge multinational conglomerates, by OPEC, by intense labor struggles, by massive unemployment, by a thousand frightening economic scenarios. Is it any wonder that the twentieth century mind makes use of the similes, metaphors, and implied comparisons of big time business and finance? The corporate infrastructure has the further positive attribute of ostensible clarity. Where else, with the possible exception of competitive sports, does one know exactly who has won and who has lost, and by how much? All that needs to be done is to examine the infamous bottom line. The one who makes the most money (or scores the most countable points) wins. There is little concern for subjective judgment; you get no points for how you go about the task.

Profit is a convenient, manageable mode of measurement; everyone can count, the units are all part of a common metric, and there is little room for argument. Clearly, this is an attractive trait. It appeals, in tidiness, to our rational side. Much of life is nebulous, subjective, clouded by value judgment, ambiguous, and complex. There are precious few times in an individual's life when a clear, concise, comprehensible bottom line exists. Hence, we are attracted to corporate metaphors and we infuse them into, or impose them onto, other areas of human activity, where they may or may not achieve a proper fit.

This chapter argues, in part, that this is the case with the notion of accountability in education, especially as accountability is operationalized in the form of minimum competency tests. We contend that we have been subverted by what Scriven (1972) calls the "logician's perennial temptation: Make the portrait neat and perhaps the subject of the portrait will become neater."

It is perhaps worth emphasizing that the central issue which follows is accountability, rather than minimum competency tests (MCTs). These tests are an overt response to the accountability issue and, to measurement specialists, an especially important one. MCTs, though, are a symptom, or an index, of the proliferation of an orientation toward accountability as a "wholly appropriate" model for schooling. But there are certainly other correlatives: change scores, gain scores, criterion scores, the ubiquity of specific scale scores—all are important issues in the examination of accountability, as are many of the proposed schemes for merit pay for teachers, and perhaps even our national mania for standardized test results.

It is interesting that accountability, as it is currently conceived, represents a kind of thinking that has been historically alien to education. As Ravitch (1983) has suggested, corporate metaphors have rarely been considered appropriate for education until the present generation. It is important, therefore, to keep accountability, MCTs, and other corporate metaphors in context, while simultaneously being aware of how they shape our schools, our curriculum, our instructional agendas, and our testing practices.

General issues in competency testing

At the present time, a majority of states have legislated programs of minimal competency testing, and there is little reason to believe that the movement is dead or even slowing down. It is a movement with profound social implications, profound problems, and powerful advocates. Minimal competency testing is with us, probably for many years to come, and in this chapter we propose to examine it and discuss more specifically some of the issues associated with the movement and the testing of minimal competence in reading.

Some advantages

As has been demonstrated (Farr, 1985), the trend toward minimal competency testing is rooted in historical and political forces of which we are generally unaware. There is good evidence, in fact, that several major urban centers in the United States engaged in something very much like MCT more than a hundred years ago (Jaeger, 1982).

The MCT movement has much in common with the history of the IQ test in that it has served, and tends to serve, many of the same social goals. As tests go, the MCT types are relatively efficient in terms of time and money. They are mass produced, mass administered, and mass scored. They supply relatively quick and clean answers to a number of very messy social problems. They are particularly useful as public relations devices for state departments of education and other educational systems and institutions. They attract attention in both local and national media, and they provide policy makers with some "data" for making decisions about public education.

These are the advantages, or at least the perceived advantages, of the movement toward widespread use of MCTs. These are the acknowledged reasons for their existence and continued use with literally millions of children, adolescents, and teachers.

Some disadvantages

This section will be a bit longer, but let us summarize at the outset the central arguments against MCTs by quoting Glass (1978) on the same topic:

> A common expression of wishful thinking is to base a grand scheme on a fundamental, unresolved problem.

And that is the problem. Minimal competency tests reflect society's misguided but probably sincere attempt to make education "accountable." There are, however, staggering technical problems with the tests themselves and serious flaws in the wishful thinking that has engendered them.

It may well be that our "mania for testing" (Hipple & Kaplan, 1983) has led us to the use of MCTs which some critics say have "wreaked major havoc" (Lazarus, 1981) on our entire educational system. The difficulties with MCTs are many, but their major problems are encapsulated below.

1. MCTs assume a "critical list" of facts, concepts, or skills which everyone must know or possess.
2. MCTs put great emphasis on learning only those things which are easily measurable.
3. MCTs inhibit educational improvement by focusing on the "minimal."

These are all significant problems, and none is really discrete. When considered as a group, however, they form the basis of most nontechnical arguments against MCTs. Most critics tend to view the technical problems of MCTs as red herrings anyway (Glass, 1978). The most damaging criticisms of the movement are at the "assumptive" level. MCTs represent a kind of "assumptive testing," analogous to the "assumptive teaching" Herber (1970) has warned us about for years.

Epistemological problems

In Chapter 2, we noted that many tests of comprehension are built upon a framework of unexamined assumptions. For example, any reading test has an implicit theory of comprehension, of language, and of learning. This is a special problem, some would say weakness, of MCTs. It has been called the problem of the "critical list" (Wolf, 1981).

This is an especially interesting problem because it goes right to the heart of epistemology (that part of philosophy which seeks to examine Knowledge: where it comes from, how it is to be valued, and how we come to know). MCTs are necessarily built upon the assumption that there are some few pieces of knowledge, some structured domains of human intellectual development, which are indispensable; i.e., the "critical list." This is the conventional wisdom. Most of us do, indeed, assume that there are some things everyone has to know to get through life, or school, successfully. This is a comforting thought, perhaps, but it falls apart upon rigorous examination. There may be processes or strategies, or even discrete facts, that most persons in our society share, but they have not yet been isolated, and it is not likely that they will be in the near future. Chances are quite good that the things we perceive to be on the critical list are the things *we* know. In other words, there is an inherent subjectivity in deciding what the content of an MCT will include.

It is sometimes amusing to compare the MCTS from several states. Apparently, the Constitution and the Federalist Papers notwithstanding, it takes very different kinds of knowledge and radically disparate skills to live in different states, even neighboring states.

The MCT movement is, perhaps obviously, only one aspect of the widely touted "Back-to-Basics" movement in American education. The problem is that the basics await definition, although some educators, only half in jest, have proposed that *children* are the basics. As most philosophers of education would agree, there is no critical list. As a consequence, all MCTS are fundamentally subjective. They represent the opinion of a particular individual or particular group about what it is essential to know. Even when these tests are developed by a committee, as they often are, it is not probable that all the potential critical lists are subsumed.

Measuring the critical list

Nevertheless, the assumption continues to be made that there is an indispensable domain of knowledge that students should have "minimally mastered" at a given grade level. It is also assumed that the schools are accountable for this minimum competence, or that the students are.

Consider this notion in tandem with its twin, also borrowed from the corporate world: cost effectiveness. One of the alleged virtues of MCTS is that they are efficient instruments, in terms of both time and money, for obtaining large amounts of data. This means they are always pencil and paper tests. As a consequence, most MCTS attempt to measure only those aspects of the critical list which are amenable to easy quantification.

A number of problems arise from this practice, not the least of which is the notion of "indirect assessment." Many MCTS were developed to evaluate an individual student's "life skills" competencies. Often these skills are substantially different from the kinds of skills which might be called "school competencies," yet students are expected to have somehow developed and honed these life skills and to demonstrate them on a pencil and paper test.

In the first place, it is worth questioning the proposition that there is a direct relationship between the ability to perform well in life and our ability to measure that performance on a conventional multiple choice test. French (1966) suggests a high correlation between the two. Other researchers suggest a low correspondence between, for example, performance on the STEP (Sequential Tests of Educational Progress) Writing Test (in which the examinee is asked to respond to multiple choice questions about errors in a given passage) and actual writing ability (Madaus & Rippey, 1966).

Second, questions of curricular and instructional validity come into play. To what extent are schools charged with the responsibility to prepare students to perform well on specific life skills (e.g., income tax preparation, filling out a job application) as opposed to the supposedly valued skills of critical thinking or creative application? If schools spend their time teaching to tests of life skills, will they realistically be able to devote much time to the higher level cognitive domains?

The question of fairness to both the students and schools also arises. If the schools do not spend a preponderance of their time on life skills, is it fair to make them or the students accountable for the learning of these skills? Nathan and Jennings (1978) have compared this kind of testing to the bait-and-switch method of fraudulent advertising, in which an inferior or different product is actually available at a store, although a superior product has been advertised at an unrealistically low price.

In addition, this question of curricular relevance (i.e., does the school teach what the test tests?) is allied to the notion of cost effectiveness. Despite their alleged efficiency, MCTs contain a number of important hidden costs. The greatest of these is probably the requisite remediation for students who fail to prove their competence. The tests themselves have been determined to cost between fifteen cents and thirteen dollars (Haney & Madaus, 1978), but this cost does not include the expense of "fixing" the problems after they are uncovered. There is also the potential problem of costs resulting from legal challenges to the entire MCT system (Harper & Kellarr, 1978; McCarthy, 1983).

The solution to these costs in some states has been to use commercially developed and validated instruments. Unfortunately, this raises the spectre of an MCT which is technically robust in reliability and norming groups, but of questionable validity for local curriculum and instruction.

Setting standards

To this point, it has been suggested there are grave problems with: 1) determining what *should* be tested, and 2) determining what *can* be tested. For the moment, let us consider that those problems have been solved; we have established the "critical list" and are able to measure it with relative success. The problem now is to determine the minimally acceptable performances on the test we have developed.

Most competency tests have evolved into *minimum* competency tests. Thus, we have a questionable equation of competencies and minimal abilities. Are they the same thing (Haney & Madaus, 1978)? It seems likely they are not. Green (1978) has suggested that, in social practice, the "goals" we establish as competencies function as "measures of failure rather than standards of success."

Nor is there much consensus about miminal acceptability. "In practice, the setting of minimum scores seems to be the result of compromise between judgments of what minimums seem plausible to expect and judgments about what proportions of failure seem politically tolerable" (Haney & Madaus, 1978).

A popular, if controversial, way of setting these standards has been the grade equivalent. It is not uncommon, for example, for a decision to be made that high school graduation (grade twelve) be tied to an MCT on which a given student must perform at a minimum grade nine level. The immediate problem is often a political one: "We're paying for twelve years of schooling and only getting nine" (Nathan & Jennings, 1978).

This problem is important, but it overlooks the source of the scale used in determining grade equivalents, which are derived from a norming pool. If the local schools were to set the standards for high school graduation at the twelfth grade equivalent level, 50 percent of the students taking the test would automatically fail. This would no doubt please some critics of public education, but it can hardly be called a workable approach in the real world of politics. Nor is it especially fair to the students, the school board, school administrators, or teachers, all of whom are to be held accountable for such performance.

In general, attempts to use norm referenced grade equivalents as criterion levels have failed. Higher than expected failure rates have been the norm rather than the exception (Greenbaum, 1977). "At present, there is simply no scientific foundation for deciding what 'minimum' points should be; the decisions involved in setting them are political rather than scientific" (Haney & Madaus, 1978).

This aspect of the problem, however, does not even address the technical problems which beset "standard setting." This notion is a function of our fascination with the "technology of assessment" (Carey, 1983), which echoes Black's sentiment that we often confuse the rigor of the mathematics with the rigor of the conceptual underpinnings of those mathematics (1962).

Guthrie (1980) questioned the validity of state ordained minimum essentials tests in reading. An important validity question is whether answering a given percentage of a test's items is equivalent to the actual reading required in everyday life. Particularly important is whether a score below the cut score, or criterion level, validly identifies a reading ability level that would result in potential failure in life for the examinee scoring at that level. There appears to be little educational validity, or decision making user validity, in a test with the admitted ultimate purpose of arbitrarily attempting to enforce the teaching and acquisition of some percentage of selected reading behaviors. This seems particularly true if the test results in instructional neglect of any behaviors it did not, or could not, include.

The use of criterion referenced tests for dichotomous decisions has been questioned by numerous educational researchers. Glass (1978) notes Glaser's proposal (1963) that criteria should represent a continuum of proficiency and not a yes/no approach. Glass also cites Mayer (1962) who suggests that cutoff score indicators rather than specific cutoff scores are more reasonable.

In the debate on cutoff score indicators versus cutoff scores, Popham and Husek (1969) discussed "response patterns" and "percentage performance," while Glaser and Nitko (1971) favored performance standards for "some domain of tasks," but not for single objectives. Although many researchers still resisted cutoff scores (Harris & Stewart, 1971; Iven, 1970; Lindvall & Nitko, 1975), the dichotomous cutoff score prevailed by the mid 1970s (Glass, 1978).

Numerous models have been developed that attempt to make criterion setting less judgmental but, in the final analysis, setting a cutoff score that separates mastery from nonmastery and competency from noncompetency cannot be made a scientific operation (Koffler, 1980; Shepard, 1980). Rowley (1982) wrote a delightful and illuminating parody on the problems of setting minimum standards. He contrasted the problems in setting test criterion levels to those that would be encountered in establishing standards for determining "minimal beardedness." Rowley contends that the search for minimal criterion scores will continue because it allows educators, and the public, to blame the victim for his performance. Regarding minimum criterion levels on competency tests for high school graduation, Rowley states:

> None of us seriously imagined that the withholding of a high school diploma would directly benefit the person so denied. We could think of no benefits that would flow to a person denied a high school diploma, and if there were benefits, they must accrue to somebody other than the person to whom the diploma is denied. But to whom? (1982, p.91)

Glass (1978) examined in some detail each of the major approaches which tries to make it scientific to conclude that criterion referencing can be achieved through mathematical formulations. Glass concluded that criterion referencing is a concept that is "ill-prepared for mathematical treatment." "To my knowledge," Glass writes, "every attempt to derive a criterion score is either blatantly arbitrary or derives from a set of artibrary premises" (p. 258). Any pretense that criterion setting can be made scientifically independent of arbitrary judgment provokes, from experts like Glass, assertions that setting criterion levels is "capricious," "authoritarian," and "foolhardy." Glass suggests that a logical first step in making the criteria less arbitrary would be to collect performance scores on a criterion referenced test to establish norms.

Minimum competency in reading

The vast majority of MCTs developed so far have rarely gone beyond testing performance in reading and mathematics. A few states have developed competency examinations in other areas and many individual schools and school districts have long employed what are essentially MCTs as promotion or graduation requirements in a number of disciplines. But most large scale competency testing programs have focused on math computation, problem solving and reading, usually vocabulary and comprehension.

This is significant for a number of reasons discussed throughout this volume. Clearly, there are major problems in testing practices associated with reading. Most professional reading educators have grave doubts about both the data derived from standardized reading tests and the uses to which those data are put.

Consider that at least half, and probably more, of any MCT is a reading test. Any weaknesses or problems in reading measurement, good intentions notwithstanding, remain and are probably magnified in a competency testing program. Flaws in reading measurement do not go away simply because the test is labeled an MCT rather than a reading test. Combine problems in reading measurement with the conceptual and technical problems in minimum competency testing, and one is confronted by a measurement maze of potentially profound proportions.

At the very least, it seems fair to say that the issues surrounding MCTs in general and reading competency tests are parallel. There is, quite clearly, no critical list of reading skills. The tendency has been to measure those aspects of the reading process which lend themselves to easy quantification, despite considerable evidence that reading is much more than a

Reading: What Can Be Measured?

magic synthesis of discrete subskills. The technical and conceptual problems with standard setting are virtually identical to those which pertain to MCTS in general.

These problems have occasionally proved embarrassing for agencies developing and administering minimum competency tests in reading. One state recently developed an MCT which assessed reading and mathematics performance. The reading test was, as usual, divided into several subtests: phonics, vocabulary (word identification), and reading comprehension (multiple choice). The test was piloted and generated very respectable numbers in terms of item p-values and split-half reliabilities. The test was finally administered to about 40,000 children throughout the state, with considerable fanfare. The results were duly reported and it was generally agreed that the results were encouraging, with a few nagging exceptions. However, one enterprising graduate student at the state university conducted his own analysis of the data and uncovered one dismaying statistic: a significant and persistent *negative* correlation between a combination of the phonics and vocabulary subtests and the comprehension subtest. In other words, students who did well on phonics and vocabulary were unlikely to do well on comprehension. Students who did well on comprehension were not likely to do well on phonics and vocabulary.

Clearly, this was an inconvenient finding. It suggested significant problems with either the test or the traditional concept about the relationship between phonics and comprehension. It also added to the problem of setting minimum standards for competence in reading, which were to have been developed post hoc. Did the residents of the state really want to certify as "minimally educated" students who could "bark at print" but who could not understand or respond to the substance of what they were reading? It was perhaps more embarrassing when another researcher suggested that more than 80 percent of the reading instruction in the state's public schools tended to focus on things like phonics and vocabulary. Could it be that this focus actually impeded the students' comprehension? Almost no one in the state's educational hierarchy wanted to contend with this question, and the test died a relatively quiet death.

The point of this narrative is that problems in reading measurement may well be reified in minimum competency testing programs. The problems with conventional assessment may actually loom larger when they are not contended with early in the development of an MCT. And this does not really speak to the most serious aspect of test abuse, the uses made of test results. It would be difficult, for example, to justify promoting or not promoting children on the basis of their performance on the test just described.

Reading management programs

An important aspect of reading education which is often overlooked in the debate over competency testing is what has come to be called the "reading management system." These management systems or programs, going under a variety of labels, have become a dominant force in the organization of reading instruction in the United States. They are really little more than a minor variation on minimum competency testing, although they have certainly not been subject to the same rigorous examination or criticism as the MCTs.

Like MCTs the instructional management systems have a long, and generally respected, history in reading education. Both Smith (1965) and Mathews (1973) suggest that these systems were a part of reading instruction from the earliest attempts at direct, systematic instruction. But they have certainly blossomed in the past two decades, perhaps in part as a function of the trend toward something akin to corporate accountability in education.

Perhaps the most important model for these instructional systems, or one of the most popular, was the approach to reading offered in the Individually Guided Education (IGE) program, often referred to as the Wisconsin Design because it was developed at the University of Wisconsin. This model has been adopted, modified, and implemented in many school systems. Offshoots of the approach have been re-created in a number of districts, and some have been "validated" and offered for direct implementation by agencies such as the National Diffusion Network.

Indeed, virtually any instructional system featuring a diagnostic/prescriptive view or a scope and sequence chart, or a programed learning system owes something to this systems approach, although not necessarily to the IGE model. The approach has become more important, though, as publishers of basal reading series have adopted it virtually en masse. Basal series clearly dominate reading instruction in the United States (Anderson, 1984; Farr, 1984) and, if publishers of these series employ this approach, it automatically becomes a formidable part of how reading is taught.

In essence, this approach emphasizes mastery of discrete, and usually isolated, subskills, all of which have been clearly identified at the outset and for which a variety of individual drills, exercises, and tests are provided. The skills have been placed in a clear and common sense hierarchy and students contend with the next higher skill once they have demonstrated their ability to master a lower skill or skills.

The approach is in many ways a cookbook for the teaching of reading. For the most part, instructional decisions are made by the designers of the system and the teacher becomes the manager of the system. Ideally, the teacher is alleged to be able to pinpoint exactly where every student is in terms of skill mastery. Also, the teacher should be able to provide a list of skills that have been mastered and describe the likely progress of any student based on rate of past performance.

The problems with such an approach have been dealt with at some length elsewhere in this volume. But they can also be examined from the viewpoint of their role as MCTs.

These systems have a number of advantages. They are considered by many to be cost effective. Also, many teachers are pleased with the systems: They are perceived as commonsensical, ordered and sequenced, and offer the individual teacher a sense of security about the progress of each student not available in more holistic approaches. The data generated by these systems are likewise intuitively comprehensible. A child either has or has not mastered a skill. If not, there are backup exercises which the child can do before once again attempting to demonstrate mastery. Again, this is often perceived as a commonsense and very businesslike approach to a subject some teachers believe is too often discussed as though it were a mystical experience.

However, the systems tend to have many of the same disadvantages as MCTs in general. Despite the lack of consensus among experts and researchers, developers of these systems clearly think they have developed the "critical list." This naturally ignores the subskill controversy, but it also ignores the fact that there is little agreement, even among those who subscribe to a subskill point of view, as to which skills are critical. These problems are not addressed in these systems, and the confusing decisions do not have to be made by teachers.

Also, these systems tend to measure what it is assumed can be measured, and consequently tend to ignore the higher order skills. Many do include instruction in critical thinking or making inferences, but this is not necessarily considered important in terms of instructional emphasis. These skills, which are also taught as discrete entities or processes, are treated like dessert and are available only after a child has demonstrated mastery over vowel digraphs or some other low level skill.

The problem of standard setting, so important in the development of MCTs, also does not disappear in reading instruction management systems. A number of these systems use 80 percent as a convenient mastery index for a given skill. Generally, this means that the test for the skill, provided as part of the system package, will be a ten question multiple choice test on which students are considered successful if they get eight correct. It remains a mystery, though, how the 80 percent mark was set (or 70 percent in some cases, or 90 percent in others). In assessing comprehension, for example, is understanding 80 percent of a story a reasonable demonstration of "mastery"? The problem here is analogous to the problem with Informal Reading Inventories, as suggested by Powell (1971). It seems that we do not know quite enough about either the process or the measurement of the process to be able to affix a specific number to it. As noted earlier, Glass (1978) has called criterion referencing "a concept ill prepared for mathematical treatment."

We should not be too quick to accept the alleged advantages of the instructional management programs. The cost effectiveness of these systems, for example, is dubious. In many cases, record keeping is the major enterprise in which the instructional staff is engaged. Do we wish to pay teachers to function as clerks? One large midwestern city abandoned its instructional system when it was determined that approximately $1 million a year in salaries for teacher aides was paid to persons who kept marvelous records, but who rarely, if ever, came in contact with a child.

It is possible, then, to view these systems in light of their functional equivalence to MCT programs. They form an important component of reading instruction in America, but they are heir to a number of flaws which often go unexamined and which have an impact on literally millions of children.

MCTS in context: Some recommendations

The movement toward minimum competency testing has clearly been fueled in recent years by the publication of what are now lumped together as the Commission Reports. These are essentially a series of reports by nationally recognized groups and agencies which have been markedly critical of education in the United States. In some cases, these reports have called directly for the implementation of minimum competency tests at the state or national levels.

Despite generally favorable media attention, many educators were not impressed by the quality, insightfulness, or recommendations of these reports. The reports garnered a great deal of publicity and in general were reported favorably in the press, but some of them, especially that of the National Commission on Excellence in Education, were regarded by some experts as both naive and elitist (Goodman, 1984). Some specific studies, such as the Libertyville report published by the National Academy of the Humanities and Arts, were criticized as "incompetent" and "cavalier" (Carey, 1984).

It is important, therefore, for reading educators to consider the recommendations of these reports within the boundaries of their discipline. Despite some ardent and scholarly support (Popham, 1981; Pullin, 1981), MCTs have rarely been acclaimed as the answer to whatever educational ills our society faces. This is even more the case with MCTs in reading, for some of the reasons outlined previously.

The International Reading Association, as well as other professional organizations, have seriously questioned the role of MCTs in reading instruction, especially the advisability of using test results for curricular or instructional decision making. The abuse of MCT results is especially insidious when it occurs in conjunction with schemes for merit pay for teachers. It behooves all of us as reading educators to consider the minimum competency movement in a critical light. A moratorium on MCTs is unlikely to occur soon and, frankly, it is questionable whether such a ban would be advisable. Perhaps conceptual and technical breakthroughs will occur which will render MCTs more acceptable. In the meantime, reading educators have a professional responsibility, implicit in International Reading Association's Code of Ethics, to raise questions about competency testing in reading and to inform parents, students, and administrators about constraints on the use of the test results.

At the very least, the results should never be considered out of context. Again, a corroborative framework (Page & Vacca, 1979) is called for. MCTs are simply not good enough at this point to be used as the sole source for making decisions about a child's life or a school district's performance. Other test results, as well as qualitative data such as teacher observation and judgment, should always be used as a context within which to interpret MCT results.

At the same time, we should encourage further research in the area of minimum competency testing, especially research in the quest for alternatives. Support for MCTs is often uninformed. It is our responsibility to change that situation and provide those responsible with the wherewithal to make informed choices in this area.

References

Anderson, R.C. *Report of the National Commission on Reading.* Paper presented at the annual meeting of the National Reading Conference, St. Petersburg Beach, Florida, 1984.

Black, M. *Models and metaphors: Studies in language and philosophy.* Ithaca, NY: Cornell University Press, 1962.

Carey, R. *Measurement and mythology.* Paper presented at the Conference on Reading Research for the Center for the Study of Reading, Long Beach, California, May 1983.

Carey, R. Libertyville study: Superficial, cavalier investigation. *Providence Journal,* February 23, 1984.

Farr, R. Reaction to "Do basal manuals teach reading comprehension?" In R.C. Anderson, J. Osborn, and R.J. Tierney (Eds.), *Learning to read in American schools.* Hillsdale, NJ: Erlbaum, 1984.

Farr, R. Can minimum competency tests have a positive impact on education? In J. Osborn, P.T. Wilson, and R.C. Anderson (Eds.), *Reading education: Foundations for a literate America.* Lexington, MA: Lexington Books, 1985.

French, J. Schools of thought in judging excellence in English themes. In A. Anastasi (Ed.), *Testing problems in perspective.* Washington, DC: American Council on Education, 1966.

Glaser, R. Instructional technology and the measurement of learning outcomes. *American Psychologist,* 1963, *18,* 519-521.

Glaser, R., and Nitko, A.J. Measurement in learning and instruction. In R.L. Thorndike (Ed.), *Educational measurement,* second edition. Washington, DC: American Council on Education, 1971.

Glass, G.V. Standards and criteria. *Journal of Educational Measurement,* 1978, *15,* 237-261.

Glass, G. Minimum competence and incompetence in Florida. *Phi Delta Kappan,* 1978, *59,* 602-605.

Goodman, K. The solution is the risk: A reply to the report of the National Commission on Excellence in Education. *Slate,* 1983, *9,* 1-4. Reprinted as "A critique of the NCEE report," *Education Digest,* January 1984, 6-9.

Green, T. *Minimal educational standards: A systematic perspective.* Paper presented at the Education Commission of the States/National Institute of Education/Carnegie Corporation Regional Conference on Minimum Competency Testing, 1977.

Greenbaum, W., Garet, M., and Solomon, E. *Measuring educational progress.* New York: McGraw-Hill, 1977.

Guthrie, J. An assessment of educational policy research. *Educational Evaluation and Policy Analysis,* 1980, *2,* 48.

Haney, W., and Madaus, G.. Making sense of the competency testing movement. *Harvard Educational Review,* 1978, *48,* 462-484.

Harper, R., and Kilarr, G. (Eds.). *Reading and the law.* Newark, DE: International Reading Association, 1978.

Harris, M.L., and Stewart, D.M. *Application of classical strategies to criterion referenced test construction.* Paper presented at the annual meeting of the American Educational Research Association, New York, 1971.

Herber, H. *Teaching reading in content areas.* Englewood Cliffs, NJ: Prentice-Hall, 1978.

Hipple, T.W., and Kaplan, J.S. A carefully researched argument against competency tests. *Phi Delta Kappan*, 1983, *65*, 148-149.

Ivens, S.H. *An investigation of item analysis, reliability and validity in relation to criterion referenced tests*. Unpublished doctoral dissertation, Florida State University, 1970.

Jaeger, R. The final hurdle: Minimum competency achievement testing. In G. Austin and H. Garber (Eds.), *The rise and fall of national test scores*. New York: Academic Press, 1982.

Koffler, S.L. A comparison of approaches for setting proficiency standards. *Journal of Educational Measurement*, 1980, *17*, 167-178.

Lazarus, M. *Goodbye to excellence: A critical look at minimum competency testing*. Boulder, CO: National Association of Elementary School Principals, 1981.

Lindvall, C.M., and Nitko, A.J. *Measuring pupil achievement and aptitude*, second edition. New York: Harcourt Brace Jovanovich, 1975.

Madaus, G., and Rippey, R. Zeroing in on the STEP writing test: What does it tell a teacher? *Journal of Educational Measurement*, 1966, *3*, 19-25.

Mager, R.F. *Preparing instructional objectives*. Palo Alto, CA: Fearon, 1962.

Mathews, W.M. Narrative format testing reports and traditional testing reports: A comparative study. *Journal of Educational Measurement*, 1973, *3*, 171-178.

McCarthy, M. The application of competency testing mandates to handicapped children. *Harvard Educational Review*, 1983, *53*, 146-164.

Nathan, J., and Jennings, W. Educational bait and switch. *Phi Delta Kappan*, 1978, *59*, 621-624.

Page, W., and Vacca, R. Toward a corroborative framework for reading comprehension. In R. Vacca and J. Meagher (Eds.), *Reading through content*. Storrs, CT: University of Connecticut, Reading/Language Arts Center, 1979.

Popham, W. The case for minimum competency testing. *Phi Delta Kappan*, 1981, *63*, 92-94.

Popham, W.J., and Husek, T.R. Implications of criterion referenced measurement. *Journal of Educational Measurement*, 1969, *6*, 1-9.

Powell, W.R. The validity of the instructional reading level. In D.L. DeBoer (Ed.), *Reading diagnosis and evaluation*. Newark, DE: International Reading Association, 1971.

Pullin, D. Minimum competency testing and the demand for accountability. *Phi Delta Kappan*, 1981, *63*, 20-22.

Ravitch, D. *The troubled crusade: American education, 1945-1980*. New York: Basic Books, 1983.

Rowley, G.L. Historical antecedents of the standard setting debate: An inside account of the minimal beardedness controversy. *Journal of Educational Measurement*, 1982, *2*, 87-96.

Scriven, M. *Objectivity and subjectivity in educational research*. Monograph no. 1. Chicago: National Society for the Study of Education, 1972.

Shepard, L.A. Technical issues in minimum competency testing. In D.C. Berliner (Ed.), *Review of research in education,* volume 8. Itasca, IL: Peacock, 1980.

Smith, N.B. *American reading instruction.* Newark, DE: International Reading Association, 1965.

Wolf, R. *Is there a critical list?* Paper presented at the Henry Lester Smith Conference on Educational Research, Bloomington, Indiana, 1981.

7
Issues and trends in reading assessment: Summing up

T here are so many vital issues facing reading assessment today that it is impossible not to appear pretentious for attempting a summary of them. Measurement affects almost every aspect of education. The issues range from the determination of a useful definition of reading to the development of unbiased and valid tests, from the influence of test results on classroom planning to their influence on the politics of schooling, and from the use of test results to influence school bond votes to their use in affecting national elections. Most educators are not apt to forget the role education played in the 1980 Presidential election when the decline on the Scholastic Aptitude Test became a major political issue.

If summarizing issues in this broad topic area seems pretentious, then attempting to explain trends may be downright foolish. Trends in education generally, and in educational measurement specifically, are affected by myriad events outside education. Perhaps the public's opinion of the success or failure of education is nothing more than its broader opinion of the success of American society. It has been suggested, for example, that in times of national economic difficulty criticism of education rises to a crescendo (Tyler, 1982).

This was the persuasive, if unconvincing, message of *A Nation At Risk* (1983), a report which emphatically endorsed the use of tests:

Standardized tests of achievement (not to be confused with aptitude tests) should be administered at major transition points from one level of schooling to another and particularly from high school to college or work. The purposes of these tests would be to: a) certify the student's credentials; b) identify the need for remedial intervention; and c) identify the opportunity for advanced or accelerated work. The tests should be administered as part of a nationwide (but not Federal) system of state and local standardized tests. This system should include other diagnostic procedures that assist teachers and students to evaluate student progress.

There are other discernible and more immediate factors which influence the use of tests in schools, including the vagaries of funding for both educational research and the establishment of special programs. For example, the passage of the Elementary and Secondary Education Act (ESEA) in 1965 brought about the development of more diagnostic tests to be used with students who have been tracked into special remedial/corrective reading classes of one kind or another. In addition, the ESEA stipulations regarding program evaluation increased the use of testing to determine the success of programs established under this act. The state administrators for most ESEA Title I Programs (later called Chapter I) mandated that pre and postprogram test results be submitted to state education agencies.

No wonder that tests are often in the educational spotlight. They are seen as both the bane of education and the bellwether of our schools' achievement. As critics blast tests for their cultural bias, their lack of validity, and their constricting influences on the curriculum, others champion their use as the most significant indicators of the success of our schools. President Ronald Reagan, speaking before the Education Department's Annual Secondary School Recognition awards gathering in 1984, said that the first goal of education is to "regain at least half the losses of the past twenty years" on combined Scholastic Aptitude Test (SAT) scores. This is a "big challenge," Reagan said, but it can be done "if we try."

It is certainly heady stuff for proponents of testing when the President of the United States suggests that the primary goal of education is to improve test performance. One wonders if President Reagan was aware that the SAT is taken by about only 45 percent of the high school seniors in the country. If so, does this mean that what the college bound students achieve is all that should concern us. More importantly, one wonders if he thought that a single test could be used as the total indicator of the success of American education. It is even more disconcerting that Reagan never discussed the improvements in education that test score increase is supposed to reveal. Rather, he seemed to suggest that the goal of education is the improved test scores themselves.

Local politicians are equally enamored with test performance. In Indiana, as in many other states, a legislative bill was passed by the state Senate in 1984 decreeing that "Student test scores would determine a school by school ranking of Indiana's school corporations." The bill's sponsor told his Senate colleagues that with his bill, "At least you would know and your constituents also would know how well your corporation is doing..." (UPI, 1984).

Educational decision makers, in particular, seem to accept the notion that test scores are all that matter. Madaus (1985) makes the point that "policy makers have created the illusion that test performance is synonymous with the quality of education." Madaus argues if test scores increase, policy makers will argue "more and more pupils are therefore competent to face the demands of our society; that meaning has been restored to the high school diploma; and that we at last have truth in labeling in education."

The extensive use of tests is more than an argument about the technical considerations of test development. The argument extends to whether some aspects of education generally, and the most significant aspects of reading specifically, ever can be measured. The argument also concerns whether the ultimate goals of education have anything to do with specific learning outcomes. These arguments are often swept aside when tests are mandated by policy makers eager to reform education and provide concrete evidence to taxpayers and voters that their reforms are getting the job done.

Salganik (1985) discussed the control of education that resides in the use of test scores to judge the quality of education. She believes that the reliance on test scores "[has] helped to weaken the authority of professional judgment and to centralize school governance." Her discussion concludes with the belief that we can expect an even greater reliance on testing:

> Thus we can reasonably expect that increased reliance on technical evidence, decreased reliance on professional judgment, continued use of test results to assess the quality of schools, and increased regulation of local school districts by the states will continue and that they will be absorbed into the set of norms that govern the assumptions of both educators and lay people about how the U.S. system of education should work. (p. 610)

Concern about the use of test scores to judge educational quality was emphasized by Eisner (1983), who declared that test scores are causing educators and policy makers to focus on the wrong problems, and more importantly, on the wrong solutions to those problems:

I have little confidence in the educational significance of the use of standardized achievement test scores. It's not that the scores have no meaning, it's simply that they tap much too slender a slice of what I believe is important in education. Neither standardized achievement tests, nor the Scholastic Aptitude Test, nor the tests used for advanced placement adequately represent the kind of criteria that should be used to appraise the quality of schooling or their effects upon students. (p. 49)

Eisner's point is nicely traced in the concerns of Anrig (1985) who describes the progress that black children have made in education. Anrig cites a number of test score indicators, including their performance on the Scholastic Aptitude Tests and the National Assessment of Educational Progress (administered to national samples of 9, 13, and 17 year olds). He notes that the gap between the test performance of white students and black students is being closed. Anrig also cites as evidence for the academic improvement of black students their increased enrollment "in demanding academic courses—especially in mathematics and the physical sciences...." Anrig points out, however, that there are disturbing nontest data related to the general academic improvement of black students: The percentage of black students completing high school has declined; the number of black students enrolled in higher education has also declined; and the high school dropout rate for black students has increased slightly.

One would have an incomplete picture of the academic progress of black students by merely reviewing test data. In addition, an examination of the tests themselves and of the kinds of instruction in the schools might suggest that test score improvements are achieved as the result of instruction focused narrowly on the types of behaviors included on the tests. It may be that some test score improvements are masking the fact that black students are not progressing in curriculum areas that are less amenable to focused instruction but more important to producing educated citizens.

The preceding comments are not meant to disparage any test score gains by black students, nor to suggest that the test scores are not valid. Rather, they are intended to emphasize the importance of collecting a broader range of information and of carefully considering the types of behaviors assessed by the tests we use.

When test scores are interpreted in a broader context, some startling conclusions emerge. Howe (1985) has provided an interesting observation on the interpretation of the SAT scores. He argues that the decline on the SAT is a positive sign of the improvement of education. He believes that the twenty year change in the composition of the population of examinees is the result of a more egalitarian view of education and increased opportunities for minority students to take advantage of postsecondary education. Howe summarizes this belief as follows:

> Given our national ideals, we can do no less than to take on the task of educating an ever larger proportion of our population. That is why I have titled this article as I did: "Let's Have Another SAT Score Decline." The 1977 report of the College Board Advisory Panel clearly demonstrates that educating a larger proportion of our population poses fewer risks to the quality of schooling than widespread misinterpretations of the recent SAT score decline suggested. The risks we run by accepting a dropout rate of more than 40 percent in our central cities are infinitely greater. (p. 602)

We continue to misunderstand the limited value of tests. They are only estimates of student achievement of some of the goals of education. Even if all politicians, educators, and citizens understood this, there would be many important issues related to testing that would need to be examined. The need for an even closer examination of testing issues is mandated as long as misplaced overreliance on test scores continues.

Where are we in reading assessment?

Tests are administered to literally millions of children every year. Reading is probably the most frequently tested behavior in schools. The importance of reading in the school curriculum is reflected in the importance of reading in assessment. Almost all of the state minimum competency tests include a reading test. Many schools administer only standardized reading and mathematics tests to elementary students. The Scholastic Aptitude Test: Verbal is primarily a reading comprehension and vocabulary test.

As testing and reading scores become more popular among those making major decisions about the schools, the uses of tests continue to be generally the same as they have been for several generations. Most states, school districts, and individual schools rely on norm referenced achievement tests for student placement, policy decisions, and the diagnosis of individual student performance.

A recent survey of test usage in one state (Carey, 1984) reported that the average student in that state can expect to take between twelve and fifteen major standardized achievement test batteries during a normal K-12 public school experience. This represents a considerable expenditure of time and money, yet many teachers and administrators in the study said they had no clear idea why the tests were being administered, other than the political need for reporting test scores.

A second, more indepth study of one school system (Carey 1985) was unable to discover a single teacher who used the test results for any curricular or instructional purpose. In fact, the only person in favor of the test and the testing program in the school district was the superintendent, who had a functional need to report test scores to the local school board and, for certain groups of students, to the state.

One has to assume that such confusion about the potential application of standardized test results does not occur with the informal testing that teachers often design themselves and is increasingly recommended by educators. Yet the use of informal assessments in reading is seldom studied.

Classroom teachers are also encouraged to use various observation forms, to collect anecdotal records, and to record each student's oral reading behaviors as a basis for planning instruction. There is a paucity of research on how often this kind of assessment activity takes place, how reliable or valid it is, and what use is made of the results.

A type of reading assessment which falls between formal standardized tests and informal observations made by a classroom teacher is the basal reader tests that accompany all the basal reader programs in schools today. These tests are typically administered to pupils at the end of each book and/or at the end of each unit in the book. In some schools, the results of these tests must be submitted to the principal, and they are often filed in each student's cumulative record. In addition, the test results are usually used by teachers at parent conferences to explain a student's progress in learning to read. Basal reader tests are probably the driving force behind classroom reading instruction.

Since basal reader tests are so common in classrooms, it is legitimate to ask about their validity and reliability. An examination of most directions for administering and interpreting basal reader tests reveals very little evidence regarding either their validity or reliability. Inquiries to the test publishers usually result in a general statement that all the instructional materials that are part of the reading program are "tried out" in classrooms, but little information is provided about the specifics of the tryouts.

Are reading tests changing? The evidence presented in previous chapters of this monograph suggests that reading tests have not changed significantly in the past fifty years. There have been numerous advances in the statistical areas of validity and reliability. The invention, development, and extensive use of test scoring machines and computer summaries of test information have radically changed the speed with which test results are returned to schools and teachers. The use of computers to generate a variety of test score reports for teachers, administrators, and parents has also developed extensively in the past decade. However, the tests themselves look very similar to those developed in the 1920s. The use of short passages followed by multiple choice questions is still the predominant format for assessing reading comprehension. The word recognition tests used on both norm and criterion referenced tests have not changed in any significant way.

Does the lack of change indicate that nothing has been learned about the reading process or the skills of reading since the first reading tests were developed? Does it mean that while we may have learned much about the reading process, the product of that process is still what we thought it was decades ago?

Is the lack of change because those who author and publish reading tests have not paid attention to new developments in reading theory? Is it the extremely conservative nature of the test producing industry that prohibits significant change? Is the industry concerned that tests which reflect change will not sell a valid image of an educational market that is indeed intolerant to change?

Is the lack of change the result of general indifference toward testing on the part of educators? Does the lack of change reflect our determination to test what can easily be tested and what results in the least amount of teacher and administrator effort, such as machine scored multiple choice tests?

The reality is probably some combination of the factors these questions suggested. Clearly, with the exception of the advances in measurement science, there has been little change in the actual format and structure of reading tests.

Some would argue that the development of criterion referenced reading tests has been a significant change (see Chapter 6), but this change has been in the development of the general structure of the tests and the interpretation of test scores rather than in the format of the test items themselves. For example, criterion referenced tests are generally very specific regarding the domain to be tested, the number of test items to be developed for each test objective, and the relation of test objectives to curriculum objectives. In addition, a criterion referenced test score is interpreted in relation to some "absolute standard" while a norm referenced test is interpreted in relation to how others perform on the tests.

Despite these differences, an examination of the test items themselves reveals no observable differences between those used on criterion referenced and norm referenced tests. Not only do the test items on norm referenced and criterion referenced tests generally look the same, but the test items on both types of tests look much the same as those used in the 1920s and 1930s.

Informal reading assessments have been proclaimed as a more valid and useful approach to learning about students' reading behaviors. Despite such statements there has been a paucity of development in this area. Moreover, there has been little research into the validity and reliability of the informal approaches that have been suggested. A decade ago there was a spurt of studies on informal reading inventories. Most of these studies attempted to identify the most valid criteria for determining instructional placements, but even this kind of research has faded away.

Defining purposes for reading was suggested in the previous version of this monograph (Farr, 1969) to improve reading comprehension tests. This emphasis might not only aid in assessing reading ability, but also improve the teaching of reading. Descriptions of readers' behaviors indicate that readers do not alter their reading patterns unless they have had guided practice in doing so. If teachers discover that students can increase their reading comprehension by establishing specific purposes for reading, then tests which promote the use of purposes for reading will have provided a springboard for improved instruction. Several reading tests have now begun to use purposes for reading (Metropolitan Achievement Test, 1986; Tests of General Educational Development, 1986).

Using qualitative levels of responses for multiple choice questions was also suggested in the first edition of this monograph (Farr, 1969). Measurement specialists have always suggested that as much can be learned from an incorrect response as from a correct response. For example, a particular incorrect choice on a reading comprehension test might indicate a lack of appropriate background information, another incorrect response might indicate a failure to recognize the antecedent for a pronoun, and a third might mean that a student failed to recognize the cause for a particular event. Similar developments of this type may be possible for word recognition tests. At least one reading test publisher has been pursuing the development of multiple choice items along this line (California Achievement Test, 1986).

A third development which seems to have gained some momentum since the last edition is reading skills tests that assess those skills as they are actually used in classrooms. One example is reading vocabulary tests in which words to be defined are imbedded in reading text. Despite the apparent logic of this approach, many reading vocabulary tests still present words in isolation and ask examinees to select the most appropriate synonyms from a group of alternatives.

The cloze procedure, discussed in earlier chapters, continues to be an intriguing testing approach. Though this approach appears to resemble "real reading" more closely, cloze techniques do not seem to allow the test developer to examine the inferential reading/thinking abilities of students as well as multiple choice techniques. We have not had adequate study of the construct validity of cloze reading tests even though the approach was popularized almost thirty years ago.

How are decisions made about using tests? The use of tests is certain to be affected by how decisions to use them are made. Test selection seems to have evolved over the past sixty years in two ways: 1) The first tests used in schools were selected primarily by testing specialists and school administrators, and 2) the emphasis of test development and selection was on producing and using tests that reflected curriculum. That emphasis has now shifted to selecting tests that drive curriculum.

The emphasis of early tests, like the trend today, was on their value in determining the success or failure of the schools. Only after tests were widely used to determine school success did they begin to be used for collecting information for classroom decisions. This meant that, in the beginning, tests were selected primarily on the basis of technical and statistical characteristics. Only in the past decade has the emphasis of test selection been on curriculum considerations. Early test committees (when such committees existed) were typically made up of school guidance counselors, test specialists, perhaps an educational statistician from a nearby college or university, and several school administrators. The single most significant recommendation in large school district test adoptions came from the director of testing; the final test selection was made by the school superintendent.

That pattern still exists in many school districts, but it is now becoming common to find large test committees made up of classroom teachers, curriculum specialists, and even parents. The school district test specialist serves as an advisor on technical matters, but often is not a key decision maker. The school superintendent or board of education still makes the final decision to purchase the tests, but with such large and open committee reviews, the committees' recommendations are usually followed.

Greater involvement of classroom teachers and curriculum coordinators has resulted in tests that more closely match the local school curriculum. Test publishers are now attempting to match their test content of basal reading systems. Several of them provide relatively detailed reporting formats which are keyed to basal reader objectives.

The narrative reports produced as a result of a student's test performance at one time included such statements as: "Student X is deficient in making inferences and in drawing conclusions." With the emerging emphasis on matching basal readers, the report might now state: "Student X should probably review lessons seven and eight in workbook A of the Y reading series (Y reading series being the series now used in the school district). The student might also complete the exercises on pages 34 and 37 in the book at level G. Also, see teacher's manual, page 108."

Obviously, this approach is attractive to many teachers because of its apparent specificity. This approach, however, may be leading us to a national curriculum in reading rather than a stronger emphasis on local curriculum. The initial response to the basal reader emphasis has been positive; however, it appears that test publishers are going to be expected to continue, and even expand, this kind of linkage.

The emphasis on curriculum/test match has, until the phenomenon discussed at the beginning of this chapter, been an encouraging indication that educators and the public were at last understanding what tests can do and their limitations. But lately there has been a burgeoning reverence for tests as the ultimate accountability instruments to comfort politicians, the press, and much of the public who believe the schools are failing. This strongly pronounced trend has led from the selection of tests that reflect curriculum to selecting tests that direct curriculum. This emphasis has evolved primarily at the level of the state department of education in just the past ten years and seems to follow a consistent pattern in all those states and school districts where it has been adopted. This emphasis is often encouraged, if not instigated, by state legislators. The pattern, although discussed earlier, bears outlining here:

- *The public becomes disenchanted with education*. Often this disenchantment is based on news reports of declines on tests such as the SAT and the NAEP. (The NAEP tests often show as many increases as declines, but the declines capture the headlines.) The test score declines are used by politicians as campaign issues, and are accompanied by promises of educational reform.

- *Reform efforts are focused on discrete, measurable education outcomes*. A task force of educators and lay people is asked to produce a framework for education in the state. This framework includes statements of the state's broad aims and goals of education which are followed by lists of specific behavioral objectives.

- *Tests are then developed to assess the specific objectives*. The legislatures and department of education officials argue that they need to know the status of education and need outcome measures to determine whether their reforms are effective.

- *The school systems are told to emphasize the frameworks (objectives) that have been developed.* Often the schools and teachers do more than that. They find out the content of the test and make sure that their students receive intensive instruction and practice on its objectives, content, and format.
- *As a result of the focused instruction, test scores go up.*
- *The education policy makers and leaders proclaim that their reforms have improved education.* They counter the claims that teachers have just taught to the tests with statements that suggest this is all they wanted to have happen in the first place. They argue that, as long as trivial objectives are avoided in the education frameworks and on the tests, objective focused instruction is appropriate.

In a recent article, Popham, et al.* (1985) proclaimed the correctness of instruction that is directed by assessment. The title of the article states its approach succinctly: "Measurement-Drive Instruction: It's on the Road." In the article, brief scenarios are provided for such reforms in Texas, metropolitan Detroit, South Carolina, and Maryland. The focus for these reports includes the following statement:

> The belief was widespread in the late 1970s that too many students were being promoted for "seat time" rather than for their academic accomplishments. So legislatures installed competency testing programs to force educators to produce tangible evidence that students had actually mastered the basic skills.

The introduction goes on to emphasize the importance of the tests as the focus for instruction:

> The competencies that are covered by the test will become curricular magnets that draw instruction toward themselves. If the competencies are significant, rather than trivial, they will have a decidedly salutary effect on the instructional program. The notion of measurement-driven instruction is common to all four of the programs discussed in the remainder of this article.

Following the description of the four programs the authors describe what they feel the success of these ventures has been:

> Four success stories are certainly not enough to declare a total victory for measurement-drive instruction. However, these four accounts do reveal

* Excerpts reprinted from W. James Popham, et al. "Measurement Driven Instruction: It's on the Road." Copyright © 1985, *Phi Delta Kappan.* Used with permission.

that a carefully conceived measurement-driven strategy can yield improvements in student basic skills. When future historians look back on the competency testing programs in Texas, Detroit, South Carolina, and Maryland, they will find solid evidence that measurement-driven instruction can work.

Similar descriptions of the importance of tests in determining curriculum and in pushing schools and teachers to emphasize what the tests test come from Florida (Turlington, 1985) and Connecticut (Tirozzi, 1985). It seems clear that at the state level and in some large city school districts, education leaders are turning to tests to do more than just assess the curriculum. They are using tests to control what is taught in schools. This fairly recent phenomenon will bear close watching in the next decade. It may become an even greater influence on curriculum. The fear is that schools will be nothing more than test preparation academies where the curriculum becomes what can be tested.

Where are we going in reading assessment?

The safest projections about the future of testing are those based on a linear progression of what now exists. They are the most acceptable projections because they are based on currently accepted practice. They are also usually the most inaccurate projections because they fail to take into account the variables about which we are most ignorant. Many of those variables are apt to become the most significant.

Rather than linear extensions, this section will consider three issues we think may shape the future of reading assessment. One issue concerns rethinking basic assumptions about reading and whether it can be assessed. The second issue deals with whether reading assessments can be developed to respond to the specific decision making needs of educators. The third is concerned with advances in measurement theory and technology which have great influence on trends in the field. These sections will not only discuss each basic issue but will also suggest research and development to shape the future of reading assessment.

Do the assumptions on which reading assessment is based need to be reconsidered? Major decisions and technical improvements regarding the development, selection, and administration of reading tests continue to be

Reading: What Can Be Measured?

contingent on fundamental philosophical issues, such as how reading is defined and whether certain aspects of reading can be measured.

Consider, for example, that some theories of the reading process simply preclude traditional measurement modes. A narrower, although still important, problem is that some reading theories, despite being "measurable" in a broad sense, suggest that any cost effective means of measuring reading performance is patently improbable. Whether some great synthesis of models and theories will, or can, occur remains to be seen. The point is that these questions are worthy of pursuit.

As has been consistently maintained throughout this volume, the unexamined assumption is the most insidious influence on educational practice. There is little reason to believe that the measurement of reading differs in this respect from any other intellectual endeavor.

Fundamental philosophical issues continue to be the major decision points in the development, selection, and administration of reading tests. Some technical issues in test development are truly important within a given sphere of activity and focus. Moreover, these technical issues are interesting and worthwhile problems in and of themselves. But we must emphasize that by the time one has come to grips with a fascinating problem, in sampling design for example, several basic and important decisions already have been made. This progressive refinement of focus continues on into the classroom, where questions of instructional emphasis are often decided on the basis of a test developer's perspective on the larger questions. A brief outline follows of some conceptual issues or points of departure which are emerging in the field of reading and which have direct and indirect implications for the future of reading assessment.

Research methodology is evolving. Even a cursory review of reputable research journals and the proceedings from major national conferences leads one to conclude that an increasingly large number of educational researchers are employing research methodologies significantly different from those used in the past and new to education. These methods of inquiry probably cannot be lumped together, but words like *naturalistic, ethnographic*, and *ethnomethodology* capture their essence. These approaches suggest fundamental changes in attitude concerning the study of the reading process and, perhaps, concerning the process itself.

The research concepts and attitudes these methodologies represent seem to be gaining little emphasis in the publications and conferences on measurement and measurement theory. The implications of this potential divergence seem obvious. Measurement theorists and at least some reading theorists seem to be moving in different directions. A rapprochement seems unlikely, but it may be possible that the new modes of studying reading will inevitably be quite different from the ways in which the process is measured.

The specifics are in doubt, and so are the trends we can expect. It does seem obvious that the two disciplines are evolving in different ways. Reading research and theory may be moving away from academic psychology while measurement moves more toward its center. Research directed toward a study of these changing patterns would be timely and valuable.

A parallel development to new approaches to studying reading has been the evolution of a sizeable body of theorists and researchers who, for want of a better term, represent a movement toward a more holistic view of reading and, consequently, toward the measurement of reading. Frank Smith and Kenneth Goodman are two of the most noted leaders in this movement. Their work has received much attention and has succeeded in influencing the perceptions of many researchers of a younger generation that reading must be viewed as a total language behavior. Whether Goodman and Smith advocate "top down" or "inside out" models is moot; it is important that they are clearly critical of traditional reading tests' ability to assess their conception of reading. Neither they, nor those who adhere to their views, have had much good to say about issues central to the traditional canons of measurement. Holistic theorists are, for the most part, "antitest," and they cannot be ignored with impunity.

Using the assessment of writing as a metaphor is potentially valuable in understanding this issue. Until recently, writing tests have tended to be little more than indices of individual or group abilities of the more superficial aspects of writing mechanics and English language usage. The recent burgeoning interest in the writing process, however, has caused most writing researchers to take the position that the assessment of writing must be the assessment of the composing process itself. This cannot be achieved successfully with a conventional pencil and paper, multiple choice test of writing mechanics. In effect, writing tests must employ a more holistic assessment mode if they are to be of much value in assessing the actual process of writing.

Perhaps tests of writing ability never received much attention and, as a consequence, entrenched beliefs never attained the degree of confidence that has tended to surround reading tests. The rise of holistic theory in reading, just as with writing, may well interfere with our current preconceptions of acceptable measurement of the process.

Another basic assumption which continues to go unexamined in the development of reading tests is the existence of the "critical list." Since no one can, at present, provide an assured, validated list of the critical skills for proficient reading, it is appropriate to ask about the origin of the critical list of skills upon which reading tests are now based.

When considered in concert with the prior issues in this section, this concern further erodes the foundation of many existing reading tests. At the very least, we should keep these problems in mind and examine tests and test results with a critical eye. Large scale testing, both with norm referenced and criterion referenced tests, is obviously going to be with us for a long time, but there is no reason we cannot be highly skeptical of its use.

Reading assessment must be responsive to the needs of those who plan and carry out reading instruction. More research is needed concerning the functional uses of tests. Tests are devices for collecting information — information that is needed for making educational decisions. The validity of a test depends on whether it provides the information needed for considering a particular instructional decision.

We need continued research on the types of decisions made by teachers, curriculum supervisors, and administrators to plan and carry out instruction. We also need to know the kinds of information they require to make those decisions, the format in which the information should be provided, and how this relates to the timing of decisionmaking. Such research most likely will reveal that educators need a wide variety of information for decision making, much broader than that which could be provided by any reading test. Moreover, these information needs probably cannot wait until a test is administered and scored and a set of packaged results are returned to the teacher or administrator. We know that information needs for planning instruction are often immediate. Such immediate needs necessarily rely on informal evaluation carried out as part of ongoing instruction, an area of reading assessment which has already been described as woefully underdeveloped.

Guthrie and Lissitz (1985) have provided a framework for assessment and decision making. They argue that there are different types of instructional decisions made by different decision makers, and that each of these necessitates different information.

> Mismatches or discrepancies between types of assessment and generic categories of decisionmaking may be counterproductive for schools and children. Distinctions among the uses for tests set the stage for the employment of different assessment strategies. That is, qualitatively different decisions that will be made from test scores require qualitatively different approaches to measurement and interpretation of tests.

In regard to the use of traditional standardized tests for making classroom decisions, Guthrie and Lissitz state:

> Decisions about what to teach, how long to spend on a topic, and whether it has been learned to a level adequate for independent performance by the student are indispensable to a teacher and are probably impossible information to obtain from a standardized test. Consequently, using formal standardized tests as a basis for instructional decisions raises the hazard of ignoring the causes of successful learning, which is the only basis for enhancing it.

The issue of how test results are reported is especially potent. Despite wide professional outcry concerning the abuse of grade equivalent scores, for example, most publishers still make them available, and although no industrywide figures are available, it seems likely that the majority of school districts still request them. New types of test scores which are less subject to misinterpretation must be developed.

An issue which goes beyond the utilization of a specific scale is that of implied (or explicit) comparisons in the public reporting of test scores. States and large school districts which conduct census testing often publish scores by school, and sometimes by teacher. In some states, whole cities and school districts are implicitly compared in achievement test performance.

It is not an uncommon event for initial test results to be reported at a school board meeting and for the press to play up the scores. This attracts attention and the inevitable comparisons of schools and teachers are made. Qualifiers and conditionals tend to be lost in the public discussion which often follows. Clearly, socioeconomic differences and other differences between schools are given lip service, but the upshot of these "competitions" can scarcely be viewed as productive for understanding the achievements of the schools or what is needed to improve them. More research is therefore needed on alternative reporting models and formats.

Continued efforts must point to the development of new techniques for developing tests, alternative test formats, improved statistics for analyzing test scores, and more usable test reports. While we must not lose sight of the importance of more fundamental issues discussed earlier in this chapter, we need to continue research and development efforts to improve existing reading tests. New forms of assessment may evolve from present tests rather than from the development of totally different alternatives. The history of education seems to be one of gradual evolution rather than dramatic revolution.

The following brief discussion highlights some of the technical, statistical, and logistical solutions to problems in reading test development and scoring. Collectively, these constitute what might be called the "technology of assessment." This is where the field of reading measurement has made the most progress in recent years. Some truly startling innovations have made tests fairer, more accurate, more complete in their representations of human knowledge and behavior, and generally more efficient.

Tests have gotten better. Test developers have begun to draw on new areas of scientific knowledge which allow them to fine-tune tests at a level heretofore thought impossible. Techniques from branches of higher mathematics, statistics, engineering, and artificial intelligence have been adapted for use in specific problems associated with constructing and using tests and test results. Advances in topological theory, computer simulation, econometric models, and even catastrophe theory have contributed to recent editions of some large scale tests.

Consider, for example, some of the recent improvements in the technical design of the National Assessment of Educational Progress. The power and value of the data collected through this new design will significantly enhance the utility of the NAEP results. Analyses of the data, for example, are no longer "booklet bound" as they have been in the past. To accomplish this seemingly minor task the test developers employed an entirely new kind of design generally referred to as a balanced incomplete block spiraling variant of matrix sampling.

As Messick (1984) notes, this change will allow a variety of new analyses, so that:

- scales can be developed which have common meaning across exercises, population subgroups, age levels, and time periods;
- performance scales can be correlated with background, attitudinal, and program variables to address a rich variety of educational and policy issues; and,
- various kinds of "composite" exercises can be analyzed for coherence and even for construct validity.

These are major testing improvements. They will render the results of the NAEP tests considerably more useful to test developers and policy makers at many levels; all this becomes more important as some states opt to tie in with the national effort for local assessment programs, even for census testing in some states.

The application of Item Response Theory (IRT) to the process is among the more exciting recent advances in test construction and analysis. IRT has been the focus of considerable research in psychometrics and has fully evolved in two forms—the one parameter model and the three parameter model. The three parameter model is more powerful because it can take more variables into consideration. However, the one parameter model has found many adherents because of its simplicity and arguments that the additional parameters do not add enough to understanding the underlying variables to offset implementation difficulties.

The three parameters used in the selection of items are item difficulty, item discrimination, and "guessability." When these factors are taken into account simultaneously during test development, the test constructor has a more complete understanding of the factors which comprise test performance.

Perhaps more important, both one parameter and three parameter models can be used for scoring and analyzing test results. This produces a fairer, and presumably more accurate, scale for each pupil. While IRT is not without its problems or its detractors, it represents a major advance in the technical realm of test development. Perhaps one of these two models will become dominant in the next several years.

Several approaches to assessing functional reading levels have evolved in the past decade. These approaches commonly attempt to relate an examinee's reading test performance to specific levels of materials the examinee would be expected to read. The Degrees of Reading Power (DRP) uses a modified cloze procedure to determine functional reading performance and relates that performance to materials for which the reading difficulty has been determined with a readability formula. The Metropolitan Achievement Test: Reading (MAT) uses traditional reading passages and multiple choice test items to determine functional reading levels. The MAT passages and items are carefully developed so that the readability of the passages and the difficulties of the test items form a scale of reading difficulty. Educational Testing Service is now developing a functional reading scale for the National Assessment of Educational Progress Reading Tests. This scale will be based on an analysis of the items used on the test.

All these functional reading tests have in common that they attempt to relate test performance to a criterion of reading level rather than to a norm referenced scale. The attempt may provide a more objective answer to the continuing question: "Exactly what does the reading test score say about materials the examinee can be expected to read successfully?"

Reading: What Can Be Measured?

Other developments in assessment technology are important to test consumers. New and predicted techniques for the performance assessment of limited English proficient students are eagerly anticipated, especially in areas of the country with large and recent immigrant populations, such as the Southwest and Northeast.

These and other measurement advances represent progress in the development of more accurate, valid, and useful reading measurement. While researchers and test developers continue to make progress on questions of this sort, we hope they will not lose sight of basic questions about what should be measured that have been raised throughout this monograph.

In summary it must be stated that the basic ways in which reading tests are used is consistent with the ways they were used fifty years ago. The fundamental assumptions and conventional wisdom regarding testing continue to go largely unexamined. If anything, the recent wave of calls for more accountability and going back to basics has tended to correlate with an upsurge in some kinds of achievement testing. Excellence is often implicitly equated with high test scores, and major conceptual issues still go begging in the marketplace of ideas.

Future research and development in reading and language may, in time, provide more satisfying answers to some of the more basic conceptual questions about what reading is. In the meantime, research will have to concentrate on how to use current tests effectively and avoid the most flagrant misuses. Hopefully, this monograph will provide some assistance with that task.

References

A Nation at Risk. The National Commission on Excellence in Education. Washington, DC: U.S. Department of Education, 1983.

Anrig, G.R. Educational standards, testing, and equity. *Phi Delta Kappan,* 1985, *66,* 623-625.

Carey, R.F. Program evaluation as ethnographic research. Providence, RI: Department of Education, 1985. (mimeo)

Carey, R.F. Selecting a test for the state testing program. Providence, RI: Department of Education, 1984. (mimeo)

Eisner, E.W. The kinds of schools we need. *Educational Leadership,* 1983, *4,* 48-85.

Farr, R. *Reading: What can be measured?* Newark, DE: International Reading Association, 1969.

Guthrie, J.T., and Lissitz, R.W. A framework for assessment-based decision-making in reading education. *Educational Measurement: Issues and Practice,* 1985, *4,* 26-30.

Howe, H. II. Let's have another SAT score decline. *Phi Delta Kappan,* 1985, *66,* 599-602.

Madaus, G.F. Test scores as administrative mechanisms in educational policy. *Phi Delta Kappan,* 1985, *66,* 611-617.

Messick, S. *NAEP: A decade of change.* Princeton, NJ: Educational Testing Service, 1984.

Popham, W.J., Cruse, K.L., Rankin, S.L., Sandifer, P.D., and Williams P.L. Measurement driven instruction: It's on the road. *Phi Delta Kappan,* 1985, *66,* 628-634.

Salganik, L.H. Why testing reforms are so popular and how they are changing education. *Phi Delta Kappan,* 1985, *66,* 607-610.

Tirozzi, G.N., Baron, J.B., Forgione, P.D., and Rindone, D.A. How testing is changing education in Connecticut. *Educational Measurement Issues and Practice,* 1985, *4,* 12-16.

Turlington, R.D. How testing is changing education in Florida. *Educational Measurement Issues and Practices,* 1985, *4,* 9-11.

Tyler, R.W. Comment. *Educational Researcher,* 1982, *11,* 9-11.

United Press International. Bill would rank schools by test scores. Bloomington, Indiana, *Herald Telephone,* February 14, 1984, p. 12.

Test References

California Achievement Tests: Reading. Monterey, CA: California Test Bureau, 1986.

Degrees of Reading Power. New York: College Entrance Examination Board, 1980.

Metropolitan Achievement Tests: Reading. Cleveland, OH: Psychological Corporation, 1986.

Tests of General Educational Development. Washington, DC: American Council on Education, 1986.